from Buzaglo to Balis

Chris Lepkowski

[handwritten: Best Wishes]

[signature]

Shareholders for Albion

First published in Great Britain in August 2020
by Shareholders for Albion

ISBN 978-0-9574229-1-9

Shareholders for Albion

Printed and bound by TJ International, Padstow, Cornwall

Contents

I dedicate this book to the memory of those who have passed away from Covid-19 and to the many key workers who have cared for us and kept us safe, watered and fed during 2020.

Foreword

By Bob Taylor

When I was asked to write the foreword for this book, I didn't hesitate. It took me back to a wonderful and important time in my career. It was one of the most special periods of my life – a journey starting in the Third Division and ending in the Premier League.

I remember early 1992 well. Sadly, my mum had just died from emphysema. She was only 47. It wasn't unexpected but it did hit me hard. I had a week away where I could attend the funeral in the north east. When I went back to Bristol City, my club, they told me there was interest from Bobby Gould and West Bromwich Albion. Little did I know what an impact that conversation would have on my career and life. Bobby was living in Portishead, so apparently he used to come and watch me play. I've since heard he might even have signed Paul Williams thinking it was me? Seriously! Keep reading if you don't believe me…

By the time Gouldy wanted to sign me, I was up for a fresh challenge. I didn't even know where West Bromwich was. All I knew was that I lived near junction 21 of the M5 and I was being asked to drive in one straight line north to junction one. From there, it was right at the roundabout, with the stadium just half a mile up the road. That sounded simple enough for me. Oh, and it was two hours nearer the north east. I was happy with that. I knew a little about the history of West Brom – being a former Leeds United player, I knew that my manager Billy Bremner still wasn't happy about THAT Jeff Astle goal. Even then, some 17 years later, he mentioned it.

The first person I met at Albion was Gary Robson. He was to become my best mate and still is. I was staying at the Moat House Hotel just up the road and remember Earl Barrett was there too, as he had just signed for Aston Villa. Being able to chat to someone was good but Gary was the person I really bonded with. I can only thank him for helping me when I first joined because I was nervous. Who wouldn't be when starting at a new club? Putting on that no 9 shirt was just incredible. I came to the club and the fans didn't know who I was. They got rid of one of their best players, Don Goodman, for just under £1m and ended up signing a striker for a third of the amount…so it was understandable if people were worried. But it was a challenge and I had something to prove. I scored on my home debut against Brentford, scored twice on my away debut against Birmingham. Not a bad start, I thought.

By 1992-93, the club was emerging from a downward spiral. Supporters had been losing interest but under Ossie Ardiles, we suddenly found a sparkle. There was such a brilliant feeling around the club. That was a breath of fresh air for everyone.

I learned about the boots I was filling. I got to meet Ronnie Allen, I met The Tank (Derek Kevan), I met The King, Jeff Astle. They were all wonderful. Jeff was a humble window cleaner at the time – a terrific man. And then I met big Cyrille Regis as well as getting to know a legend from a different shirt number, Tony 'Bomber' Brown. The names roll off the tongue and it was humbling to be mentioned alongside such people after I had scored 37 goals in a season. That 1992-93 campaign made me at West Bromwich Albion. It felt like I was at a special club.

I remember feeling how lucky I was. I'd been a kid in the north east, going down the mines, being on the dole, watching cup finals, wishing I could be at Wembley…and there I was, representing West Bromwich Albion on that huge stage. The old Wembley was the proper Wembley. I remember counting every step when Darren Bradley led us up to the Royal Box at the 1993 play-off final after we had beaten Port Vale. Thirty-nine. To do so with Albion was amazing. When I walked up out of the tunnel, I thought there was nobody there. I could hear people but I couldn't see any fans. All I could see were empty seats. And then the noise hit me as we walked out – all those fans behind the tunnel. Unbelievable. The hairs still stand on the back of my neck now, just thinking about it. There was no way we would lose that day.

I played for seven of the eight permanent managers of this book's period – I'm more fond of some than others. But they were all part of the fabric of my career and part of West Bromwich Albion history. I remember leaving for Bolton in 1998 and wondering if I'd ever come back… and then I returned when Gary Megson was boss in 2000. I got a contract of three and a half years but had absolutely no idea what was awaiting us. I actually came back to West Brom because it was Albion. Bolton had an FA Cup semi-final coming up against Villa and I'd had my pictures taken with Lofty the Lion, the Bolton mascot, and the Cup – just before the semi-final at Wembley. All the press were there. I took that as meaning I would be playing. Then, Mike Phelan, who was good mates with Megson, asked me if I would go back to the Albion. You're damn right, I would! I ended up watching the semi-final on TV, remember Dean Holdsworth side-footing over the bar and thinking I'd have scored. Against Villa, too. Imagine that!

Never mind, I was back at Albion, my club. We enjoyed the (first) great escape in 2000, the play-offs of 2001 and then the drama of 2002. Just as Albion won an advantage when Port Vale's Peter Swan was sent off for fouling me at Wembley, along came the penalty at Bradford. I was way too injured to take that penalty – honestly! I missed the first one that season against Grimsby. We had others missing a few. I really didn't fancy it. Thank you, Igor. And, let's be honest, From Buzaglo to Taylor doesn't sound as good, does it? All I remember was Andy Myers catching me. I just kept looking at the fans. My mate's wife and daughter were in the stands and I was smiling at them, thinking there's no way I'm taking this. And then Igor stepped up. Igor? What the hell? I remember him telling us he took them for his country. Turns out it might not have been true. My God. He didn't say much but, when he did, it was a drama. The stoppage felt like about 20 minutes. The penalty was perfect. Then he turned and ran back. Igor was the coolest man in Bradford that day.

The following week, wow! I didn't think I would play against Crystal Palace. But I did. Gary Megson said he wanted someone for the big occasion. Derek McInnes said to me: 'It's all set up for you…you're going to score.' He kept saying that. During training, it became clear I would be playing. On the day, Darren Moore scored, then I scored. I remember Scott Dobie running through at 2-0…everyone is egging him on to put the game beyond doubt and I'm thinking: 'Ah no… please don't score, please don't score, please don't score'. I'm sorry for being so selfish. But I wanted that moment. I am a goalscorer, after all…

That day was special to me. It was my daughter Chantelle's 11th birthday and it was our first time in the top flight for 16 years. West Bromwich Albion is so much more than merely a club I played for. I have friends in the Black Country, I live in the area, I am settled here. This is my football club. A football club is bricks and mortar. Players, managers, coaches come and go. Football clubs are down to the supporters. That's what it's all about. They breathe it, they live it, they go through every emotion during a game. West Bromwich Albion fans are what make West Bromwich Albion. I've always thought the West Midlands was like the north east. The people are so similar. When people hear my accent, they ask: 'Are you Newcastle or Sunderland?' But I'm not black and white, nor red and white. I'm navy blue and white. This is my home. This is a football club supported by my kind of people. I'm West Bromwich Albion through and through.

I go to games as a fan now. I remember as a player when we lost 13 on the run under Alan Buckley. The fans could have turned. They didn't. This is my way of repaying them. It's in my blood. I have been here nearly 30 years and so proud to be part of this football club. I've been Bob Taylor the footballer, now I'm Bob Taylor the West Bromwich Albion supporter.

Enjoy the book.

Bob Taylor

Introduction

The story begins with embarrassment. The story ends with euphoria. First, some context.....

This book began in 2017 – in theory, if not in practice. And it was all down to Gary Megson. I last wrote a book about West Bromwich Albion in 2012. Since then, I've contributed to several other football publications but certainly didn't envisage writing another one about the Baggies. Then Megson returned. He came back to The Hawthorns to briefly become Tony Pulis's assistant manager. I was out shopping when a friend texted the news of his appointment. Immediately, I was in work mode. The man who could tie up several loose ends was back on our patch. I could have called him at any point before then but now he was back on the manor, it made this a very real pursuit. I had no excuses.

Megson and I were hardly the best of friends. We had a difficult relationship during his time as Albion boss and my spell on the Birmingham Mail. Still, let bygones be bygones and all that…

I had deliberately left him out of *In Pastures Green*, my previous book, on the basis that I wanted it to be about the players. The dynamic was now somewhat different. I wondered whether Megson might wish to go on the record, if only to respond to the strident views offered about him by certain players. I sent a text sounding him out. Within a few minutes, he replied: 'Yes'. We were in business. Bygones were definitely bygones.

When we met, Gary and I spent several hours poring over stories, players, coaches, directors and so many other matters, not least the working relationship with two chairmen. He was good. Very good. He was brilliant. My initial thought was to rebrand *In Pastures Green* with an altered title and the words 'Extra Time' stamped across the front – the same book, but with an extra chapter. A reissue of an old story if you like, with a new feature attached. That idea was quickly scrapped. Would enough fans have wanted to read old stories, with one new chapter?

It became clear – in my mind at least – that the man who started my last book journey might actually be better as a conclusion to a new book. Hell, if Star Wars can do prequels, so can the rest of us. Thankfully, Shareholders for Albion were more than willing to back this project, as they had done my first one. An outline was drawn up. The book would be about West Bromwich Albion over the years leading up to 2002. But where to start? That was easy. Let's begin with Albion's lowest, darkest point. Yes, January 5, 1991. This project was always going to be a darker, earthier and less corporate experience. It was about capturing a period of time. The irony is that, to try to convince yourself to step back into a particular journey, you're asking yourself to go somewhere you would rather forget. We might as well start in the deepest of dips. Woking. Tim Buzaglo. I make no apologies for this. Let's start it with Buzaglo. And let's end it with Balis. Alliteration is our saviour: From Buzaglo to Balis works, yes?

In the 1980s, I used to travel past The Hawthorns every weekend. I would see the billboards outside the stadium advertising forthcoming matches – Liverpool, Manchester United, etc. I would cast an envious eye on the magical stories evolving behind those corrugated metal fences. I always wondered whether I was missing out on something. I would hear the tales, read the reports. I wanted to be part of it but, with hindsight, I'm glad I wasn't. Back in the mid-to-late 1980s especially, football was a dark place. Fans were regarded like animals, penned in behind metal fences, herded like cattle, treated with utter disdain. Albion were hardly blessed with huge crowds as it was, with their descent gathering pace. At The Hawthorns, like everywhere, football was becoming increasingly stigmatised. Hooliganism, racism, societal breakdown and depravation. The national game was the go-to blame sponge for the country's ills.

By 1991, football was starting to embrace change, mainly out of necessity. Four tragedies from 1985 to 1989 were to shape the game forever. Bradford underlined the utter devastation of inadequate facilities in old-fashioned, wooden stands. Heysel and St Andrew's highlighted the desperate need for supporters to improve their own behaviour, along with the hope that one day we could watch football from safer arenas rather than the crumbling, dilapidated grounds of that period. And Hillsborough, where 96 were to perish, was to embody all that was bad about football during the period – no longer could we allow the sport to treat supporters with such derision and disrespect. By the start of the next decade, stadia were beginning to change and money was starting to dominate the sport's future in a way it had never done before.

Italia 90 had been the crucial reset button. It was the much-needed departure from the 1980s and a symbolic arrival into a new decade. Another leg-up into a brighter era came with the creation of the Premier League in 1992. Surely, nothing could be as bad as the 1980s? From football's point of view, it probably did never reach those depths again. It also meant football became more expensive to watch. Slowly, the demographic of fans was changing. Traditional fans were being priced out of the game. While football waved good riddance to a grim decade and looked ahead to the prosperity of the 1990s, Albion merely sat back, slumped against the settee of mediocrity. They had entered the 1980s as a club of ambition but, ten years later, were one of the slobs – unhealthy, lacking any prospects or ambition and seemingly heading towards further decay. Albion, back in 1991, were alive but not doing much kicking – theirs was no more than an existence. For too long, they had been playing Snakes and Ladders, only without the ladders.

Back then, there were no pre-match handshakes, no pomp, no ceremony, no squad numbers or names on shirts. It was a place where footballers – generally with British names – were on much more modest wages than today, even at the foot of the Second Division. And, by Second Division, I mean the next level down from the top tier. All very simple. Terraces were in the process of being phased out, ticket prices were relatively cheap, no more than two substitutes could be used and the managers your club appointed were generally people you didn't need to google. Not that you could have googled them then, of course. If you wanted your latest news fix, you would reach for the Express & Star or the Evening Mail – Albion fans were lucky to have two prominent newspapers covering their club because most had only one. Elsewhere, you could remortgage your house to hear the five-minute snippet of a press conference or transfer speculation on a premium phone service called ClubCall. If you were really fortunate, you had Ceefax and Teletext to fall back on. Page 312 was the news-in-brief section, where you could read about Matt Carbon's latest injury setback. After a Saturday match, you'd leave The Hawthorns and hop on one of the many 74s, 78s or 79s parked outside – there was no Midlands Metro until 1999, kids – and head south to Birmingham or back to your Black Country posting of choice. At around 6pm, you'd head to the newsagents to pick up your copy of the Sports Argus or the Sporting Star. If Albion had won, you'd have to move quickly because they generally sold out rapidly. If Albion lost, you could buy as many copies as you liked. It is fair to assume there are many unsold Arguses from the mid-1990s knocking around somewhere.

Towards the end of that decade, message boards started to arrive via the Internet. Newspapers were beginning to become less popular, with much of their content now being offered for free across websites. I make no apologies: we shall be revisiting grim times, some pits of despair. But there will also be moments of joy and happiness and those games you will be telling your grandchildren about.

In the year this book starts its journey, I was a 15-year-old in the fourth year at school – they call it year 10 these days – with aspirations to pursue a career in sports journalism. By 2002, where this trip concludes, I had recently finished working for FourFourTwo, before moving into a role as West Bromwich Albion reporter for the Evening Mail; a posting I enjoyed for 13 years. Although my first Albion game was in 1987 – a 1-0 home defeat against Blackburn – I didn't become a regular at The Hawthorns until 1992. For so many readers of this book, myself included, those 1990s would have been a defining period – the last chance to enjoy some carefree afternoons and nights before mortgages, bills, spouses and children.

Back to the book….with Gary Megson on board, I set about arranging interviews. It was my view that this should be more than just about players, so I immediately contacted former chairman Paul Thompson and one-time chief executive John Wile about conducting a piece with them. Both agreed. A special mention is in order for Thompson, who I was due to meet in Sheffield's Meadowhall shopping centre for our chat. A family emergency forced him away from our meeting at the very last minute, meaning a wasted trip north for me. We met a week later and he insisted on paying the expenses of my previous trip, treated us both to a meal and presented me with his old share certificate, signed by several ex-players and framed. He had even brought a small gift for my daughter, who he knew about but had never met. Oh, and he gave me several hours of his time talking about all things West Bromwich Albion – what happened, what could have happened and what would have happened had he stayed. He remains a man of such dignity and class.

I headed east to speak to Alan Miller in Norfolk, went south to speak to Enzo Maresca at London's Olympic Stadium and over to Slovakia to catch up with Igor Balis. Denis Smith welcomed me to his Staffordshire home with warmth and kindness. The phone bill after my chat with Florida-based Jason Roberts remains one of the more sobering moments of this process but it was worth every penny. Then there was Daryl Burgess, who served under 11 bosses during his years at the club, and Darren Bradley, who lifted a trophy he then managed to lose. Craig Shakespeare succeeded in squeezing me in between jury service and heading off on holiday – and then pitching up at Watford. The Chambers lads spoke to me from their respective lounges during lockdown and Ossie Ardiles did likewise. Not forgetting Tim Buzaglo, the most reluctant of heroes who accelerated Albion's slide into their worst-ever period and, unwittingly, helped bring about inevitable change at the club. Shy, but kind, Buzaglo said he was honoured to have a book in his name. My pleasure, Tim.

Then there was Andy Hunt. You might be flicking through the pages wondering where his chapter is. It was there – or at least it should have been. His comments, stories, recollections remain floating in another universe – a cyber-ether beyond our reach, where Dictaphone malfunctions swirl without any prospect of return. Of all the interviews to be struck by major technical gremlins, it had to be the one with the guy who was only comfortable with a face-to-face chat and happened to live in the Amazonian jungle. Typical!

Bobby Gould has a brilliant book out already, ghosted by David Instone – read it if you can. Alan Buckley and Brian Little have already gone to press as well with their own memoirs while Ray Harford is sadly no longer with us. So, who should be approached for the foreword? There was only one candidate. The only man to win promotion twice during the period, having been signed by Gould at the club's lowest ebb and who scored the goal at the apex of Albion's finest moment for some two decades. It was only ever going to be Bob Taylor.

Writing about this particular period required a journey back in time and I threw myself into the 1990s. Each chapter was penned against a backdrop of the particular musical soundtrack of that period. How can you write about Albion's promotion of 1993 without Ace of Base, 2 Unlimited and Shaggy accompanying Super Bob's journey to Wembley? Likewise, The Prodigy, The Lightning Seeds, Oasis and Supergrass – to name just a few – went hand in hand with Albion campaigns during the late 1990s and beyond. Those are the ones I'm willing to admit to. I listened to these songs, so you don't have to. Some good, many bad. Much like some of the recollections you're about to read – I considered it imperative to immerse myself back in those periods through music and the common culture of the time. Player of the Year nights were held at the Tower Ballroom in Edgbaston or at King's Night Club in Hamstead. Liberty's, Stoodi Bakers, The Dome and Miss Moneypenny's Bar were among the Birmingham nightclubs where you could frequently rub shoulders with your football heroes.

More players were based in the immediate locality, too. Ugo Ehiogu lived for some time in a Hallam Street flat, Alan Miller later resided just up the road near Dartmouth Park, Igor Balis moved his family to a cul-de-sac on the Wigmore estate in West Bromwich and Gary Robson was in Great Barr – this was a period before mansions in Little Aston or Solihull became the must-have homes for footballers. I remember wandering once into Burger King on West Bromwich High Street to find Tony Ford and at least three other Albion players enjoying a meal. Imagine that now.

The kits were of mixed pedigree, produced by Pelada, Patrick, Influence and something called 'Albion Collection'. Sponsors were modest: Sandwell Council, Guest Motors, Coucher and Shaw solicitors – who didn't even last a season – and, of course the West Bromwich Building Society. Managers and players were generally British, with one notable exception in Albion's case. Foreign signings were regarded as something a little exotic, ambitious and exciting – but could they do it on the much-mentioned cold Tuesday night at Grimsby? Players were known to miss games due to oversleeping, failed drugs tests, near-death experiences and regular injuries. This was an era in which West Bromwich Albion were a model of a club who were frequently getting it badly wrong.

This is an anecdotal account of that period, not a statistical look-back or a regimented game-by-game review of those years. Nor is it a recollection of the time through the prism of supporters. These are first-hand accounts from those who were in the teeth of the club's journey through that dramatic era. This is a book that also touches on all the behind-the-scenes bits; that famous coffin at Shrewsbury, the interviewee who was a part-time 'actor' in his spare time and who once declined so badly that it was touch and go whether he would pull through, the one-time manager who survived a plane crash, the players who scrapped during a kit launch, the duo taken in for police questioning while still wearing their training kit, the boss who was desperate to berate two opposition players in a pub. Also included is the definitive story about the Paul Williams signing, the naming of the football legend who rejected the job as Albion player-manager because of a Hawthorns boardroom leak and the revealing of the guy whose name you and I have been getting wrong all this time. All of this, and so much more.

As this book was going to print, Albion's class of 2020 won promotion back to the Premier League, so a big well done to Slaven Bilic and his squad. It was the club's fifth promotion since the turn of the 21st century. But let's head back to simpler, if darker, footballing times, when promotion was something other clubs achieved, while Albion drifted along a creek of mediocrity.

One last thing. The final phases of this book were written against the backdrop of one of the most challenging and harrowing experiences we will ever go through, be it as individuals or as a society. Some of you will have lost family members and friends to Covid-19. I extend my sincerest sympathies and condolences to all bereaved by it and dedicate *From Buzaglo to Balis* to the memory of every Albion supporter – indeed any football fan – who has passed away during this period.

One day, we will all return to the frontline of football; meeting our friends in the pub pre-match, moaning about team selection, taking our regular seats in the stand and, of course, joining a chorus of tens of thousands of cheers when our side scores a goal. We will return. Until then, I hope these 240 pages bring some small comfort and relief to you all…

Chris Lepkowski

Tim Buzaglo

*"...I remember looking in the West Brom dressing room and their
players were just sitting around as casual as you like, reading
the newspapers...I thought: 'We might just win this...'"*

Graham Roberts spots a familiar face a few yards away. He hasn't forgotten. He doesn't forget a face. Nor does he forget comments. By now playing for Enfield, the former West Bromwich Albion defender recognises the old foe in the colours of Marlow. Tim Buzaglo looks back and grimaces. Roberts has long since lost his pace. His memory, however, remains sharp and potent. As do his studs and challenges.

Buzaglo hates publicity. Some three decades on, he still sighs at the mere mention of West Bromwich Albion. January 5, 1991 was FA Cup third-round day. Away from The Hawthorns, preparations were being made for that evening's Match of the Day. The BBC's main camera crew went to Ewood Park, where second-tier Blackburn were taking on League champions Liverpool. In those days, there was one featured game and a sprinkling of others, so another crew popped to Barnet, hoping struggling Portsmouth might fall victim to non-League opponents. Right story, wrong venue.

A solitary cameraman was sent to Albion's game against Woking. Planners ticked it off as a routine home victory. Brian Talbot's men were 16th in a ridiculously congested bottom half of the Second Division table. Just four points separated 12th-placed Port Vale (29) with Plymouth in 22nd spot. Albion were on 27. Woking were in the Diadora League – the sixth tier of English football. When they pitched up at The Hawthorns, they had already played five games in that season's FA Cup. A 2-1 victory over Bath City in the fourth qualifying round was followed by a three-game tussle with then Conference side Kidderminster Harriers, against whom they won at Aggborough in the second replay.

Before their return to the West Midlands, Woking saw off Merthyr Tydfil 5-1 in round two. On December 10, their fans did what football supporters everywhere did and gathered around the radio on the Monday lunchtime to listen to the draw. West Bromwich Albion would play Woking. Steve Lilwall was to join Albion from Kidderminster in summer, 1992. He played and scored for the Harriers in that defining third game. It wasn't enough. Woking still won 2-1. The future Baggies left-back recalled the game clearly: "Fuck me, they were good. I remember speaking to a couple of mates before that Albion game and told them: 'Woking will do you'. They were quick, incisive and, unusually, they played good football for a team at that level."

Back to third-round day. There was drama at Ewood Park, where Blackburn went within seconds of knocking Liverpool out. A Mark Atkins own goal instead set up a replay and Jimmy Hill angrily admonished a ball girl for returning the ball too quickly to a Liverpool player. Portsmouth battered Barnet. There was nothing to see there. What was looking like a mundane day was rescued by drama in the Black Country.

Albion went ahead through Colin West. No problem. The MOTD producers were focusing elsewhere. The Sports Argus front-page planners were also looking to other games for their splash. Talbot's malfunctioning side were ok and would presumably score a couple more. Indeed, they had the chances. Only they didn't. Tim Buzaglo, a 29-year-old computer operator from Woking, was a part-time footballer, one-time Gibraltar cricket international. He wasn't ready for The Hawthorns and all that followed. He remembers the weekend clearly.

He recalls passing up the opportunity to do a tour of The Hawthorns on the Friday night. Far from treating their fixture in West Bromwich as a winnable game, the Surrey part-timers planned in a way that suggested they were on a journey of adventure – one of gallant endeavour and industry, but one unlikely to keep them in the competition. Not all shared that view. The scouting reports from Albion's previous games had exposed weaknesses that Woking's coaching staff felt they could exploit. Buzaglo was too busy trying to keep his mind occupied....

"We went up on the Friday and stayed at the Moat House Hotel near to the stadium," he said. "I remember it was walking distance because some of the lads went on the Friday night to have a look around. We were invited but I refused. I didn't fancy it. I was way too nervous. I expected us to get a good hiding. The lads were looking forward to it but I can't say I was. I recall West Brom were mid-table and struggling a bit for form but they were too good for us, surely? Geoff Chapple (Woking boss) had them watched five times and they came back and said 'They've got Gary Strodder and Graham Roberts at centre-back…lads, this lot, they're slow. We will win the game'. He was absolutely convinced."

Albion had problems beforehand. Stuart Naylor was injured. Replacing him would be the debutant Mel Rees. Don Goodman was hurt and out of the picture, so Gary Bannister partnered West. Roberts was a former England international and partnering ex-West Ham man Strodder. Gary Robson was a seasoned campaigner, Craig Shakespeare and Darren Bradley were hugely experienced, too. Albion were hardly mugs. And yet they were making mugs of their opponents. Buzaglo wasn't impressed.

"I remember looking in the West Brom dressing room and their players were sitting around as casual as you like, reading the papers. I thought: 'We might just win this'. There was no focus. I remember thinking we might just have a chance here. You could tell they were thinking: 'Who the hell are you lot?' We were about to do our warm-up and they were there, seemingly elsewhere in mind. I found that astounding. That just made me think their minds weren't quite with it. Their hearts certainly weren't. I've never come across a team that would have done that or prepared for a game like that. Whether they were unhappy generally or taking us lightly, I don't know. But it was apparent they weren't right."

Before the mass saturation of televised press conferences, journalists would speak to managers over the phone in order to preview the weekend game. Graham Hill was carving out a career for himself at the Birmingham Evening Mail and also remembers an air of nonchalance and indifference from Albion's coaching staff during the build-up. He was hardly on the best of terms with an increasingly vulnerable Talbot. A story he had reported on sometime earlier – in which he quoted a naïve Talbot claiming Wolves had made an enquiry for an unnamed Albion player – had gone down badly at both ends of the A41. A year earlier, Hill had accompanied his pre-match preview by predicting an Albion defeat in their FA Cup fourth-round tie at home to top-flight Charlton – hardly the most malicious of forecasts given Talbot's men were a division below the Londoners. Nevertheless, Talbot had ready-made ammunition to berate the journalist following Albion's somewhat fortuitous victory, a win earned thanks to Tony Ford's slithering shot deviating ever so slightly as it struck a puddle and sneaked inside the far upright. It was enough to create a Cup shock, enough reason for a beleaguered manager to vent his spleen at the young reporter.

Fast forward nearly 12 months and Hill was preparing his preview of the visit of Woking. The telephone conversation that ensued left him feeling uneasy about Albion's mind-set. "I just remember being shocked at Brian's tone," he recalls. "He took them very, very lightly. He was basically saying: 'We're a Second Division club…we won't lose to them'. I was shocked he'd said it to be honest. I distinctly remember him being so relaxed as if Albion were simply going to go through the motions. I can understand a manager or coach might well be thinking that privately…but to say it publicly? It shocked me. And, to be honest, I think it showed the next day."

Not wishing to exacerbate their fractious relationship, Hill played a straight bat with the quotes where others might have spun them into a more incendiary back-page splash. Buzaglo, preparing for the biggest match of his career, had little stomach for breakfast at the hotel next to junction one of the M5. Those precious pre-game hours were the final embers of his life as a mere non-League footballer. What followed was to change his life.

"God, I was so nervous," he recalls. "I didn't eat anything. I'm always nervous until I start warming up. Once the game starts, I'm fine but I couldn't eat and with all the build-up before, I just couldn't look at food. Looking back, it feels strange that I was that nervous. Maybe something inside me knew we had a chance, I don't know, but I should have been looking forward to the game and been excited. But I felt very nervous, almost as if we were carrying expectation.

"Everyone expected a routine result. We were expected to lose. The BBC cameras went to Barnet v Portsmouth because Barnet were still non-League. That didn't happen because Portsmouth had a decent side. Liverpool were playing Blackburn. I honestly wouldn't have been surprised had they not even bothered sending a camera to The Hawthorns, other than to record all those West Brom goals everyone was expecting."

With Albion leading at half-time, defeat looked the most likely outcome for the visitors. But only to those who weren't present. Ominously, Woking weren't playing badly. Buzaglo remembers his side were far from disappointed with their first-half show. Albion were feeble opposition. He continued: "Albion were very lucky to be one up. We had all the play and were the better side. They were just lumping the ball up to Colin West, hoping he would head it down to Gary Bannister. It was really basic stuff and we were coping with it well. Our play was so much better and we had one cleared off the line. They hit the post before that.

"But we were in a good mood at half-time and in a really confident place. Geoff was absolutely convinced we could still get something. He told us to keep passing the ball well, to keep it on the ground. We knew that was our best hope. There was no point sticking it into the air for me because I was short and up against Roberts and Strodder, who were going to keep heading it away. They were big guys, strong and powerful. The only way I was going to get around them was on the ground. And we knew their back four had no pace. We could do them in that respect and we had a fair bit of pace in the side, myself included."

Buzaglo's equaliser from Dereck Brown's through ball exposed Albion's centre-halves, who handed the keys to the Woking man to run through the centre unchallenged. "Buzaglo…who has caused Albion so many problems, scores. And Woking deserve it," exclaimed the Match of the Day commentator. His second goal came through his own perseverance. He collected the ball in the centre circle, peeled away from the static Robson, hurdled Roberts's clumsy challenge and lashed the ball at Rees. The shot was saved but the striker reacted quickly to head into an empty net.

The third – the completion of the no 10's hat-trick – came thanks to a brilliant, quick counter-attack inspired by midfielder Mark Biggins. His cross from the right wing found Adie Cowler, who laid it across to Buzaglo. 3-1. Terry Worsfeld made it four. All of Woking's goals came through incisive, neat football played on a patchy Hawthorns pitch. Albion were brutally rudimentary. Woking's third goal, for instance, had come from a desperate punt from Craig Shakespeare on the left. The ball was nodded down by Bannister into the feet of West. His first touch bounced to the feet of a Woking man. From there, the visitors exchanged a series of passes and dummies, with their movement not being tracked by Albion's runners. Talbot's side looked unfit, ragged and lacking fight. Several passes later, the game was over.

Darren Bradley pulled one back to make it 4-2. Yet, to the untrained eye, he might as well have scored it in front of another club's set of fans. A static Birmingham Road End didn't celebrate – footage on YouTube shows a crowd frozen, seemingly rooted through utter shock and delayed trauma. There was silence. And then came the jeers; the boos; the whistles; the boos; the heckles; the boos. A growing ripple of noise. None of it joyous. It was perhaps the only time a Baggies goal has been roundly dismissed. In all honesty, Albion might as well have lost 4-1, for Bradley's sake if nothing else.

Buzaglo, by now into the teeth of his money-can't-buy afternoon, struggled to grasp the utter farce around him. "It was totally surreal," he said. "Bradley pulled one back and got booed. I wondered whether it had been ruled out and the fans were booing the decision…but no, they were booing the goal. Our every touch and goal were being cheered. We had two pitch invasions, Roberts had to remove a couple of fans. We didn't want to leave the pitch at the end but the fans came on and we were moved off quickly. As I was about to go into the changing room, Geoff Chapple told me to go out and applaud the Albion fans. I said: 'Geoff, we've just beaten them and you want me to go down and applaud them? No chance. I'm not doing it on my own, that's for sure. You're coming with me.' And so out we went. I couldn't believe the reception. The fans were amazing. Those who came on to the pitch carried me off it, chanting: 'Sign him up'.

"There were no barriers or fences, so I was nervous that the West Brom fans might want to lynch me. They didn't. They weren't interested in that. They must have been hurting, angry, but they were amazing with me. I'll never forget that. The one thing I'll always say is that we weren't lucky. It wasn't a fortunate win – we outplayed, outfought and out-thought them in every way. And we weren't even the equivalent of a Conference side back then. We were below that. That made our win even more special in my view."

By 5pm, The Hawthorns was a rubber-necker's paradise, the scene of a major breaking story. By quirk, Albion's defeat meant they were the final remaining Football League club to succumb to a non-League club. Manchester United, Liverpool, Everton…all had fallen at some point. On this January afternoon, it was finally Albion's turn to lose to a club outside the 92. The Baggies were headline news for all the wrong reasons. In the absence of any shocks elsewhere, they were going to be headlining Match of the Day for the first time since Jimmy Hill was presenting the show in his pomp back in the 1970s. But not for any good reasons. This wasn't the publicity Albion fans had in mind.

Woking boss Chapple was forced to deliver his media obligations wearing a pair of borrowed shorts and t-shirt, Albion's laundry lady having kindly offered to dry his suit after he was thrown into the bath by celebrating players. Buzaglo wasn't given time to cut loose with his team-mates. "People who know me will be aware I'm a private person," he says. "I hated interviews and people making a fuss. I was just a non-League footballer who liked a game on Saturday and went back to working with computers on Monday.

"But, after that game, everything just went mad. I had people coming up to me saying I was to go on Match of the Day and I said: 'No way…get someone else to do it'. I had no chance. I was about to have a shower when I was sent straight to do Radio 5 at the top of the stand. I was freezing. It was January and there I was being interviewed in nothing more than a pair of shorts and my sodden shirt. I got back to the dressing room and was told to hurry up with the shower because the BBC car was already waiting for me. The rest of the lads went home on the coach and had a good time. Me? I was heading down to London with our coach, Fred Callaghan. I was whisked down to the studios and, actually, it was brilliant. Des Lynam was on with Trevor Brooking. It was the first time I'd ever been on TV. Thankfully, Des told me what the questions would be, which really helped. He was a charming guy."

Having started 1991 in anonymity, Buzaglo was thrust in front of the rolling cameras and waited for the questions. Back pages were devoted to his exploits, with most focusing on his achievements rather than the opponents' utter malaise and chaos. 'Woking Class Heroes' and 'Tiger Tim's Tricky Treat' were just two of the headlines. Before the game, Woking had been 5,000-1 to lift the FA Cup. Now they were the story of the competition. Only in the West Midlands media did the focus shift to Albion's deficiencies and failures. The Evening Mail, the Express & Star and BBC Radio WM were ready to draw blood.

For Buzaglo, gone was any semblance of privacy. It wasn't helped when Woking were drawn against Everton in the next round. Far from enjoying it, this unassuming individual found himself weighed down by being in demand – to the extent he had to go ex-directory. These were the days when people scoured public phone books to trace folks. There was no safe-house. Pursued at home, hounded at work, Buzaglo was sent home by his employers due to the number of calls to his company's switchboard. It gave him a brief insight into the life of a public figure – one he didn't relish. You could almost forgive him for wanting somebody else to score a winner against the Toffees in the fourth round. In the event, Everton, League champions just four years earlier, won 1-0 at Goodison Park, where an astonishing 10,000 Woking fans were present. Buzaglo's story was concluding as quickly as it had started.

"You have to remember I was just an amateur," he said. "I was a computer operator in Woking. For two or three weeks until Everton, my life was hell. I got to work on the Monday after the Albion game and someone had got hold of my work number and circulated it to the media. I was sent home because every second the phone rang. Someone had even given out my home number, so that didn't help. Nor did the fact I was the only 'T Buzaglo' in the phone book. It was interview after interview after interview. It was a team achievement but, because I scored three, I got the publicity. Those goals were fabulous but I don't think I stopped for weeks. Everyone wanted their bit of me.

"I hated the fuss. I could play football against anyone but it was the rest of it afterwards I didn't like. I wasn't used to the exposure. I started late as a player, when I was 25. I had offers from Northampton and Exeter but I was getting paid more for my work and what I was getting at Woking. By the time I played at The Hawthorns, I was nearly 30, so it was too late to turn pro. Had it happened a few years earlier, who knows..?"

Buzaglo's fame came at a further cost, albeit some time later. From the many post-match interviews he gave, he was to learn about the need for measured comment. His superiority on The Hawthorns pitch inevitably prompted questions about the decline of Graham Roberts, who had been assigned the task of marking the hat-trick man. Roberts, by then 32, had a successful career on his CV. FA Cup wins with Tottenham, SPL title success with Rangers and several England caps. Yet such was his performance against Buzaglo that his fitness and durability drew criticism and scrutiny. However, as poor as Roberts might have been on this mid-winter afternoon, his hearing and memory remained in fine working order, as Buzaglo was to find out.

Some years later, they were reunited during a non-League game and the one-time England man ensured he wasn't going to be humiliated again. "I remember putting my foot in it, big time," Buzaglo added. "What was funny is that I thought: 'Well, there's no way I'll play against him again'. So, in all the interviews, I said it became easy because Roberts wasn't very quick. That was a mistake. I had moved to Marlow and he went to Enfield, so you can guess what happened next. We ended up on the same pitch. I honestly hadn't realised the significance of it until just before the game. He saw me and shouted over: 'I heard what you said on the radio'. There's me thinking: 'Ah…he's recognised me then.' I got a good kicking from him in that game. I made sure I didn't say anything about him afterwards."

Injury saw to it that Buzaglo's career never again reached the heights of that 1990-91 season. He continued: "It says a lot about West Brom's spirit that none of the players really said anything to us after our win there. Why weren't they angry with each other, or at each other's throats? Their spirit wasn't right at all. They didn't say a word to me during that game, which is so strange. Maybe they were in shock, I don't know. It was a life-changing 45 minutes for me. My daughters are all in their 20s now. They love it when the FA Cup third round comes on because it means Dad will be on TV and I'm like: 'No, Dad will NOT be on TV'. I dread West Brom drawing Woking again because I know what will happen if they do. I did Football Focus in 2009 and my daughters loved it. When you've got a name like Buzaglo, they still get asked about it. When people say 'Woking', my name gets mentioned. I find it all a bit embarrassing unless they mean my brother, who also played for the club but unfortunately missed that West Brom game through injury. So I try to avoid all interviews if I can.

"I still, now and again, look at the goals on YouTube, but I avoid my interviews because I don't like them. In any case, that seems a lifetime away. That was then. Football has changed, The Hawthorns has changed…I still have those memories, but it's in the past. It was funny coming out of the dressing room before the game that day. I asked a ball boy what the score would be. He said: '5-0 to the Albion'. I never saw him after. I just hope West Brom don't draw Woking any time soon because it's my past. To be honest, I just found those couple of weeks an absolute bloody nightmare."

More than 14,500 supporters saw Albion's afternoon of embarrassment.

Their side was: Rees, Shakespeare, Roberts, Strodder, Harbey, Ford, Bradley, McNally, Robson, West, Bannister. The following days and weeks were to shape their short-term future. Away from the pitch, shareholders were already looking into reshaping the club's constitution. That was more of a long-term plan. The rebuild was under-way as key shareholders, directors and influencers looked to find a solution to end Albion's decay. Fans were hoping Woking would very much be the low point and it would be an upward curve from there. If only…

Craig Shakespeare

*"....We saw these fans carrying a coffin past the window with a photo
of Bobby attached – all the lads were sat there nudging each
other going: 'Bloody hell, look at that'. Bobby stood up and said:
'Right, lads, today we're going to walk to the ground'..."*

Summer, 2019 is as good a time as any to grab Craig Shakespeare. Last week, he was called in for jury service. Tomorrow, he flies off on holiday. Next week, he might well be in a new job. Such is the life of an out-of-work football coach.Shakespeare is hoping that, at some point, the phone will ring. He wants to go back to doing what he does best these days – working as a coach or manager. Ordinarily, he would be knee-deep in pre-season preparations, developing team shape or finessing those rough bits that need smoothing over before the real stuff starts. But not now. He switches his phone to silent during our meeting in Lichfield. Any missed calls will be checked afterwards.

Shakespeare has pretty much done the lot within the congested confines of the technical area. He had a lengthy spell as youth and first-team coach at Albion, stints at Hull and Everton, he was right-hand man to Claudio Ranieri at Leicester when they won the Premier League title in 2015-16 and he was a top-flight boss in his own right, not to mention having one-game stints as caretaker manager of Albion and assistant manager with England. "And we won both," he reminds me with a grin, adding that Crystal Palace and Slovakia were the opposition, just in case I'd forgotten. I hadn't – at least not the Palace bit. 'Shakey' has been a busy man.

I'm here to ask about work on the other side of the touchline for a man born and raised within a mile or so of Albion's current training ground just over the Great Barr/Walsall border. After joining the Baggies in 1989-90, he made 112 appearances and scored 12 times, playing predominantly in midfield or defensive roles. His excellent goal ratio owes much to him being a safe bet with penalties – six of his dozen came from the spot. A move from Walsall to

The Hawthorns had looked on the cards before Sheffield Wednesday, then managed by Ron Atkinson, moved in but his stay at Hillsborough lasted only 17 games before injuries set in.

He finally joined Albion for £275,000 on Brian Talbot's watch and his debut was in a 1-0 victory at Oxford, where he scored the winner. A week later came Albion's buoyant and spirited defeat to Villa in the FA Cup on his home debut. Yet it was another tie that he will be remembered for – the notorious home defeat 11 months later that was examined in detail in the last chapter. Yes, that one. His most vivid memories of the nightmare, though, are of the utter resignation of Albion's coaching staff.

"Walking back to the car after the Woking game was pretty scary," he says, with a hint of understatement. "Everything about that weekend I just tried to blot out. Whether the team selection was right, I don't know. But fans were banging on the windows baying for us. I just remember looking at Brian Talbot and Sam Allardyce and thinking: 'That's that then'. I was watching Sam and it's almost like he knew what was coming for them…and he was correct. Funny how things work out, isn't it? I ended up working with him when he was England boss some 25 years later, yet here I was watching him and Brian probably facing up to the sack."

Talbot left, Bobby Gould arrived. And while the former Coventry manager's name was above the door, Shakespeare enjoyed some of his more memorable times with Albion. "It was inevitable Brian would go," he added. "Bobby came in and all the fun started. I knew there was some animosity with the fans but I hadn't realised how bad it would get. They didn't appreciate the style of play he was associated with, so I can understand why they never took to him. Add relegation and some of the incidents during his time there and you start to build a picture...

"The emotions during the relegation period were horrible. It was an awful day when we went to Bristol Rovers. We heard this rumour that Leicester had conceded. It filtered around the dressing room but it wasn't true. The week or so leading up to it was a nightmare, too – we lost Simeon Hodson during training following a challenge with Gary Hackett. Bobby's team selection maybe wasn't right either. We kept drawing, which maybe made it worse. We were neither winning nor losing, plus it was a horrible pitch at Twerton Park, with the fans on top of us….a really awful experience.

Shakespeare continues: "But, actually, to play for Bobby was ok. He was a decent guy, genuine. And despite his reputation, he introduced a sport science programme, he introduced a sprint runner, he introduced eating together. But he had that stigma and fans never took to him. He was never accepted. The perception of him was as a long-ball man but he had some very good ideas and, early doors, he was keen to get the last few per-cent in terms of nutrition and fitness. On a personal level, he also made me captain, which was enjoyable. You tend to worry about your own performance but if you're in the team, you're happy. If you're not, you want someone to blame, rather than look within yourself. You see the manager as the reason you're not there, despite the fact it might be your own performances or training. I was playing as the central midfielder at the time and in a decent place."

Albion's failure to maintain their Third Division promotion push in the last third of 1991-92 was chipping away at Gould's reputation. Supporters had grudgingly accepted winning football, even if the quality wasn't the best. But once results started to slip away, the venom returned with a vengeance and several flashpoints culminated in the manager's dismissal. In a week in which the Fingerpost fanzine was banned by club officials for a 'blistering attack' on the board, Gould raised eyebrows by expressing a wish to re-sign Frank Sinclair. He had been sent off and subsequently banned for nine games following a clash of heads with referee Paul Alcock in Albion's 1-1 draw at Exeter – a game in which Shakespeare scored from the spot. Although video evidence showed the contact to be accidental, Sinclair was found guilty by the FA and also fined £600.

"I remember that incident," Shakespeare says. "Frank had come on loan from Chelsea and was athletic, no-nonsense. But it didn't end well for him with us. Other players tend to not get too involved in those incidents. Frank had made a mistake and was punished. It was unfortunate for us because he was clearly talented and eager to do well. And he went on to have a very good career."

It got worse for Albion. In February, they lost 2-1 at Bournemouth and tempers were fraying. Gould, upon hearing a commotion of angry away fans outside the dressing room window, investigated and confronted one Mick Coldicott, then asked him to deliver his thoughts to the squad. Shakespeare wasn't impressed. "I'd rather a manager let rip into us than allow the press or fans into the dressing room," he added. "Yet Bobby did both. He invited the press into the dressing room after one game, then he called the fan in. You lose some respect for the manager when he does that. As that guy came in, I remember him and Graham Roberts having a stand-up row. Graham Roberts... the nicest thing I could say is that he'd been there and done it, so the respect was there. But I always felt Graham was looking after Graham. I had no issues with him. He was a big-money signing under Brian. And, that day, he really wasn't impressed with a fan giving us a dressing-down. There is never going to be anything constructive to come from allowing a fan in. The players won't put up with that. It got sensationalised and I would rather the manager have a go at us, we maybe have a go back and we learn from it."

Coldicott remains a season ticket holder to this day. He recalls the bizarre incident with clarity: "I was stood outside with the lads moaning about another terrible performance. It was typical Albion humour, asking if Stuart Naylor would be catching the coach, because he hadn't caught anything during the game, that kind of thing. It was just fans being fans – my mates chatting away, moaning and fed up that we'd gone all that way to see us lose again.

"Bobby spotted us, came over and said: 'You've got something to say, have you? Well come and say it to the players.' So I did. Most of them just sat there in shock – Graham Roberts gave a bit back. Fair play to him, he shook my hand some time afterwards when the dust had settled and said it had been nothing personal. That's fair enough because it wasn't for me either. You've got to remember we'd spend most of the day getting there, taking time off work in some instances, spending loads of money and I felt the players weren't bothered. So Graham having a go back was fair enough. I didn't look for any of it but it quickly went mad. Malcolm Boyden on WM, Radio 606 or whatever it was called then, the local press...they all wanted to speak to me. That wasn't me. I just wanted to have my say about my club."

The following week, Albion hosted Torquay in a game clinched by Roy Hunter's only Baggies goal and scarred by homophobic chanting against visiting striker Justin Fashanu – an all-too-predictable response following the player's decision to come out as gay. The drama hadn't ended for Mick Coldicott. He was again granted an audience with Bobby Gould, albeit in the more serene landscape of the manager's office before the match. Evening Mail journalist Graham Hill was hauled off normal match-reporting duties to shadow Coldicott at what was the first match since Gould's bizarre access-all-areas decision.

Hill said: "My boss, Leon Hickman, told me to seek out Mick and stand with him – he thought it would be great to get his views from the terraces. I met him and it was still very toxic. Fans clearly weren't having Bobby Gould and the next thing I know, it's kicking off between supporters near us and the police. I'm there trying to take notes while fists are flying around me. After the game, I leave with Mick and we go our separate ways. A couple of days later, I get a call from the police bollocking me and saying: 'Do you realise the chaos you've caused?' I hadn't done anything, I was just there trying to do my job. Leon Hickman absolutely loved it. He thought it was a brilliant story. It was certainly one of the more interesting games I'd covered."

Yet it was Hill's Mail colleague, Steve Tudgay, who was of greater concern to Gould. He had described the Albion manager as 'eccentric' in one piece, leading to Gould blackballing him. The Mail reacted by leaving a white space at the top of the back page, with the words 'This is where the Albion story should have been' to symbolise the withdrawal of access. Gould had tried to foster an NFL-style access-all-areas environment, with local journalists bizarrely allowed to walk around the dressing room interviewing players the day before games, just moments after the team sheet had gone up. Frequently, they rubbed shoulders with those angry at being dropped from the side, so awkward and stilted answers often punctuated interviews.

Tudgay, however, remained unwelcome within Gould's circle – a clash that Shakespeare recalls. "I remember Steve Tudgay was an up-and-coming reporter and, as you might expect, he was keen to get on in the industry. You can't blame anyone for that. In the afternoons, we sometimes did yoga or pilates and Steve had been invited along. It was great in terms of stretching and so on. He got involved with us but he also had a job to do – to report what was happening. And what I would say is that if you'd said there was going to be a clash between Steve and Bobby, I'd have put a tenner on it – a reporter trying to make a name for himself versus a manager who's spiky... how do we think it's going to end? You didn't need to be a rocket scientist to work it out. It all got very messy."

In March 1992, the Sports Argus issued a damning feature on the state of play at The Hawthorns, featuring a tumultuous week of activity. Gould had that week suspended popular assistant boss Stuart Pearson and announced the sacking of physio John Macgowan, leading to a farcical situation where the club were hiring physios on a game-by-game basis. The same piece also mentioned former captain Steve Parkin's decision to hand in a transfer request, with future chairman and then director Trevor Summers stating 'Albion would be better off playing behind closed doors' rather than in front of their fans. Pearson's suspension was then converted into dismissal – despite initial reports of mediation – with Albion citing a 'lack of loyalty' to the manager. While all this was going on, the players and directors were in Gibraltar, where chairman John Silk hailed a 'tremendous' 4-0 victory over a local side, adding: "We'd win all the time if it wasn't for all the back-biting back home." Charming.

Over a hectic 23-day period in March and April, Albion didn't win once, drawing three and losing three. By the time they beat Preston 3-0 in the final home game of the season, it was too late. They then won 3-1 at Shrewsbury to finish seventh – a game more synonymous with supporters invading the pitch with a coffin, intended to depict the death throes of Gould's Baggies career. Shakespeare remembers a particularly hostile end-of-season dinner, hosted at Kings Club in Hamstead by Radio WM's Malcolm Boyden.

"Bobby came in for some fair criticism at times but also some that wasn't fair," said Shakespeare. "We went for our pre-match meal at Shrewsbury. We were sat by the hotel window and saw these fans carrying a coffin past with a photo of Bobby – all the lads were sat there nudging each other going: 'Bloody hell, look at that'. Bobby then stood up and said: 'Right, lads, today we're going to walk to the ground, we're not going on the coach'. When we asked: 'Gaffer, have you seen that outside?', he said: 'Yes…we're walking'. He was willing to front it up. So we walked the 15 minutes to the stadium, passing these coffins.

"The away fans were terrific in terms of numbers but I remember they ripped the goal down that day. We won and there was talk of Bobby losing his job. Anyway, we went to the Kings Club with our wives and girlfriends. Bobby was very protective that night. We'd had stick and I get that because we'd been crap for parts of the season and the fans weren't happy with Bobby. But then Malcolm Boyden proceeded to tell jokes that, obviously, Bobby didn't agree with or like. He then started on players, so Bobby stood up and asked us straight: 'Are we listening to this?' So we all got up and left. I felt for the fans as it was their night but Bobby was protecting us, especially in front of our other halves. He took us to the pub, bought us all a drink and apologised, although he hadn't really done anything wrong.

"Mind you, he did some odd things, too. At one point, he put us all on the transfer list. None of us actually left, yet he then never ever called us back in either to remove us from that 'list'… so we kept thinking we might get sold any time. West Brom was never a straightforward club."

Off the field, Albion are being strongly linked with a 'mystery bidder'. A 45-year-old multi-millionaire is in discussions about buying the stake belonging to Jersey-based John Hill, which would immediately make him a majority shareholder. Of the 450-plus shares at the time, 332 were owned by single shareholders. Mr Hill owned 66, with the Everiss family having 26. Albion's constitutional structure had not been updated since the mid-1970s when Sir Bert Millichip, whose family owned 13 shares themselves, was chairman. In short, the club's constitution was unfit for purpose.

Albion's status as a public limited company, along with the share structure, meant they were restricted to a maximum overdraft facility of £500,000 – offering little incentive to a multi-millionaire interested in taking charge. Nevertheless, boardroom changes were afoot. John Silk stood aside as chairman, paving the way for Trevor Summers, who owned a shed business in West Bromwich and became affectionately known as 'Trev The Shed'. He was proud to take over the governance of his beloved club. "My mom can't believe it," he told the local media. "She said she never knew a little ball of cotton wool could cause so much trouble."

Described by the Sports Argus as an 'outspoken shed tycoon', Summers was not the favoured candidate among many shareholders, with Mike McGinnity, who was to become a Coventry City chairman during their Premier League stay, deemed more suitable. Yet the strident Summers was robust from the off. "I know my promotion to chairman will not go down well in all quarters of West Bromwich and the Midlands…but I want to get on with the business of putting Albion back in the big time," he said. His next decision proved more popular, with Ossie Ardiles sworn in as Gould's replacement.

The Argentinian brought fresh ideas, new impetus and left a lasting impression on Craig Shakespeare. The style of football was eye-catching. This was an era in which percentages concentrated less on dominance of possession and more about getting the ball down the field quickly. Ardiles was the absolute antithesis of that, bringing an elegance not seen at The Hawthorns since the late 1970s.

Albion introduced a barcode shirt which, while of its time, is now regarded as a modern-day classic, possibly because of its quirky nature, but perhaps also due to the fond memories of the panache of that side. It was a team Albion fans could finally have an affinity with. On the opening day, Albion rolled over Blackpool 3-1 in front of more than 16,500 – some 5,000 up on the final home game of the previous season. The side looked the business.

Players were arriving, not just for career progression, but because of the attraction of the manager; a man of gravitas and international repute. Simon Garner, then Blackburn's record scorer and Ardiles's former team-mate at Ewood Park, was one of the first in, with Ian Hamilton and Steve Lilwall bringing craft to midfield and defence respectively. Others of varying experience – but all of football pedigree – checked in. Signing permanently during the season were Kevin Donovan, Nicky Reid and Micky Mellon. Loanees included experienced campaigners Luther Blissett, Alan Dickens and David Speedie. Andy Hunt also signed on loan initially and injected plenty of firepower during a spell in which Albion were beginning to look weary. His fine record of 11 goals in 13 games ensured his permanent move from Newcastle for £100,000.

Shakespeare was impressed by the shift of dynamic. "Ossie was totally different. It was a big coup for the club. Ossie was about the shape and playing through midfield. We made some good signings like Simon Garner. He was definitely a players' manager for all of us. You'd come into training knowing you'd enjoy the sessions, enjoy listening to Ossie. If you won 5-4, he'd be delighted while Keith Burkinshaw would be behind him trying to remind us about our shape. It wasn't just the football. Ossie brought a real excitement to the place."

Shakespeare has had an enviable career as a Premier League coach since swapping his boots for an initialled tracksuit. He looks back at his time with Albion through the eyes of a tactician, not just a former player. At a time in which third-tier clubs were more likely to adopt pragmatic hammer-and-nails football, Ardiles was happy to leave the taps running in every single room, with little thought for the consequences. He just assumed somebody, somewhere, would mop up any spillages. Sometimes they did, sometimes they didn't. Albion lost 5-2 at home to Plymouth and 5-1 at Stockport. But, more often than not, they won. And won handsomely.

They lined up with two orthodox central defenders and full-backs with the ability to produce moments of potency. Left-back Lilwall had previously been a left-winger at Kidderminster, while, at right-back, the experienced Wayne Fereday (also a former winger) or veteran Nicky Reid, were given the same licence to attack. The midfield diamond was effectively a 1-2-1, with an anchor man supported by two playing narrow (Hamilton and Bernard McNally, or Mellon, for instance) and a conventional no 10 (typically Gary Robson initially, followed by Donovan) behind the two strikers, Bob Taylor and Garner, and later Hunt. Providing the width were the full-backs, with a big onus on the deepest midfielder to prop up the two centre-halves (generally any two from Gary Strodder, Paul Raven and Daryl Burgess). It is of some significance that wingers Carl Heggs and Gary Hackett, players of pace and no little ability – one of whom could easily have been regular fixtures in any other system – were afforded so few opportunities in the starting XI simply due to their instinctive nature to drift out wide. Both had to make do with regular spots on the bench. This wasn't a team for wingers.

"The shape we used caused teams problems because nobody – certainly at that level – was used to coming up against that system," said Shakespeare. "We'd have full-backs high up, which meant the central defenders would be banking on the deepest midfielder tucking in. The movement and rotation of teams nowadays in the Premier League…well, we were doing it back then. Players make a system work. But you also need that licence from a manager to say: 'This is our style, this is what we're doing'. Ossie did that with us. He not only had the confidence in his own principles and convictions. He had the belief in us as players. And there is no better feeling as a player than to have that from your coach. It gives you an immense energy and confidence.

"I'm of the view that if a team stops you from playing a certain way, you need to find another way but we managed well that year without doing so. We were really well-drilled into roles and responsibilities. I know people said Ossie was quite attacking and, yes, he was, but he and Keith made sure all of us –

especially those of us in midfield – were disciplined in our roles. We had to be to make it work. As a no 6 as we'd now call him – in front of the defence – I was told that if the centre-halves split, I had to try to get the ball and play the strikers into space. So we could play through midfield, or have myself or Darren Bradley putting the ball into space for the strikers. There was nothing wrong with me putting the ball into the feet of Andy Hunt or Bob Taylor running behind because if it took one ball instead of six, fine, but you had the licence and shape to cause the other teams problems if you needed to keep the ball that little bit longer. It enabled us to change the pace of our play and the intensity. You could keep the ball far better. Not only were we good in those roles, we had players who could adapt and players who worked their nuts off for a manager they respected."

Shakespeare started the season as the 'anchor', straddling the area in front of his defence. Albion won seven of their opening nine games, scoring three in a match four times. Sadly, an injury was to ruin his season. Following the 2-1 defeat at Burnley on the opening day of October, he was to make just three more starts and one appearance off the bench. His place was taken by Darren Bradley, who assumed the same role and was also asked to take over as captain. "I never recovered from that heel injury," Shakespeare added. "I was out of form because I wasn't comfortable playing with the problem. Ossie and I had some disagreements, too, but I always had respect for him because he was trying to get us up and was trying to get us up playing the right way.

"The disagreements were never personal as such. They were more about me coming to terms with loss of form, not having a place in the team and being injured. It was like a growth under my heel. I couldn't wear boots, I was struggling to jog and run. It was horrible. They sent me to Cyprus for several days at Christmas, having been someone who had played 46 games a season previously. I just couldn't come to terms with it. I was trying to get back to fitness yet it felt like I was being judged. I just couldn't get going again – it was a hindrance. I was part of the squad for the play-off final but never got into the 13, as it was then. That was hard because I'd been there for the beginning.

"I appreciate now as a coach that you often have to make tough decisions for the good of the side. But you are easily forgotten as a footballer – or at least that's how it seems. As an individual, you think of yourself but actually it's about the team. You understand, with hindsight, that the players are performing better and he was right."

Garner, who went on for Hunt, was the only substitute used by Ardiles at Wembley. Surprisingly, the boss didn't give Robson a run-out, although the midfielder was due to leave on a free transfer for Bradford soon after. There was no sentimentality on Ardiles's part. "I couldn't believe Gary didn't get on when we were two or three up," said Shakespeare. "He was a great servant. I had spoken to the press before the game and I was pleased for Gary when we found out he'd be involved because he was a stalwart – a good lad who deserved to be part of it. I knew why he'd chosen Gary because it was basically me or him and Ossie will have his reasons for not putting him on. I kept thinking he would put him on... but he never did.

"I was delighted for the lads but on the coach afterwards, I didn't feel the same. I didn't get involved with the civic parade because I didn't feel part of it. I felt out of it completely. I knew I wouldn't be staying, so I stayed low-key and let the lads enjoy it."

Shakespeare is already in holiday mode as he shares with me his plans for the coming days. In the meantime, we haven't quite finished talking Albion. "It was up and down, I guess," he added. "I would have preferred it to have been more balanced. But it shaped me as a player and person. I had the down times of Woking and Bristol. The pinnacle of my career would have been to captain the team at Wembley but injury and loss of form cost me that. But it was a club I knew. I grew up in Great Barr – I lived around the corner from the Scott Arms.

"I remember first playing at The Hawthorns – it was in a youth game before the Ray Wilson testimonial in the mid-1970s – and being shocked at how far away the goals were from the corner flag. Fifteen years later, I was back as a player. I've got fond memories. We had some good lads. The one I remember was Steve Lilwall – he was a great character. He never looked like a footballer, never walked like a footballer, but he was great value. I remember he came in the once and said: 'I've lost my tortoise'. We were like: 'What? Tortoise, what tortoise?' He was adamant this pet had been stolen, so we were trying to convince him to put an advert in the paper. And every morning he'd give us an update, basically saying there was no sign of it. Then, months later, he came in and told us: 'I've found it' ... it had been bloody hibernating in his shed. He was a good lad, very well liked – not sure I'd have him looking after my pets, though.

"I had fond memories of Bruiser, Stuart Naylor. Christ, he could moan! He got a 'Moaner of the Year' t-shirt at one end-of-season do and he really wasn't impressed. But he was a good goalkeeper. And Simon Garner. After one game, I remember thinking: 'What's that smell?' There was smoke coming from the toilet – he was in the cubicle having a fag. I remember saying: 'Simon, you're one of the best goalscorers in English football' …which he was… 'did you ever think you might get another five if you didn't smoke?' He just smiled – half his teeth were missing – and carried on smoking. He liked a pint or two as well, come to think of it. Yet on the pitch he was brilliant and scored some big goals. He really was a big player for us in that season.

"It didn't end for me how I would have liked and I left on a free after Wembley, having started the season as captain. But I made some great friends along the way. And obviously I then returned to the club and had many more good times. It's a club I've had a long affinity with over the years and one I'm still very fond of."

Ossie Ardiles

"...I would tell them: 'Attack, attack, attack'... The players grow in confidence,
they become bigger footballers...Some of the things they had been told
before I arrived: 'Kick it long, hit it to the corner'.
That is your manager saying: 'You are not good enough'"

Sir Bobby Charlton sighs. He shakes his head, picks up his pen and strikes a line through Ossie Ardiles's name. The Argentinian was supposed to be one of several former footballers meeting for an annual golf day. Not anymore. He has another pressing engagement. The Bobby Charlton Golf Day will have to make do without him. Instead of teeing off at Formby, Ardiles would be heading down the M6 and M5. Destination West Bromwich. A job interview awaits.

March, 2020. Osvaldo Ardiles is on lockdown. We all are. The wretched Covid-19 pandemic has forced us into unprecedented peacetime territory. These are frightening times. Ardiles is okay. He says he is in good health and is more than pleased to chat about happier times some three decades ago. We all need happier times. Thankfully, one particular season springs to mind. Much like football in 2020 seems to have struck an era-defining milestone, Ardiles turned up on Albion's doorstep at the apex of a monumental shift in the landscape.

The 1992-93 season was the first of a restructured English province. Gone was the 92-club Football League. Replacing it was a League of 70 clubs, with 22 shifting to a new competition. The breakaway had been discussed for years but it wasn't until 1990 that talks were accelerated when Greg Dyke, managing director of ITV's London Weekend Television, met representatives from the big five (Manchester United, Liverpool, Everton, Tottenham and Arsenal). Football's elite were seeking a greater share of TV rights money to help compete against Italy's Serie A powerhouses and help with the necessity of bringing stadia up to the requirements of the Taylor Report post-Hillsborough.

It happened. There were handshakes. The meeting closed with a decision that would change the English game forever. The big five bought into Dyke's idea and began the process of change. Two years later, England's top-division clubs resigned from the League immediately and joined the newly-formed FA Premier League. Although Dyke had played a significant role in the creation of the new format, ITV would lose out in the bidding for broadcast rights. BSkyB won with a bid of £304m over five years, with the BBC awarded the highlights package on Match of the Day. The previous deal with ITV had been worth only £44m, with the leading clubs claiming three quarters of that pot. These were clearly going to be lucrative times for the top flight.

BSkyB's bid crept over the line thanks to a last-ditch call to the TV giant's representatives by Tottenham's newly-installed chairman, Alan Sugar. ITV offered £205m for the rights and later went up to £262m but were outbid by Rupert Murdoch, who saw the chance to lure new customers to a loss-making satellite service. It was during this process that Trevor East, head of ITV's football broadcasting, overheard Sugar telling Murdoch on the phone to 'blow them out of the water'. That Sugar's Amstrad computer company had just branched out into the production of satellite dish transmitters was probably no coincidence but, with no challenge forthcoming, BSkyB's pitch prevailed. Sugar was the only one of the top-five chairmen to vote for their bid. The computer mogul soon took over Tottenham – a move that had significance in the Black Country several months later.

New Baggies chairman Trevor Summers, meanwhile, wanted a piece of the action. "We need to be back in this Super League as soon as possible," he said. "To play the likes of Manchester United and Tottenham, like we used to when we were at the top of the First Division, has to be our aim. I hope it won't be too long, for everyone's sake. We have to find a way to be part of it." So far, so good but first came the small matter of sourcing Bobby Gould's successor. While Premier League fever grew during May, 1992, Albion were still manager-less.

Effectively, it was a shortlist of two, with Ardiles as first choice and Wycombe's impressive young boss, Martin O'Neill, as the fall-back option. The Sports Argus mentioned Grimsby's Alan Buckley while Bruce Rioch was also linked, the former Middlesbrough and future Arsenal boss ending up at Bolton. Ardiles's credentials were impressive, befitting of a manager wanted by a club chasing the Premier League dream. A World Cup winner with Argentina in 1978, he moved to Tottenham that summer and became the darling of White Hart Lane, barring a brief secondment to Paris Saint-Germain during the Falklands conflict. He then led Swindon to promotion to the top flight, only for the club to be demoted due to financial irregularities from before his time there. His spell at Newcastle was less successful but his commitment to attacking football made him an attractive prospect for Summers. And, crucially, he was available.

The appointment was a masterstroke, not least as Albion secured him on a salary of just £50,000, compared with his £120,000 annual wage at Newcastle. Again, it was Albion's good fortune that Ardiles was tied into a deal with the Tynesiders that ensured he was still being paid by them for 12 months after his exit. That arrangement propped up the Baggies wages of a celebrated football personality who was also an FA Cup winner and recognised as an elegant, stylish midfielder when pitched into the battleground of mid-80s English football. He had even appeared alongside Pele, Sylvester Stallone and Bobby Moore in the Hollywood movie, Escape to Victory.

Ardiles, be it the footballer, World Cup winner or film star, was the most unlikely saviour. By 1992, Albion had let themselves go, yet here they were flirting with a legend. This was one hell of a coup. Ardiles reveals that he was convinced by Summers's ambitions for the club, rather than the financial package. "I remember it was a Tuesday and I'd agreed to play in the Bobby Charlton golf day on the Wednesday," he said. "I received a phone call from Mr Summers asking whether I'd be interested. I said: 'Yes, of course.' So I didn't play in the golf and went to see him. I had the impression there was nobody else in the picture and I got the job. But, before I met him, I felt it would be a good job for me, so I already knew in my heart I would be accepting. West Bromwich was a big club even then. I had a bad time at Newcastle and appreciated that I may not get a job in the top division. West Bromwich was a big challenge for me. It should not have been in the Third Division, so I jumped into it. I had this feeling I would love it.

"It wasn't the West Bromwich I had remembered. I was used to playing against Bryan Robson, Laurie Cunningham, Cyrille Regis – an outstanding team. They were in this ridiculous position. From their point of view and mine, I knew it would work. Our meeting at the stadium lasted no more than an hour and they told me before lunch they wanted me. It was all very quick. They didn't need to sell the club to me. I knew what Albion was."

The period leading up to the appointment was some week. On the Monday, Albion convened an emergency board meeting to discuss Gould's future. On Tuesday, they announced his sacking, the resignation of chairman Tony Hale and the installation of Summers as his successor – all delivered by fax to key stakeholders, including the media. Gould used his departure to settle old scores with the press: "I would like the people who write about the game so much, Mr (Leon) Hickman, Mr (Steve) Tudgay [both of the Evening Mail] and Mr (Malcolm) Boyden [Radio WM presenter] to have a go at the manager's job because it's not as easy as it looks." The claws were out. With a swift volley, a Sports Argus comment piece returned with a dig both at Gould and rival publication, the Express & Star, who had pushed for his appointment back in 1991. It read: "So now we know. The man who landed the job on the back of a CV written up under the guidance of a Wolverhampton newspaper, blames his eventual demise at their media rivals." Thankfully, silly season was soon over.

On the Friday, Ardiles was unveiled and said: "I wouldn't have joined any other Third Division club. This is a club where we can achieve success." Albion fans finally had something to grab on to. Summers described the manager's availability as the 'biggest stroke of luck I've ever had, or am ever likely to have, in football.' Ardiles's first objective was to rid the club of the lingering, toxic stench of the Gould regime. Fans were desperate to leave behind the coffins of Shrewsbury for some Champagne football. Perhaps now, they had the man to provide that change.

Away from West Bromwich, Italia 90 felt like a seminal moment in English football – the chance to wave off the desperate, tragic 1980s. Yet it wasn't until the inaugural Premier League season that the game felt ready to embrace change. Those opening two years of the decade felt like a holding period between a declining sport rediscovering itself following the horrors of the previous ten years, and one imposing itself on a new audience fit for the 21st century. It wasn't until the first Premier League campaign, in 1992-93, that it felt like the 1990s really arrived in English football.

Significantly, it felt like Albion had checked into a new era, too. The end of one epoch, the beginning of another. Baggies fans could finally draw a curtain across the latter half of the 1980s. The club had been in decline for years and descended deeper in the Gould era. Ardiles emerged not only as a quick fix but also as potential scaffolding to help build a brighter, more structured future. By appointing him, Albion seemed to be surfing a wave towards a new culture, a progressive outlook that might, just might, see them pushing for a place in what Summers insisted on calling the Super League. He had barely been in the chair for two days, yet he was already earning praise for his bombastic, strident approach. Fans now seemingly had a chairman who was not only on their wavelength in terms of ambition, but also spoke like them. Here was a shed mogul who had attracted Osvaldo Ardiles to a third-tier club.

Staff and players were still needed. Keith Burkinshaw arrived as assistant manager, with former Tottenham right-back Danny Thomas checking in as physio. Burkinshaw was an intriguing addition. The Yorkshireman, 17 years older than his boss, had been successful in his own right as Spurs manager and was the man who had brought Ardiles and compatriot Ricardo Villa to England, en route to winning successive FA Cups and a UEFA Cup. Ardiles felt his former mentor would be the ideal man to have alongside him. He also thinks the energy and chemistry was exactly right. The perception was of a union of warmth but Ardiles now claims the two frequently clashed despite a clear mutual respect.

"I knew Keith would be a good assistant," said Ardiles. "He is much more… how can I put it? He is much more down-to-earth than me in terms of football. I am the one that flies around in the air too much. I would often think about things and Keith would try to bring me back down. I am flying away and Keith is chasing after me, trying to stop me! Sometimes I can be too ideological. I was a football purist. I wanted football played one way and one way only. Keith would calm me down. That was brilliant. But I only say that now. He would always make his position clear and we had many clashes – many, many clashes. I wasn't always happy with him and sometimes he wasn't happy with me. But I didn't want to compromise. Keith said we needed to – I said I wouldn't do that. I won the argument but maybe I should have listened to him more."

On the pitch, Ardiles needed to make vast changes. And quickly. Around a dozen players were out of contract. Arriving were Simon Garner, Ian Hamilton and Steve Lilwall, joined in the autumn by Kevin Donovan. Ardiles recalls that period of manic activity: "Ian Hamilton was Keith Burkinshaw's idea. He had seen him and liked him. I saw him and straightaway I liked him. I knew he was for us. He was very talented. I thought he could have played higher. Then there was another player – I'm not going to name him. Ronnie Allen was the chief scout at the time. He was telling me about this wonderful player. I went to watch and he was terrible. Keith and me were sat there and this player wasn't for me…but then I saw another footballer. That was Kevin Donovan. I liked him straightaway. Keith wasn't sure and I said: 'Keith, are you sure? He is a wonderful, beautiful player.' I knew immediately. We got him for very little and Kevin did so well for us.

"Simon Garner… yes, he was a different personality. He was experienced, knew the game and was Blackburn's record goalscorer, a wonderful footballer. I played with him at Blackburn for two or three months, so I knew he would score goals. He did very well." Garner was a throwback to a different era. He would remove his front teeth before games, he drank pints and often went walkabout during pre-match preparation. So often, Ardiles and Burkinshaw would deliver team talks and find themselves a man down. At which point tobacco smoke would drift across the dressing room…..

"Simon…he made me smile. Often before matches or at half-time, we could smell smoke but didn't always see it," Ardiles laughed. "I didn't really want to know or care about that because I knew he could play and score. Then there was the left-back, Lilwall. He was so cheap, it was as if they (Kidderminster) had paid us to have him. He was brilliant. One of the most honest players I have ever had. A very hard-working, lovely guy. He was the kind of footballer I want. He played it on the floor, he played with heart – I really liked Steve Lilwall. He had an instinct of when to attack and when to defend. That isn't easy. For me, he worked brilliantly. He had that balance."

Hamilton signed on the same day as Lilwall and remembers with fondness the way his transfer from Scunthorpe unfolded. As a White Hart Lane regular, albeit as an Arsenal fan, he saw it as a huge selling point when he discovered that two Spurs legends wanted him. As was the lure of leaving behind a perennial lower-League club for one in the advent of building for the future. "I went on holiday and returned to find a letter from Scunthorpe," said Hamilton. "We didn't have mobiles then and there was no way of getting hold of me because I was out of the country. The letter said Scunthorpe had accepted an offer from Albion of £175,000. I remember being sat there, reading in disbelief. I managed to get hold of our assistant manager, Bill Green. I told him I wanted to move and he drove down with me to West Brom as a kind of agent. Keith had been watching me for Swindon when he was scouting for Glenn Hoddle. I walked into The Hawthorns and that was it – I was as good as an Albion player.

"In Stevenage, you're either Arsenal or Spurs. I was Arsenal but my mate was Spurs and we used to get free tickets, so I'd often end up on the Shelf terrace watching Ossie, Glenn Hoddle, Ricardo Villa and, of course, Keith as the boss. The money was ok, too. I didn't even question it. I got in the region of £750 a week, which included a signing-on fee of about £11,000 up front and a further £11,000 after six months. I agreed a three-year deal and was told I'd get a new contract if I did well after a few months – which Ossie honoured. They even paid for the insurance for my Golf GTi. Being a young lad, that saved me a fortune. And, being a central midfielder, I cannot tell you what it feels like to hear that someone like Ossie Ardiles wants you to play that role for him. It was like a dream."

In many ways, Hamilton was to showcase Ardiles's love for football, becoming an important fulcrum of the side – capable of carrying the ball from the back to the front. Ardiles rebuilt the club on and off the pitch, including seeing off a fitness coach who wanted the players to run, run and run some more, with no emphasis on ball work. He didn't make it beyond the second day of pre-season. There was also a need to change the style of play. Albion's modus operandi under Gould had been rudimentary, reliant on percentages – getting the ball into the corners and crossing, with the aim of a tall striker heading it in. That wasn't Ardiles. Albion players were to play on the front foot, with confidence and, crucially, to play it on the ground.

"The day I walked in, I changed everything," Ardiles continued. "It was immediate and had to be immediate. I arrived and told them we would not play long balls into the wings. We were going to play every single ball on the ground. That long football is not football. I wasn't prepared to have my team playing that horrible way. They understood very quickly. I would tell them: 'Everything is with the ball. Pass it, pass it, pass it. Attack, attack, attack. And attack, pass, pass, attack, pass, attack.' I had to do the same at Swindon. When you allow your footballers to do that, they become better players and start to believe they are better players. They grow in confidence, they become bigger footballers when you make them think they are good footballers and attack teams. Some of the things they had been told before I arrived: 'Kick it long, hit it to the corner'. That is your manager saying: 'You are not good enough'. I wanted my players to think they were good enough, to think they were the best. Defenders, midfielders…everyone. My players came in early and didn't want to go home after training. We enjoyed it that much."

He admitted the culture between the club and supporters also needed to change. "Everyone seemed to be at war – the management, the board, the players, the supporters, the media. The players were afraid to go out and play. They knew that if they made a mistake, the crowd would go mad. And I discovered they even fined players at one time for missing penalties. Can you imagine the pressure the next player would have? I said that the problem with English football was that winning was all-important. It could have been the best in the world if there was more emphasis on technique. We had a good squad there and I had every confidence we could play well…and win."

Albion began the season by convincingly beating Blackpool and won seven of their opening nine games, lining up with a back four and a front two. In between, in a narrow diamond, were a defensive midfielder, two central midfielders and an attacking one, tucked in just behind the strikers. There were no wingers, with full-backs Lilwall and Wayne Fereday encouraged to attack. The centre-halves were also urged to do so – some three decades before Chris Wilder was telling his own central defenders (albeit in a different formation) to do the same. The system meant one unfortunate outfielder would have to take one for the team. Enter captain Darren Bradley, Ardiles's insurance policy. Yet the manager claims his favoured formation was due to personnel, not down to his own philosophies.

"The diamond was because of what we had," he added. "I didn't think at that time we had any wide players who made us better, so I chose a system using the players I had. And I signed players for that system. We didn't have much money, so I had to make do with what I could get for the value. I didn't have normal wide players. I relied on the right-back and left-back attacking a lot. People think I invented this at West Brom. I didn't. I had used it before at Swindon and I didn't even think the 'diamond' was the best system in the world. Not at all. It was because my players suited that. Kevin Donovan, for example, was made for that no 10 position. He did that well. Ian Hamilton was a clever player. Darren Bradley was my insurance. Everyone was allowed to go forwards: the right-back, the left-back, even the centre-backs. But not Bradley. Bradley made sure we had someone there for insurance. He was a very good captain. He had to be."

By mid-season, Albion were promotion challengers but increasingly inconsistent. Of 13 games between the first weekend of October and New Year, they won only four. Teams were finding a way to combat their free-flowing style. Bob Taylor led the way by scoring 12 times in the League by the season's mid-point and would go on to score 30 in the 46 games – the first Albion man to do so since Tony Brown in 1970-71. Ardiles offers an interesting take on Taylor's return during the first half of the season…..

"Bob could play in any system and he scored goals," he said. "But I thought he was one of the most reluctant with the way we wanted to play, not because he didn't enjoy it but because he had done well before I joined. Perhaps he felt he wouldn't have the same impact. I don't know. But I have to say he was so in love with it by the end that he was one of the best footballers I worked with. He became a much better player for it. Before, he would score goals and maybe no more. But during that season, wow! He suddenly became this lovely footballer and got better and better. I really thought he was made for the system whereas at first I did wonder if he would be able to adapt. Every player while I was there seemed to enjoy training. They knew they would improve and we were playing well. It was a happy team."

Off the field, Albion had a new majority shareholder. Graham Waldron had bought out Jersey-based John Hill's 14 per cent block for £250,000. His proposal was to install a chief executive to work alongside Trevor Summers. The candidate he had in mind was former Albion right-back and PFA assistant secretary Brendon Batson. The idea was supported by the club's long-time secretary and former director, Alan Everiss, who told the Sports Argus: "Most successful companies in Britain today have a chairman and a chief executive. I would support this move." The proposal never materialised. It wasn't until 1997 that Albion installed a former player, John Wile, as chief executive, although Batson did eventually join the club in an administrative role when he arrived in 2002 as managing director.

Waldron was trying to force Albion to revamp their financial structure in time for summer, 1993, regardless of whether promotion was achieved. Across the city, Birmingham had spent £700,000 bringing in new blood to boost their own second-tier survival prospects while Albion had pegged their transfer budget at a modest £100,000, which ended Ardiles's pursuit of Villa right-back Dariusz Kubicki. Waldron's plan, as revealed by the Express & Star, was to create an issue of an additional 495 shares at around £1,000 each, raising an immediate £500,000. His words fell on deaf ears. Albion's board had ignored the calls in the autumn of 1992 and were in no mood to change their mind. The Redditch-based millionaire said: "I'm convinced we could have found the bidders for 495 shares, with in-built safeguards against a one-man takeover if necessary, and raised half a million pounds overnight. We could have had this settled by now if the board had taken up this idea four months ago. It wouldn't make a scrap of difference even if we were whistling away ten points clear at the top."

Albion certainly weren't ten points clear. By March 10, they were lagging behind in fifth spot, having lost four of their last seven games. Ardiles had tried to revive his squad with the few resources he had available. Nicky Reid was brought in from Blackburn, with Luther Blissett, David Speedie and Alan Dickens making 12 appearances between them on loan – and totalling three goals (Speedie two, Blissett one). Micky Mellon was signed for £75,000 from Bristol City to add steel to the midfield. Wayne Fereday, a right-winger used as a full-back by Ardiles, was struggling with injury, so Bernie McNally and Reid filled the no 2 shirt at various periods. Mellon's arrival at least allowed Ardiles the luxury of pitching McNally into that defensive role.

Yet results were still nowhere near the levels of those opening two months. In the final days of March, Ardiles tried to sign Middlesbrough striker Bernie Slaven, who eventually joined promotion rivals Port Vale. But Ardiles made one last signing that was to define Albion's season and his own future. Andy Hunt had played for him at Newcastle and while Albion couldn't afford the £100,000 transfer fee, the Magpies allowed him to leave on loan. "We needed quality," the manager added. "I was always reluctant to sign players on loan because they don't tend to commit in games. But they did ok. And then there was Andy Hunt. Wow! Now he was a really bright footballer, with pace and technique. With him in the team, I knew we wouldn't need anyone else. He wasn't that sharp when he arrived but he got fitter and was ideal for us. He made a huge difference and it was reflected by results."

Indeed it was. Hunt scored nine goals in the final ten League games, with strike partner Taylor contributing ten of his own over the same period. Albion finished fourth, earning themselves a play-off semi-final against Swansea. Crucially, they were in form. Taylor wasn't to score another goal that spring, yet his overall contribution was a defining factor to the club's success while Hunt seized the moment goals-wise.

Ardiles was confident, although a poor display brought a 2-1 defeat at Vetch Field in the first leg before Hunt and Hamilton ensured Albion's aggregate victory and trip to Wembley. "I was very confident as soon as we made the play-offs," the manager added. "There was a belief in the team we were not only going to get to the final, but win it. I knew we would do it. I think the players did. I wanted my players to enjoy themselves. And the atmosphere at West Bromwich was the best. Wembley was even better but as far as our own stadium was concerned, Swansea was amazing."

Hamilton, scorer of Albion's second goal, has only fond memories of that semi-final and also remembers it for domestic reasons. He reckons the outcome saved him a fortune, courtesy of Colin West's sending-off following Micky Mellon's earlier dismissal. "We were shit in that first game – utter garbage," he said. "So I knew we needed something big. But we controlled that second game. I took the ball into the box, which was nose-bleed territory for me, and as Des Lyttle came flying at me, I just cut inside him, carried on running and smashed it in. It was brilliant. The whole place went absolutely mental."

He continued: "Anyway, I had a problem. Micky was sent off and it was all getting a bit tasty, then Westy gets sent off after stamping on my chest. He had a lovely big house in Shenstone and was going to do me a dea. We'd even spoken about it before the game but I never heard from him again. I have him to thank for saving me a few grand. There I was wondering where I was going to live when suddenly I heard from Carlton Palmer via Craig Shakespeare. They lived by each other in Lichfield and Carlton was happy for me to live in his place while he played for Sheffield Wednesday. So I accepted it and had a lovely gaff. This was before direct debits. I was wanting to pay him cash into his bank account, kept calling him but could never get hold of him. It was a five-bedroom house and I was living there for a year rent-free. So, yeah, I did okay from that semi-final. From buying Colin West's house, I ended up living rent-free in a nicer, bigger house in Lichfield."

For Ardiles, it meant another return to the twin towers. He had experienced mixed fortunes at Wembley, where his first final came in the 1981 FA Cup and he charmed his way into the competition's folklore with a one-line contribution to Chas and Dave's FA Cup song 'Ossie's Dream (Spurs are on their way to Wembley)'. Tottenham beat Manchester City 3-2 at the second attempt, thanks to a stunning solo goal by Ricky Villa. Ardiles was on the losing side in the 1982 League Cup final against Liverpool, though, before missing the FA Cup final the same season after returning to Argentina early to prepare for the World Cup at a time when the Falklands conflict was looming.

In 1987, he was on the receiving end against Coventry before returning as the victorious manager of Swindon in 1990, only to have that promotion withdrawn. Happily, there was to be no such problem with Albion in 1993. The Baggies gave him the most comprehensive Wembley result of his career. "It was a proud and brilliant day," he added. "For all our confidence, it was a tough day. You are at Wembley and that brings pressure. When you win, it is like heaven – the best place on earth. But you must never lose at Wembley. The match was very competitive until we scored the first goal. After that, we were only going to win. They tried to attack us and we were able to counter-attack. I knew we would win. The sending-off (of Peter Swan, for denying Bob Taylor a goal-scoring opportunity) didn't matter. It was that first goal that changed the match.

"My idea was to take all the pressure away from the boys. I didn't want them to feel any weight. We knew we were West Bromwich Albion trying to get out of a division we should not have been in. But I wanted to be taking that pressure, not the players, and I knew if we played good football, we would win."

Substitute Simon Garner was the last player to touch the ball as referee Roger Milford blew the final whistle. His fellow substitute Gary Robson wasn't given an opportunity to play any minutes in what would have been his final outing for the club. Ardiles now clears up any suggestions that his decision was driven tactically or even through malice. "Yes, I have one regret: Gary Robson. I am really sorry for that. It was a mistake and I wish I had allowed him on. The problem is that when you're a manager, you are so in the game that you block everything out around you. For a long time, I didn't realise he hadn't gone on to the pitch. There is no time for sentimentality – which people say and is true – but if I had realised then, I would have put him on. He was a lovely, great guy. He was not a regular but he was a wonderful man, always positive and a very good player. So, yes, I can only say sorry to Gary."

September, 1992. Trevor Summers was interviewed by the local press. About half-way through his chat with the Evening Mail's Steve Tudgay, he released a nugget of information that appeared at the time to be without significance. "Let me put one thing straight," the chairman said. "I know the fans are already starting to get worried about Ossie and Keith being poached by other clubs. It's natural that envious eyes will be cast in our direction because our pair are achieving results – and in some style. But I've shaken on a three-year deal with Ossie and do not expect him to leave. Keith has a similar contract and has said publicly he would never walk away."

That very quote was to have repercussions following Albion's promotion. On May 14, two days before the semi-final first leg at Swansea, Terry Venables had been dismissed as Tottenham's chief executive following a 'clash of personalities' with owner Alan Sugar. Venables managed to overturn the decision briefly through the High Court. Although he hadn't been manager for two years, he had played a key first-team role alongside the managerial team of Ray Clemence and Doug Livermore. His exit effectively spelled the end for them as well and Spurs were looking for a new manager.

In an era in which few clubs pursued overseas managers, Spurs limited their search to those based in England, which was not good news for Albion. There was a further narrative troubling supporters. During the late 1980s and early 1990s, English powerhouses Liverpool, Everton and Arsenal had appointed former players as managers. Liverpool replaced Kenny Dalglish with Graeme Souness, George Graham went in at Arsenal and, at Goodison Park, Howard Kendall was succeeded by his former Toffees team-mate, Colin Harvey, and later returned for another spell. It was looking ominous for Albion. The obvious choice for the Spurs job would ordinarily have been Glenn Hoddle but he had guided Swindon to the Premier League the day after Albion won promotion and was quickly appointed as Chelsea manager.

Crucially, Ardiles was on a particularly ordinary contract – and it wasn't watertight. His £50,000-a-year salary was being supplemented by the final payment of his contract at Newcastle, albeit at pro-rata. For taking Albion up, he was also given a £50,000 bonus but he had not signed an improved deal. Sugar, showing the same opportunism he had demonstrated during the protracted broadcasting rights negotiations, made his move. Summers didn't hold back, firing back at his counterpart: "If that Sugar wants a battle, he's got one. I'll send Exocet missiles down the M1 and blow up his computers."

It was all a little bit crude, all a little bit panto and Ardiles grimaces when reminded of the episode. "Trevor Summers and I spoke after Wembley," he added. "It was time to relax and enjoy it. But, yes, I was happy with the club, the club were happy with me and we knew we would need two or three players. I didn't think we needed many. Andy Hunt signed permanently and the other few I knew we could buy and improve us. I had a contract but that was irrelevant in many ways. I was still being paid by Newcastle and was actually on more up there than I was at West Bromwich, so basically I was paid by two clubs. Money wasn't the issue for me. But then I received a phone call from John Lacy, who was a friend of mine from my Tottenham days, when I was in Argentina for about two weeks. He said the chairman of Tottenham wanted to talk to me. I said I had a job. But he came back, then came back again and, yes, eventually I agreed. So, yes, my mind was made up."

A few weeks after guiding the Baggies to promotion, the Argentinian had returned to his spiritual home. Spurs finished a disappointing 15th in his first season in charge. The second season didn't go too well either and he was sacked in October, 1994 following a poor start. Among the criticisms for his demise was his failure to grasp and deal with Tottenham's defensive frailties as he pursued an outlandishly adventurous style of play. In some games, he effectively fielded five attacking players.

Ardiles remains scarred by that phase of his career. He even feels the Baggies might have pushed for Premier League promotion on his watch. "You know… it isn't something I'm happy with. I shouldn't have done what I did. I look back and I wonder what might have happened," he admits. "I had said publicly I was going to stay with West Bromwich but this was Tottenham. It proved to be a big mistake. I had been so happy at West Bromwich. We had won promotion and I knew we would have a good chance of maybe going to the new Premier League. So there were no problems with West Bromwich. I was more than willing to take this very happy team forward. But Tottenham were the one I knew I couldn't say no to. When I'd finished playing, I always said that I would want to go back to Tottenham one day. When they offered me the job, I knew the opportunity may not come up again, so I said yes. It was a very, very bad decision on my part.

"West Brom did everything they could to keep me but my mind was made up. Trevor Summers said a lot of things in the press – and I can understand his anger – but I had spent ten years at Tottenham as a player. It was my club. The lure was too much. I didn't speak to Trevor again after that. With hindsight, I gave a lot up because we might have gone up with that team. We were confident, we were happy and I think we would have done well. It was a wonderful time for me."

Keith Burkinshaw replaced Ardiles. The new Spurs manager opted against taking his no 2 back with him to London, choosing to appoint Steve Perryman as his assistant. Although he appreciates why Burkinshaw took the Albion job, he believes his former mentor wasn't the man for it. Despite success in the 1980s, Burkinshaw cut a down-beat, tired figure while trying to balance Albion's lack of resources and a failing side. "Keith was not the manager he had been before," added Ardiles. "He wasn't on the same level as me for wanting to play attacking football. And maybe the job just came too late for him. I knew – because people told me – that a lot of things changed. I was extremely relaxed, whereas Keith was more old school and disciplined. We complemented each other well as manager and assistant but maybe it changed for all of us. I'm not sure anybody did well out of my decision to leave. Albion didn't, Spurs didn't, I didn't, I don't think Keith did either. I'd made my decision that I wanted Steve Perryman, who was a very good friend of mine. That left Keith with nowhere to go. And maybe he shouldn't have taken the West Bromwich job."

Time has passed. Ardiles looks back on his Albion career with pleasant memories, albeit tinged with regret. Was it his finest season of club management? He agrees it was. There were suggestions Albion tried to bring him back in the late 1990s. "There were rumours but the call never came to go back – I didn't hear anything," he said. "But that's okay. It isn't always the right thing. But 1993…yes, it was an incredibly happy year. It always is when you achieve what you want to. The spirit and feeling I had with the players was wonderful – the best I've had at any football club. And when you win, you are a happy team. I think other teams were envious of us. We often won games without trying too hard – at least that's how it looked. We played without the handbrake. We passed and we pressed teams off the field. It was wonderful.

"I will always remember my excitement at joining the club. I had the call and was told to report at about 11am. I called Sir Bobby and said 'Bobby I am very sorry…I cannot come'. I told him I was going to West Brom. I didn't want him to think I was trying to get out of golf, so I was honest – not that I am very good at golf! He wished me all the very best and told me it was a good club. The next day, he phoned me and congratulated me."

Albion, without Ardiles, would need to go on. Trevor Summers's assault on the so-called Super League would have to wait.

Darren Bradley

"...He was always angry. He kept coming out with these clichés thinking he was being clever but it didn't wash with some of the lads. I just didn't like him..."

"Daz, Don…what the fuck have you two been up to?" Brian Talbot isn't impressed. Police cars have pulled up outside Albion's training venue at the Birmingham County FA buildings in Great Barr. Darren Bradley and Don Goodman are escorted out of the dressing room and not even given time to remove their training kit. Both are frog-marched into police cars and whisked off to Perry Barr police station for questioning. They're about to learn the hard way that nobody gets away with playing Brian Talbot for a fool.

Darren Bradley is enjoying the spring sunshine at Woodrush Rugby Club near the M42 south of Birmingham. It's Sunday lunchtime and live coverage from Rangers' 5-0 victory at Hamilton is creating an overbearing noise in the clubhouse. Behind him, young rugby players are folding away their kit. A dog runs through the bar area, barking, before sprinting out through a half-open exit. Bradley's family sit, patiently, nursing drinks in another part of the bar while the ex-Albion captain trawls back through good times, bad times and many indifferent periods. Then there's the Buckley era. We'll come on to that.

Rangers score another. Bradley isn't interested. His move from Aston Villa to Albion is the topic of conversation. "I went to work one day as a Villa player, came home as an Albion player," he said, as if describing swapping a can of Coke for a tin of Pepsi in a supermarket. Highly-regarded England international Steve Hunt went the other way. Bradley, a Birmingham City fan through childhood, wasn't to know it at the time of his Hawthorns arrival in 1986 but his rise into Albion folklore would be a slow-burner. Not only did he take the scenic route, but his exploration took in some of Albion's worst troughs and dramas. There were few peaks.

He added: "Ron Saunders was manager at West Brom – he knew me from his time at Villa – and it was a grim period. It was hard work. There were a few guys there on big money and the dressing room was quite poisonous. Some of the old heads didn't like Ron. We had some decent players but it doesn't take much to lose a dressing room. I was excited about being at Albion but I was young."

Asked why it took him so long to adjust and his answer needs little consideration. "I came from Villa, didn't I?" he concedes, with the despair of a man who, some days days into a holiday, has just remembered he might have left the gas on at home. "It was a huge issue with the fans. It seemed like I went through two years of being booed each time I touched the ball but slowly it got better. It seemed I played in every position for the club, including in goal against Bolton at home. I kept a clean sheet. I was like a modern-day keeper, I didn't often pick it up. People forget that game…in some ways, it might have been the one that changed things." Yet it was the Woking nightmare that changed the dynamic.

Bradley scored perhaps the first and last Baggies goal to be roundly booed by Albion fans – the second in the 4-2 FA Cup defeat against Woking. "Our confidence was shot," he recalled. "Big Sam (Allardyce) and Stuart Pearson were with Brian and all three were great footballing guys but we were on this downward spiral and just couldn't get out of it. I don't know how we allowed Woking to happen. We actually went on a long unbeaten run at the end of the season after Brian had gone but just drew too many. My goal was booed. It was horrible and Brian was sacked a couple of days later. There is nothing you can do to change the outcome. There is nowhere to hide after a defeat like that. You just want to crawl into a hole and stay there. You don't expect that to happen. But back then, it wasn't unusual. Coventry lost to Sutton, Arsenal lost to Wrexham a year after we lost to Woking. It was just a horrible day. It should have been routine. But there's being up for it…and being UP FOR IT [Bradley's rousing exclamation and fist thump on the table draws the attention of other patrons sat near the bar]. They are very different things. Swansea in the play-offs – that was UP FOR IT. Against Woking, it was just a nightmare. Maybe we just weren't up to it and, more so, we weren't up for it."

Talbot's preparations for that game have drawn scrutiny already. Speaking in May, 2019, the former boss claims Albion were rife with political agendas.

And he believes the club acted with unnecessary and damaging haste. "We'd have stayed up that year, definitely," he argues. "It was a difficult time. Mr (John) Silk was a supporter of mine but others weren't – they were against me. And that other lot won the support of the boardroom. Yes, we lost to Woking. It was a disgrace on my part and that of the players. You shouldn't lose to a non-League club but we did. We should have been three up at half-time but it was a bad day. Woking were brilliant and it was a shock to the nation. The lad Buzaglo was amazing up front.

"We were going through a bad period but it wasn't a terrible period. It was a knee-jerk reaction by the club and they got what they deserved. Thirty years on and Sam is still managing. But then he was always his own man, he was honest and strong. He had opinions. I had my opinions. In my view, the club should have kept us."

Within 48 hours of Talbot's sacking, shareholders were mobilising to discuss changing Albion's constitution. Never before had the club been in such a perilous state: a home defeat against non-League opposition, with relegation to the Third Division a real threat. Although they were still within touching distance of the top of the table, the overall feeling was one of systematic decline. Each Albion defeat carried extra weight. Talbot was clearly not the right man. A large group of shareholders including Geoff Snape, Mike McGinnity and Joe Brandrick met at the Moat House in West Bromwich. There was standing room only. On the agenda was Albion's future. Machinations were already commencing to change the club's structure and constitution. But, for now, there were more urgent matters. The club needed a new manager. Any boardroom changes could wait.

Chairman John Silk and his fellow directors met several candidates. The Sports Argus reported the clear favourite as Alan Buckley. His time would come. John Sillett, an FA Cup-winning manager with Coventry four years previously, was another candidate, as was Barnsley's former Manchester City chief Mel Machin. Arthur Cox, then at Derby, was linked, so was the former Wolves and future Villa boss Brian Little, along with Lou Macari. The Evening Mail were leaning towards Cox while the Express & Star had been championing wildcard Bobby Gould, Wimbledon's FA Cup-winning boss from 1988.

Albion fans were warming to caretaker manager Stuart Pearson. The former Manchester United striker, who was nicknamed Pancho, was committed to a freer-flowing game abandoned by Talbot. But it was Gould who was to get the nod – though not before John Silk had delivered an ominous comment during his unveiling by conceding that the former Coventry boss and one-time Albion forward wasn't his first choice. Supporters were far from enamoured but Bradley reflects on a manager he holds in high regard. Training methods were, well, somewhat different but Bradley said: "I actually quite liked him. It was odd at times but we came back super-fit the one year. He took us away to the barracks, we did a day at Sandhurst undergoing the officers' course. We were put through it big time and then CS gassed – imagine that now!

"It was a great experience, with hindsight. These guys would tell us about the horrors in the Falklands and it was humbling, also quite scary. They stuck us in a heavy tent and asked us to put on this charcoal-lined kit. You then had to take off your mask, tell them your position and put your mask back on while the gas was being released. It was interesting, especially when Colin West broke his toe. He ran out of the toilets in the barracks, completely confused as to what was going on. The poor sod smashed his little toe against something or other. Not what we needed. But that was Bobby."

Another period of inactivity, this time courtesy of Gould's team selection, left West frustrated – and dangerous! Bradley continues: "Bobby had some strange ideas. One day, he marched us all up to the big pitches off Halfords Lane, where the academy building is now. He sat us on the bank while he dragged this bin bag out and produced two pairs of boxing gloves. Then he said: 'Right, lads...anyone got any grievances, come and tell me now.' So Westy stood up, marched over and grabbed the gloves. He just piled into Bobby, smashing him to bits. After a few punches, Bobby turned to us, his nose pouring with blood, and said: 'You see, lads, that's what happens if you don't have a good defence'. We're all sat there thinking: 'Bloody hell!'"

Then there was Paul Williams, the unfortunate and somewhat disparaged poster boy of the Gould regime. The tall striker had scored 14 goals in 25 games for Stockport when £250,000 was splashed out to bring him to The Hawthorns. The interest was considered unusual, not least as his early career had hardly been prolific or befitting of a move to a club of Albion's pedigree. Nevertheless, these were bleak times, with money scarce and ambitions extremely sparse. Williams, who eventually became a one-cap Northern Ireland international, wasn't even the most celebrated member of his own family – his mother Betty, who passed away in March, 2020, was a joint winner of the Nobel Peace Prize in 1976, for her work in promoting peace in Northern Ireland. Her dedication to the cause came after she saw a fatally-wounded IRA paramilitary's car lose control and tragically veer into three children, killing them instantly.

Her son simply didn't deliver for Albion. His signing drew suggestions that the wrong player had been signed, with speculation among the manager's critics at the time that Gould had intended to sign a different Paul Williams – a short, black left-back who did eventually move to The Hawthorns on loan. The truth is somewhat less farcical, albeit no less revealing......

Sources involved at the time have told me Gould and backroom colleague Norman Bodell went to watch Manchester United's young winger Giuliano Maiorana in a reserve game at their Carrington training ground. Within 15 minutes, Gould had seen enough to decide he wasn't the man for him. With United's second team kicking off at 7pm and Stockport in action at 7.30pm, the duo dashed across Manchester to check out County striker Williams. He performed well, impressing the Albion boss who, by then, was convinced he had seen him play some time earlier. Albion were already in discussions about signing Notts County's Dave Regis, brother of Cyrille, and were desperately trying to keep that link out of the press, knowing the stir another Regis signing would cause. The striker had made a name for himself in non-League before a decent run at Meadow Lane. However, Gould had also watched Bristol City's impressive centre-forward, Bob Taylor, who wasn't unlike Stockport's Paul Williams in appearance, albeit several inches shorter, thus possibly adding to the confusion. Indeed, Williams was decent in the air, as was Taylor.

Somewhere along the line, the process became muddled and it was clear that Gould had made a different signing to the one he intended. He recruited Williams, thinking he was signing Taylor, having mistaken the Bristol man for the Stockport forward. Anyway, Williams was brought in, tripled his wages and did very little. He scored five times in 44 Albion games. The deal to bring Dave Regis to the club floundered. The second Paul Williams played five matches for Albion in 1993-94. As for Taylor, he pitched up in 1991-92 and did a little better....

Bradley wasn't impressed with the first capture. "Paul was a lovely lad but couldn't play," he said. "I felt sorry for him but he just never got going and the fans were pretty unforgiving to him. By then, we'd gone totally route one and, as a midfielder, you were picking up scraps and running round with a bad neck. Would it have been different had Stuart Pearson been appointed? Maybe. Pancho had a massive influence. He worked every day on Don Goodman's finishing and touch. Don was blisteringly quick and dangerous but his positioning and runs weren't always right. He became a real force under Pancho's influence. Had Pancho been around when Paul Williams was there, he might have made a difference. Whatever people say, we'll never know how things might have worked out. Managers do get it wrong at times. People remember Gould signed Williams. But he also signed Bob Taylor."

In summer, 1992, Bradley's fortunes were to change for the better. It was a significant transition for a player who, for so long, had struggled to get supporters on-side. Gould was sacked and the board's focus was on Ossie Ardiles, the preferred option, and the next cab off the rank – young, aspiring Martin O'Neill, who had just led Wycombe into the Football League. He was favoured by some board members, although there was opposition from one prominent director. O'Neill never did get the call. The Sports Argus suggested Alan Buckley was also in the frame but he would be made to wait a few years as Ardiles agreed within days to become Gould's successor.

Bradley's form rocketed, as did the affection from supporters. "We got called back in by Ossie," he added. "We had a whole week of matches on half a pitch at the Smethwick End. Hour after hour of one-touch football. It was wonderful, playing out from the back. If you stuck it into Row Z when you could have played it out, he'd substitute you. He demanded football. We had a fitness coach who, on his first day, had us running and running. I think he left the next day. Ossie wanted us working and running with the ball. It was fantastic and my confidence grew more and more.

"I don't think the back four were too keen but, for the rest of us, it was heaven. I remember Raves, Burge and Strodd came to me for a moan – I'd been named captain by then as Shakey was struggling with injuries. Anyway, we're about four games in and I've got a committee of defenders in front of me saying: 'We've got to tighten up at the back… can you have a word with the gaffer?' Ossie just smiled at me. It was all 'charge'. He introduced the high press. If I felt somebody on the opposition was dodgy, I'd give a code word and we'd target that weakness. It was also the first season the back-pass rule was introduced, which caused even more chaos. We exploited that – again, we pressed from midfield. We had intelligent footballers. It was brilliant. The fans absolutely loved it. They finally had some love for us. That was a great season but, seriously, how we didn't go up automatically, I'll never know. It's a bit of a disgrace that we didn't. But, in the end, it turned out well."

After the comeback win over Swansea in the play-off semi-final came the Wembley victory over Port Vale. Bradley shies away from referring to it as a cup final. Far from it, he feels it highlighted some inadequacies during an otherwise glorious season. "The build-up was hideous," he admits. "It isn't a cup final – it's a be-all-and-end-all game. The dieticians had started by then so we were getting carb-loaded. I didn't sleep much. I was very nervous for starters. We got up, had a walk, had some toast and jam at 12 and then travelled to Wembley. Incredible. It was just one big wall of Albion fans. Fucking amazing, it was!

"But, you know something, as great as it is looking back, there was nothing to enjoy in the build-up. The result was everything. Yes, they try and make it into a cup final but there you are after about 48 games and everything is down to 90 minutes. It turned out great but I only enjoyed the last ten minutes when we were 2-0 up and against ten men. I can enjoy it now. Wembley suited us. Peter Swan getting sent off helped. I knew a few of the Vale lads like Dean Glover and Paul Kerr from Villa. They had a decent side but we weren't going to lose. Walking out and trying to hold the tears back was something else. We had something like 45,000 fans there. They barely took any. It was just amazing. But we should have gone up automatically. As much as I loved Wembley, we were good enough to finish top two in my view."

Then came the small matter of looking after the trophy presented to the winning captain and, for once, Bradley wasn't watching his back. "Ossie was in the dressing room smoking a cigarette and drinking Champagne," he said. "We went back to the Midlands on three or four coaches and had a reception at the ground. They actually replayed the game there, probably on a Betamax knowing the Albion, then we just got absolutely hammered. We went to a place in Birmingham and did the bus tour around West Bromwich. We were seriously hung over. Andy Hunt thought it would be a good idea to bring a two-litre bottle of Bacardi along. There were casualties, as you can imagine, and people went missing. Travelling around on a rickety old bus when you've had a skinful isn't the best thing.

"We had the trophy with us and it was bloody horrible, like a relay baton. I remember going up to collect it in the Royal Box and thinking: 'What the fuck is that…is that it?' Then I only went and lost the bloody thing after Wembley. I couldn't find it anywhere. We were at this drinking club called Calthorpe Old Boys on the Bristol Road, just opposite the Dome, having a few beers with these Blues lads I knew. We've just won at Wembley and I've only gone and lost the trophy. I was looking everywhere and didn't realise the lads from the pub had hidden it. So I was panicking knowing we had the official reception at Penns Hall, with all the dignitaries and directors. When I got home, Ossie was on the phone to tell me to take the trophy to the civic reception and I'm trying my best to sound calm. I used my whole repertoire of lies… but I was panicking. One of the lads had remembered about the trophy and went over to Penns the next day. He saw Ossie driving in and stopped right in front of him, ran over and gave him the trophy. So I arrive and Ossie by now is playing along, saying: 'Oh dear, Braddy…what have you done, Braddy? No, no, no, Braddy…you will have to tell everyone you've lost the trophy'. I was shitting it, knowing all the dignitaries and VIPs would be there, thinking I'm an idiot. Next thing I know, Ossie's walked over to his car and taken the trophy out. It had been gone for several days but by then it had been broken and used as a microphone for our makeshift karaoke. It turns out they'd stuck it behind the bar, next to the optics. I hadn't even noticed it."

Bradley spent nine years at The Hawthorns and played more than 250 times. The season on Ardiles's watch was one of his most productive. At 27, he was acutely aware that his value would never be greater, nor would his potential for earning a better contract. The next deal could well be his final big one. And he was about to make the biggest decision of his career by turning down a move to Norwich in the summer of 1993.

"We'd played Wycombe in the Cup during our promotion season," he recalled. "We were cruising 1-0 and I came off because I wasn't feeling the best. Ossie called me in the next day and said: 'I know there was nothing wrong with you, Braddy…' I said my hamstring had been tight and he replied: 'You don't run quick enough for your hamstrings to be tight'. He said that if we were promoted, I would get the best contract this club had ever seen…and if we don't, I'd be the first out'. So you can see the pressure I was under.

"I apologised to him but I didn't throw it in. My body was simply wrecked. I genuinely felt knackered. But I was mindful that Ossie had doubted me, so I never did that again. I often played when I wasn't even 90 per cent fit. Anyway, fast forward several months. It all came crashing down. I was getting on a plane for Florida when I picked up a copy of a free paper – there it was across the back: 'Ossie for Spurs'. I was distraught. It left the whole club flat just a few weeks after Wembley. But the club honoured that deal he'd promised me – I got a couple of grand a month, which was a lot of money then. Norwich wanted me. John Deehan, who I knew from Villa, was assistant boss and said they were keen but I said: 'Sorry, Dixie, but Albion are a bigger club…and we've got big plans.' So I stayed. By then, Ossie had left – he wasn't going to turn down Tottenham – and it wasn't the same after that.

"Ossie has said many times since that he should never have gone. It was too early. Keith Burkinshaw took over. He was dour but he'd been a brilliant manager, although maybe just getting on a bit now. To go from being a no 2 to no 1 must have been tough, too, as he'd not been a gaffer for a while. We lost the 'Ossieness'."

Burkinshaw had been cast as the man applying the handbrake to Ardiles's fast-moving, free-wheeling side but he was no mug. He had managed Spurs to FA Cup glory in 1981 and 1982 and to a UEFA Cup triumph in 1984. Yet he wasn't the ebullient Ardiles and his enthusiasm wasn't as it had been a decade earlier. The loss of the infectious Ardiles charm and the leap to the second tier proved too much and Albion laboured through a difficult campaign, only achieving survival on the final day of the season at Portsmouth.

The club played the final third of 1993-94 in unbranded shirts after their sponsor Coucher & Shaw were closed down by the Law Society for improper conduct. It was that kind of season. Norwich, meanwhile, had qualified for the UEFA Cup, having finished third in the first Premier League campaign. An incredible aggregate victory against Bayern Munich in October came at a point, in mid-October, when Albion had won just twice in the League – one of them a memorable 3-2 victory against Wolves in which Bradley took aim and crashed an unforgettable goal at the Birmingham Road End. In a match screened live by ITV, Bradley's powerful shot 'came straight out of a cannon', according to match co-commentator Terry Cooper. It was the midfielder's first goal at The Hawthorns since the one against Woking.

Bradley has firm views about rejecting the move to Norfolk – Norwich were knocked out by Inter Milan in the third round of the competition – in favour of staying with the meat-and-potatoes of the Endsleigh League Division One. Did he make the wrong call? "I have no regrets," he laughs as the TV behind him shows Rangers smashing another one in. "And I will always have that Wolves game. We lost Bob to chickenpox on the morning, so you can imagine that was a big worry. And people forget that Wolves had a quality side. Geoff Thomas had come in for a lot of money and they had Steve Bull, Mark Venus, David Kelly and Paul Birch. And, of course, they had Cyrille Regis, who came on for Bully during the game. Has a Wolves player ever been applauded on to the Hawthorns pitch like Cyrille that day? I can't imagine he has...

"We'd played at Stoke a couple of games before Wolves and I'd gone close with a similar shot when I hit the bar, so I knew I could do it. And it happened against Wolves, into the top corner – it was a bit better than the one against Woking! The fans cheered this time as well. We played well in the second game, too. We murdered them at Molineux (Albion won 2-1) from memory. As poor as that season was, it was good to do the double over them."

Albion played their opening six games of 1994-95 on the road while the Birmingham Road End and Smethwick End were redeveloped so as to comply with the Lord Justice Taylor Report, which ordered the removal of terraces and fencing. Both stands were operational by the end of 1994 – the Smethwick End was ready for the late September game against Burnley, while the Brummie Road reopened on Boxing Day for the fixture against Bristol City. Albion won both. By Christmas, however, Burkinshaw was long gone.

The necessity to play so many away games early on caught up with Albion, who won just one of their opening 11. Out went Burkinshaw, in came, according to chairman Tony Hale, 'one of the best five managers in the country'. One can only imagine the surprise when Alan Buckley, not Sir Alex Ferguson, walked through the door. His appointment came three and a half years after he was first linked with a move to The Hawthorns. Where, under Burkinshaw, the club had tried to prosper with gradualism and consensus, they turned to the Grimsby boss, a revolutionary and autocrat: a man who wanted personal success as much as collective glory, a man committed to the 'my way or highway' approach. And all too often it would be the highway – in his case, usually heading back to Blundell Park to recruit his former players "Alan Buckley?" Bradley asks. "Hang on, I'm going to need another pint…"

Bradley sighs with utter resignation as he returns from the bar and begins: "I'll say this – his no 2 Arthur Mann was a lovely guy, but Buckley? He wasn't my favourite to put it mildly. What really pissed me off about him was that he thought he was more important than the club. The training was all for him and then he started buying Grimsby players. It was ridiculous and I told him. I was still captain and actually asked him: 'Why the fuck do you keep buying Grimsby players?' We're West Bromwich Albion, not some lower League club. It was embarrassing. I mean, Paul Groves? No offence but he wasn't at my level, even then. He was a good lad – and I don't mean to be harsh – but I was being moved on to bring him in. That happens, fair enough, and I was coming up to 30 but I just couldn't believe what Buckley was filling our squad with."

The manager's weakness for players from his former club did little to endear him to supporters. Eight current or former Mariners players arrived, namely Paul Agnew, Tony Rees, Paul Crichton, Chris Hargreaves, Shaun Cunnington, Dave Gilbert, Paul Reece and Groves. A further six recruits with previous Blundell Park connections included brothers Adam and Simon Buckley and assistant manager Mann. Rees, a striker, scored just twice for Albion while Crichton's performances in goal were frequently maligned, notably following one particularly poor game against Wolves. Gilbert was perhaps the most productive but lacked physicality. There was an apocryphal story at the time that the 5ft 4in winger auctioned off a man-of-the-match bike he had received as he was too short to reach the pedals. Groves, at £600,000, was the most expensive recruit but struggled for form against the expectation of his price tag and a lack of chemistry with other midfielders.

Bradley added: "He (Buckley) had 'little man syndrome'. He was always angry. He kept coming out with these clichés thinking he was being clever but it didn't wash with some of the lads. I just didn't like him. Don't get me

Superbob in action on and off the pitch......an interviewee in Chris Lepkowski's previous Albion book, he stepped into a special role for this prequel. Well, who better to ask for a brilliant foreword than a brilliant forward? In addition to showing him taking a turn at the mic while on corporate duty, our pictures capture him posing for photographers before training in the second half of the 1990s and, inevitably, with his sights fixed on yet more Baggies goals.

Battered boss faces sack in Albion showdown

Walsall t

A NEWLY formed big-money consortium is set to mount a takeover bid for Walsall FC — and if successful its first act will be to axe chairman Barrie Blower and the rest of the club's board of directors.

The consortium — five West Midlands businessmen and American multi-millionaires trying Brown — has been set up in the last ten days following Brown's receipt on Thursday of information on the club's financial state.

As well as replacing the existing board the consortium, it its takeover bid goes through, will also give top priority to buying Bescot Stadium from the developers to whom Walsall are currently paying a rent bill of around £145 per year.

Tomorrow the powerful combination

TALBOT'S CUP OF WOE-KING

By Bill Corry

Darren delight

WIGAN'S FA Cup hero Darren Patterson, who snatched a last-gasp equaliser at Coventry, was rejected by West Brom manager Brian Talbot four minutes after he took over at the Hawthorns.

Patterson had completed a

BRIAN TALBOT's future as Albion manager hung in the balance today after the his side's FA Cup humiliation by non-League Woking.

Chairman John Silk added to Talbot's worries by revealing that the Albion board would be discussing the consequences of the 4-2 defeat in the next few days.

Silk called a Press conference immediately after the game when several 4,000 fans demonstrated in front of the main stand chanting 'Talbot out' and 'Back the Board.'

He described the defeat as 'terrible' and said: 'The board will be discussing this result and its consequences over the next few days.

'I understand the fans' feelings and I accept we have been faced with a problem of considerable size.

'But I don't wish to make any statement about the manager at this moment of the moment.

'It's time for myself and the Board to sit down and think everything out calmly,' he added.

Celebrations on the first day of 1990-91 (above) as Gary Bannister and Don Goodman rejoice in the draw at Portsmouth with goalscorer Tony Ford. It was a season, though, that slid downhill amid some nightmare headlines.

FA CUP 3rd ROUND
January 5, 1991

WBA — West 34, Bradley 90 — **2**

WOKING — Buzaglo 59, 65, 74, Wyesfold 89 — **4**

WEST BROM: Rees, Strodder, Bradley, Harbey (Palmer), Shakespeare, West, Ford, Roberts, Robson, McNally, Bannister.
WOKING: Read, Pratt, Cowler, Mitchell, Baron, Biggins, Wye, Franks (Worsfold), Wye, Brown, Buzaglo.
Attendance: 14,516.

Liverpool next is Tim's dream

It has been quite a journey.....from Walsall and his Great Barr roots via several seasons at Albion and a famous Premier League title triumph with Leicester to a short stint with England. Craig Shakespeare is pictured left in the barcode kit that the Baggies wore during the successful and highly exciting year under Ossie Ardiles - a fitting send-off to the playing sector of the player's time at The Hawthorns. He returned to the club much later as a coach and then had the thrill of linking up again with an Albion colleague of the late 1980s and early 1990s, Sam Allardyce, this time at international level. We are grateful to the FA for allowing us use of the photos below and bottom.

Above: Albion's 1993 play-off final squad in their Wembley finery. This 'before' picture by Dave Smallwood was taken at an upbeat time for the club, even if captain Darren Bradley feels there was an element of under-achievement in the side having to go into end-of-season overtime at all. But supporters look back at the 3-0 victory over Port Vale with much fondness and the match programme front cover and another keepsake of the big day out are shown here (right), along with a photograph of Ossie Ardiles, taken well over a decade ago. The manager now admits he made a mistake in leaving The Hawthorns.

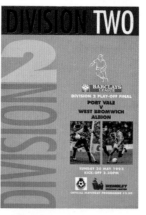

Sorry, lads.... we had a great thing going - and I really should have stayed put at Albion

ts off, let's get the buffet served! Ossie Ardiles and his assistant Keith Burkinshaw in understandably
spirits aboard the team coach following the emphatic play-off final conquest of Port Vale. The two had
ed together superbly at Tottenham as player and manager and had a good thing going in the Black
try, too. Events conspired to bring about a parting of the ways, though, and supporters and squad
bers alike were upset to learn during the close season that the genial Argentinian would not be needing
avy blue cap and club tracksuit (size: small) any longer.

It wasn't just about that belter against Wolves as far as Darren Bradley and goal-scoring was concerned. He could strike a sweet shot at times and the technique is good here (above) as he takes aim. Not that all his 13 Baggies goals were joyously acclaimed - in fact one was booed by the Birmingham Road End. Yes, honestly! Below, the former skipper, who previously served Villa and later went on to play for Walsall, is in pensive moodbut the author found him open and engaging company as he kept his glass topped up when interviewing him for this book.

◀ Burgess celebrates a 2-1 victory under Keith
︙inshaw at Molineux in March, 1994 and cosies up
﹙▸﹚ to his good pal, Ian Hamilton. Below: Don't tell
﹙﹚affer! A hush-hush game on the continent....

So mature for his years....Enzo Maresca's free-
wowed bystanders on his first day at Albion,
wonder he was on duty with this free-kick at Ip
(above). Left: Working as a coach at West Ha▮

wrong…..these players were decent lads. And I was being a bit harsh about Groves – he was a decent player, but was he an improvement? Was he an improvement for £600,000? That was a lot of money for us then. We'd lost the freedom to play. The midfield was asked to scrap for bits, we were regimented again. Going from Ossie to that in the space of a little over a year… Christ, it was hard going. And he not only wanted to control the players but the staff as well. He wanted control over everything.

"I've got a degree and I'm not stupid. But he kept talking down to everyone and misusing words. He kept saying 'echelon' in the wrong context. He just made himself look a twat. I know some other lads liked him but he wasn't for me. We were basically Grimsby. I'd turned down Norwich to stay at 'Grimsby'. There's Norwich playing Bayern Munich in the UEFA Cup and little over a year later, I'm stuck there with Mr Fucking Grimsby, who's misusing words trying to be clever. If I'd known what he was like, I'd have gone long before then. The one player of theirs we should have signed was the centre-forward (Clive Mendonca) but we couldn't afford him."

Bradley's knee injuries persisted, which didn't help. Even when he did play, the relationship was deteriorating – culminating in a sending-off in an FA Cup third-round replay against Premier League side Coventry. "I was injured and he put me on the bench for six games," added Bradley. "Every time I warmed up, the fans were cheering and wanting me on. He fucking hated it. We played Coventry away and should have won. We brought them back to The Hawthorns and tried to rattle a few people because I knew Peter Ndlovu was a threat. I got myself booked and, at the start of the second half, slid into a tackle and realised I was going to catch the player. The pitch was wet and although he jumped over the tackle, I was sent off. Buckley never spoke to me again. He totally blamed me for that. He was right, I guess. I was to blame. He called me in after the final match and said I could go. My knees were starting to go and, to be honest, I knew I'd be gone." Bradley joined Walsall.

Bradley enjoyed his Albion time, making friends – and occasional foes – along the way. His friendship with Don Goodman particularly shines through, not least one or two memorable scrapes with Brian Talbot. "The one summer, we were down on the coast during pre-season," smiles Bradley, hinting at potential mischief. "My missus was pregnant. Anyway, I could see all the coaching staff were sat downstairs having a beer – I could see them all by looking down over this giant staircase.

"So I phoned them from my room and said: 'Gaffer, my missus is in labour. I've got to go home'. I looked over the balcony and could see Brian going spare, saying: 'Bloody hell, my plans are out of the window – Bradley's got to go home'. I left him for a bit, watching them all moaning, then I shouted down: 'Gaffer, I'm only joking'. He looked up and went absolutely mental. I thought no more of it. The following season, Don and I had been away playing golf. We'd had a few nights out and Brian knew. We were at Ray Hall Lane (the Birmingham FA base), where we trained at the time, and these police cars turned up. I thought nothing of it as Hoppy [Robert Hopkins] had been with us around that time, so it wasn't unusual to see a cop car parked up.

"Brian came over: 'Daz, Don…what the fuck have you two been up to in Newquay?' We looked at each other, wondering what the hell we'd forgotten about. These police officers are there looking all serious and we were told we're being taken for questioning. We were taken to Perry Barr nick, where they put us in different cells – still in training kit, by the way – and were told there had been a call from Mr Talbot saying we must go back to The Hawthorns, then return to the station for more interrogation about this so-called allegation. We were absolutely bricking it wondering what we'd forgotten. Had Don done something I wasn't aware of? Was I that pissed that I'd forgotten something?

"We were frog-marched back in handcuffs and there are all the lads with Brian, who's just stood there shaking his head trying not to laugh. He then turns to me and says: 'That'll teach you, won't it, Daz? That'll teach you for having me on last summer in that hotel'. Fucking hell, he'd only planned the whole thing and waited a whole year to get us back! That was Brian Talbot. He got police pals of his to stage a so-called 'arrest'. Fair play to him – it was the best 'get' of all time."

In his years at The Hawthorns, Bradley became particularly close to Gary Robson and Bob Taylor. Being on good terms with the younger brother of the former England captain and Albion man would present all sorts of opportunities for mischief, not least the temptation to hook up with the legendary Manchester United drinking school. At a time when Sir Alex Ferguson was trying to change the culture at Old Trafford, Bryan Robson, a future Baggies manager, was to survive the cull of the late 1980s while Norman Whiteside, Frank Stapleton and Paul McGrath were moved on. Bradley simply shakes his head as the mind wanders back......

"Nights out could be nuts," he added. "I went with Gary to Bryan's house in Cheshire. He'd just signed a clothing contract with Lee Cooper, so that was another reason to celebrate. We're there with Whiteside and Stapleton at Paddy Crerand's bar.... bloody hell, United legends all of them. It's just drink, drink, drink and more drink. Bryan was one of the best footballers England has ever produced and he's there doing 15 pints. And yet he looks in training next day like he's not had a drink. Such quality! Gary and I had to somehow get back to training the next day. I'm pretty sure we got fined for being late.

"Nights out with Bob could be fun, too. He and I got into the PFA team in 1992-93. We played at Bradford and needed to find a way of getting to London for the awards bash. We were in a car heading south when this taxi piled into the back of us, causing all sorts of damage. The whole scene must have looked animated to people driving past. We've just beaten Bradford and we're stood on the side when a minibus full of Albion fans goes past and they thought we were being attacked. This poor cab driver was stood there not knowing what to do. Thankfully, we convinced them all was ok...and we got a lift down."

Then there was the pre-season in the Algarve under Ron Atkinson when, frankly, all protagonists were lucky to not find themselves booted out of the club. A squad featuring Andy Gray, Tony Morley, Robert Hopkins and Tony Kelly, among others, was one of potential combustion. Bradley continues: "Bloody hell... Portugal. We all got deported. Every last one of us was kicked out. Something blew up over there between a couple of the players. We were in Lagos and all the lads started scrapping – Tony Kelly, Andy Gray, Don, Tony (Kelly) and myself. Don and I were living together at the time, yet there we were scrapping.

"The mayor of Lagos sent us packing. Colin Addison found out what had gone on and blasted us. He was fuming. Andy (Gray) had gone to punch Tony Kelly. He had a ring with AG on it. He missed Tony and ended up swiping Tony Morley on the forehead. So Tony had this big AG on his forehead for a week – we were pissing ourselves. We ended up being sent to Lisbon, spent the night there and were then sent home. We'd have been front-page news these days. Thank God there was no social media then.

"We had our fun with opponents, too. Dennis Wise and I would just kick the crap out of each other. No idea why – he wound me up, I wound him up. We just kicked each other. And then there was Paul Ince. He was fucking horrible to play against."

Bradley scored nine goals in 254 games for Albion before seeing out his career at Walsall. Having started at Villa, the Midlander had no issues about staying in the area. "I don't regret anything," he goes on, taking the final gulp of his drink at Woodrush Rugby Club, two minutes from Blues' Wast Hills training ground. "Obviously the Norwich thing was one that gave me something to think about but that was a freakish run they went on. Would I have been better off? I'm not so sure. It was all a bit of an old boys' club at times really. We had one of the lowest-paid squads in the top two divisions. I had a sponsored Peugeot 405 for goodness sake. It was still the best job in the world but it didn't make you for life like it does now. And that's fair enough – no sour grapes on my part. That's how it was.

"I probably wish I'd pulled out of a couple of tackles that left me badly injured. I did both my cruciate ligaments, twice in one knee. Fourteen operations in total. The shit I got for the first couple of years made me stronger, made me a better person. Tony Morley is probably one of the best footballers I've seen and he got murdered by some fans, too. It is difficult if you come from Villa. I was 14 when I joined them. I was born in Sparkbrook. The whole family were Blues. I got courted by both but Villa were so far ahead at the time in terms of recruitment.

"You asked me earlier why it took me so long to adapt at Albion. I think the Villa thing played a part. Villa signed me in May, 1982 – a time they often mention down there. They were good for me but I loved my time with Albion. I'll always have that goal against Wolves and Wembley. Just don't leave me in charge of any trophies…"

Daryl Burgess

"...They'd be smashing these raw sausages with the cricket bat, leaving them stuck to the walls and over the neighbours' fences into the road. There was sausage everywhere, it was absolute carnage...

Daryl Burgess really shouldn't be playing football on this particular afternoon. He pulls on his striped shirt somewhat nervously and looks across the crowded dressing room to his right to where Andy Hunt is doing the same. Joining them is Dave Seaman. No, not that one. A different Dave Seaman. Likewise Andy Thompson. No, not the one from Wolves. A different Andy Thompson. Seaman and Thompson are renowned DJs of the 1990s.

The blue and white stripes, worn by a collection of dance DJs from the UK, including Hunt and part-time disc-spinner Burgess, are about to take on a team of Italian DJs at a near-empty stadium in Rimini. The match is being broadcast by MTV. This is supposed to be the close season for the Hawthorns duo: a summer break where measured fitness training is to be encouraged. Taking to the field against amateur cloggers from Italy's night scene is definitely not on any recommended programme. Discretion is paramount. Should Alan Buckley tune in to watch any hard house music channels any time soon – unlikely, we know – then all hell would break loose. Burgess knows that if word gets back to West Bromwich, he and Andy Hunt would be in serious trouble…

Autumn, 2019. Daryl Burgess is nursing a pint at the Digby Hotel in Water Orton when he spots a familiar face. He introduces me to the coach of Digby Rangers, a Sunday League side so good that nobody wants to play them. Seriously. Their story will be a Sunday Mercury front-page splash in the coming weeks, lampooning their opponents and using every feasible pun available. Try as they might, Rangers are unable to find opposition because sides have quit their division, rather than be drubbed by them. The irony of this brief introduction isn't lost on Burgess as his friend leaves us to continue our Albion discussion. We return to the more familiar mid-1990s territory of defeats. Lots of defeats.

Burgess served under 11 managers in 15 years at Albion. It was on Buckley's watch that the club went through a period of losses that would shame the worst pub team. The Albion of 1995-96 were no Digby Rangers. On October 28, they travelled to Millwall knowing a victory would take them top of the table. The hosts were also vying for top spot. The Baggies fell 2-1 at the New Den and were to lose 13 of their next 14 games, drawing just once. Burgess winces as he recalls the most horrible of runs.

"That was a strange time," he says. "We lost at Millwall and from there we slid…and kept sliding. When we walked into the dressing room, the physio Paul Mitchell was sat behind the door. He was a proper ex-Army bloke and didn't take any crap. He's trying to get all of his medical stuff out from behind the dressing room door because he's seen the gaffer isn't happy. He's there scrambling away, trying to clear everything out of the way before Bucko storms in. He's there when the door starts being banged and pushed. Bucko's on the other side, kicking, punching the door, shoving it all he can, going mental. Paul's having the door smashed into his face, blood pouring down his cheeks. Bucko walked in, looked at him, shook his head and started laying into the rest of us."

Defeats followed against Leicester, Derby, Grimsby, Norwich, Sunderland, Reading, Stoke, Huddersfield, Crystal Palace, Port Vale, Charlton and Ipswich. In between the losses at Vale Park and The Valley was a 0-0 draw with Wolves, with Albion denied a potential victory through Andy Hunt's penalty miss. The only real respite came in the Anglo-Italian Cup, with the side recording victories at home against Reggiana and at Brescia – the latter a bad-tempered game played in front of some 200 fans on a snow-covered pitch. While Albion were feeling the chilling and bruising effects of the Alpine cold, the club's directors were feeling the heat from their own supporters. Not that it mattered much to Tony Hale and his board.

Rather than turning their ire on the manager, the Baggies chairman made a more bewildering call. Where many clubs might have been issuing statements of 'confidence' or even delivering a P45, the beleaguered Buckley was instead offered a new four-year deal before the home game against Stoke. The Baggies lost 1-0, with the manager and his coaching staff locking the players in their dressing room for a full hour's post mortem into defeat no 8. Despite Albion being in the eye of their worst ever storm of defeats, Buckley now had the security of being under contract until 1999. Speaking to the Evening Mail, he said: "I didn't ask for the extension but I was happy to get it and it makes me even more determined to put the situation right. I am happy to sign the contract that was offered to me. It shows that despite all that has happened on the pitch over the last few weeks, the directors don't believe I have become a bad manager."

Hale remained increasingly supportive despite growing anger and disbelief among supporters. "It is a mystery as to why this mess has happened," he told the Sports Argus. "The players enjoy working for Alan and enjoy their training. That's a good thing and hopefully that helps to pull us round again." To his credit, Buckley wasn't about to give up easily. Lock-ins, team bonding sessions, lock-ins ….and more lock-ins. Buckley tried all he could to halt the alarming descent into the abyss of the second-tier relegation zone. He even went down the unconventional route by bringing in a mentor to preach about Rorke's Drift, where 200 Anglo soldiers stood up to 4,000 Zulu warriors and resisted attack through their resilience. The objective was to convince Albion they could go head-to-head with any side.

The Baggies still lost their next match, against Sunderland, but with a spirited performance. Burgess recalled that unusual period, not least those training sessions supposedly enjoyed by the players. "Fair play to Bucko – he somehow got a contract out of the club. I've no idea how," he said. "Each Monday, every professional, every kid, every staff member, would play across the pitch. You'd play about 25-a-side until he scored. He kept on and on and on 'I'm a goalscorer… pass me the ball' and if he scored, he'd run off celebrating. That was our manager.

"We used to get bored quite quickly and, as you can imagine during that run, it was weird to be doing stuff like that. It was a joke to have 25-a-side after we've lost on the Saturday for the umpteenth time. One day, I looked over the other side of the pitch and Hunty was in a daydream. He was in his own world until he saw me – and then starting playing 'air guitar'. Meanwhile, Bucko's there running around trying to score the goal to prove he was still a 'goalscorer'. He had his way of playing: You got it wide, played it to the front man's feet. That's why he signed Tony Rees from Grimsby, to hold the ball and play in others. It was ok but it got found out soon enough. We didn't really have a different way of playing.

"What I remember is that he would come in after games where we'd lost and he would be ranting for one or two hours sometimes. Yet he remembered everything about the game. Every little slip or mistake, every challenge that wasn't quite bang on, or header you missed – he remembered everything. He could be angry. Angry with everyone – players, staff, fans. He was just an angry man at times. We got dicked in some games but in others we were really unlucky. We played Sunderland and lost 1-0, with them scoring with their only shot. I remember Peter Reid praising us afterwards. We should have battered them but it just wasn't falling for us. We couldn't buy a break. But, yes, Bucko did okay out of it from his own point of view."

The turning point was the arrival of Richard Sneekes. The Dutchman began his football education at Ajax, a sporting version of Harvard or Oxbridge, if you prefer. Sneekes was one its undergraduates, a member of the youth finishing school that produced Johan Cruyff, Edwin van der Sar, Dennis Bergkamp, Marco van Basten and so many others. Buckley called on Albion supporters to not expect too much too soon from their new £400,000 signing from Bolton. Sneekes didn't listen. He scored ten goals in his first 13 games and went on to serve the club until 2001. That early splurge of strikes not only kept Albion in the second tier but elevated them to mid-table, offering optimism for better times ahead. By some quirk, Millwall, their opponents from that October fixture, were relegated.

As for Sneekes, Burgess lowers his pint at the mere mention of his former team-mate as he prepares his own tribute. "I can't remember how many people I played with at Albion but Richard Sneekes was the best of the lot," he continued. "That few weeks after he signed were just incredible. It gave all of us such a lift and boost of confidence at a time when we needed it most. He was a great guy off the field. He didn't drink, he didn't come out with us. He was quiet. Me, Bradders, Bruiser (Stuart Naylor), Ian Hamilton, Kev (Donovan) would go out…but Sneekes stayed at home with his wife and kids and wouldn't touch a drop. For our Christmas do, he'd pay the £50 and still stay at home. Mind you, I'm not sure he's as strict now about the no-alcohol policy.

"His technical ability used to really stand out. He could read the game better than anyone and he had grace and intelligence on the ball. The one thing Richard could do was speak his mind. If he upset you, he upset you – as I think a few managers maybe later found out. But he was bright enough and if it was said in the dressing room, you didn't mind him losing his patience and kicking off. You'd watch him play and his ability was just outstanding."

Summer, 1996. The year England hoped football would finally come home, against a soundtrack of Oasis and Blur slogging it out in the Britpop scene. England's wait was to continue. Less thrilled about coming home was Burgess, who had enjoyed a memorable summer with his good friend and team-mate Andy Hunt. The duo had been friends since the latter's move from Newcastle in 1993. Burgess was carving a niche for himself by 1996 as a part-time DJ, providing the music at various nightspots in the Midlands, including Some Place Else in Birmingham.

His connections presented opportunities to rub shoulders with some of the nation's leading disc-spinners, with Hunt being introduced to his future wife and both men being arm-twisted into playing in a match that would have had their manager back home fuming. "Andy was my room-mate and a good pal for many years – he used to stay at my house, we went on holiday together and hang out," continued Burgess. "Hunty was into most things music-wise, although I was more of a House-head. I did like Oasis and Blur. The music of both bands was great but that summer was all about Italy.

"It was around then I got to meet Andy Thompson, who was working for London Records with Pete Tong on a label called FFRR. I was doing a lot of DJing and he ended up involved with Virgin Records and setting up a dance department. They used to do a dance exhibition in Rimini. Virgin had a stand there, so they invited myself and Andy Hunt over for a big club culture week. It was just incredible. All the big names from the time were there. They'd managed to get Kappa on board, who were really going big on football kits at the time. Kappa told us they'd sort some kits out if we'd play a game at Rimini stadium against an Italian House Music team. Word got out that Hunty and myself were footballers, so we were asked to play. As professionals, you're not allowed to do anything like that. You can't do any dangerous sports or play football…but we just looked at each and thought: 'Fuck it, nobody will find out, let's do it'.

"I went left-back – my name was down on the team-sheet as Guest DJ/Defender. Hunty played up front, with people like Paul Oakenfold, Pete Heller. Dave Seaman was also involved. We beat the Italian DJs 6-2, with Andy scoring four. There was hardly anyone there apart from MTV, who had a girl called Simone working for them. She saw Hunty and thought: 'Christ, this DJ can play…' and they got together after that and have been together since. That was some week. We were partying and enjoying the Italian House scene. Incredible.

"Nothing was ever said about the game. But about a year later, I was interviewed by DJ Magazine in London. They spoke to myself, Danny Dichio and David James – we were all into our music. Next thing I know, our coach John Trewick had managed to get hold of the magazine and I could see him laughing. I thought: 'Oh shit, they've printed the team photo of that game' – Andy and I were fully kitted out with the other players in it – but, of course, Tucker wouldn't have known it was played a year earlier. Thankfully, we got away with it."

Hunt arrived as a rough-around-the-edges forward in 1993 – the final piece of Ossie Ardiles's promotion-winning side. By the mid-90s, the forward was emerging as a more elegant and stylish striker with the capacity to create space where others couldn't while capable of scoring a good 15-20 goals per season. Off the field, he looked more like the front man for a Britpop band than an elite footballer, with a mass of floppy hair, shirt nearly always untucked and a gait that was more in tune with Indie music. He gave the impression he might be more at home at Snobs than in the opposition box, yet appearances were deceptive.

Despite Albion's mid-90s indifference, Hunt's career continued to blossom. He was to become their first player to exploit the Bosman Ruling – leaving for Charlton on a free transfer at the end of his contract in 1998. He enjoyed two seasons in the top flight with the Londoners before his career was brought to a shattering end due to chronic fatigue syndrome at barely 30. These days, he lives on a ranch and owns a business in Belize, surrounded by Amazonian rainforests. Long before Central America came calling, he lived in a jungle of another kind – the urban sprawl of mid-1990s Birmingham. Burgess remembers those times with fondness.

"Andy was just brilliant," he recalled. "When he first moved here, he lived in the Moat House and had his mates hanging around, along with his brother Mark. We all hung around together. They were like students. Andy wasn't a typical footballer – he was into his music and didn't care how he looked. Buckley used to call him 'Stude' as in 'student' – 'just look at Stude...just a fucking student, pretending to be a footballer.' But Hunt knew how to play football. He was so raw when he arrived but he worked on his upper body and he just got better. The thing about Andy is that he understood football really well. He was able to adapt and was intelligent on the ball. I always said that he came to us as a boy and left as a man. That's how it felt. He developed into such a stylish player.

"As a bloke, he was so laid-back. He bought a house by the old Tower Ballroom, near Birmingham Reservoir. His mates would treat it like a youth hostel. He had a pair of decks and a mixer. We'd play music, go to clubs and every Saturday we'd end up in Liberty's on Broad Street and then go back to his. Not that you'd get much sleep. He had a sheet up against the window, rather than curtains. Those were funny times. Sometimes they'd play sausage cricket – bear with me here, it's not what you think it is – which is where you don't play with a ball. You get a pack of sausages from the fridge and use them as a ball. So they'd be smashing these raw sausages with the bat, leaving them stuck to the walls and over the neighbours' fences and into the road. There was sausage everywhere. It was absolute carnage. Like I said, Andy was more like a student than a footballer."

Burgess joined Albion as a 15-year-old and left in 2001. He is a rare case, having played for the club over a period spanning three different decades. It was legendary scout Roy Horobin who spotted the youngster playing for Birmingham following some training sessions at Villa and Manchester City. At one point, Burgess was training with Albion, Blues and Villa until a backroom change at The Hawthorns defined his future.

"I'd been at Birmingham from about 12," he added. "Roy asked me to train with Albion, then there was a clash of days when the three clubs trained, so I opted to go to Blues. Then their chief scout, Norman Bodell, went to West Brom and, as soon he went, he took me there as a schoolboy. That was in 1986. I signed a pro-contract in 1989 but loved being an apprentice, doing the kit, cleaning the boots and dressing room. That might sound weird but it was a great craic with the other lads and really made me appreciate the potential move to the first team."

Brian Talbot was Burgess's first main manager, alongside Sam Allardyce. He missed the game that sealed Talbot's exit – "I was injured, thank God" – but believes the Albion manager's fate was decided long before the Woking defeat by a chance meeting with another coach. It started a sequence of events that completely refocused Talbot's vision about the Baggies' style …and not necessarily in a good way.

"Brian was my first manager and at first it went well for him after he replaced Ron Atkinson [in 1988]," said Burgess. "But the dynamic changed. He swapped Stuart Pearson and Sam Allardyce around, so effectively Pearson was 'demoted' to the reserves and Sam stepped up. He (Allardyce) could be deemed a bully these days if football now was the way it was. He didn't hold back but you accepted that no-nonsense approach back then. But, equally, I'm not sure that swap-around of staff helped Brian. The story goes that he had gone on holiday in the summer of 1989 and bumped into Dave Bassett, who was doing a great job with Sheffield United. They had a bet about who would win the opening game of the season (Albion v Sheffield United) and they absolutely thumped us, with Tony Agana and Brian Deane running us ragged.

"That game really had a big effect on Brian. It made him rethink how we played. I suspect bumping into Dave Bassett had a significant impact because he was doing so well playing a very direct way. So when Sheffield beat us so convincingly, that persuaded Brian we needed to go the same way. That wasn't Stuart Pearson's style but Sam Allardyce was more of a Bassett sort of a guy. He was loud, brash and more outgoing than Brian and Stuart. Would it have been better under Brian and Pearson? I think so. What I did know is that the lads in the reserves loved playing under Pearson – it was all sharp, one-touch games, passing, movement. It was fun. Then you'd come into the first team and it was more methodical and pragmatic, certainly much more regimented. The reserves and first team were completely opposite experiences for a player."

Having played for so many managers – nine, not including caretakers – Burgess inevitably has his favourites. Ossie Ardiles and Ray Harford feature highly. He said: "Ossie was brilliant. He just loved training, especially the circle where you keep the ball. Whenever we played five-a-side, if someone hit a long ball, you'd hear him shout: 'Vim-ble-don, Vim-ble-don'. He was top class.

A lovely, intelligent guy and a breath of fresh air. Ray was the best coach I've worked for. He only came in Mondays and Thursdays. He would do the teamwork then and leave the coaches to it. He treated people like men. He wouldn't rant and rave but there was a purpose to all he said and all we did. Every exercise we did in training had a meaning. On Saturday, it was all structured to how you wanted to play, so you knew exactly what you were doing. Once when Paul Raven and Paul Mardon were playing and I wasn't in the side, Ray caught me up while I was walking back after training. He said: 'Daryl, don't worry, you'll get your chance'. He didn't have to say that but at least he was thinking about it. That's good management."

Featuring less favourably with Burgess, were Harford's three immediate successors, Denis Smith, Brian Little and, his final Baggies boss, Gary Megson. "Smith was just fucking horrendous," recalled Burgess. "He was the worst I've ever had. He couldn't coach. He needed Malcolm Crosby but couldn't get him in for six weeks, so all we did during that period was practice games. He also had a problem with the senior players for some reason; a real mistrust of them. I ended up out of the team and in the reserves playing on Wednesdays, which meant Tuesdays became my Fridays. I hated that. And one of the few times I played in the team, I went on against Sheffield United and smashed into Nigel Spackman. After that, Denis made me captain, and I have no idea why. Mind you, I did like John Gorman, who was his no 2 for a while. He was an amazing guy. It's 20 years since my old man died and John came to his funeral – that's the sort of guy he was. I remember he had his old France 98 folder with him that he'd had with Glenn Hoddle at the World Cup. He had the England bits crossed out and was still using it!

"Brian Little was a lovely man and an ex-coach of mine from when I was a kid. But it was just the wrong time for him as he had a fair amount going on in his personal life. He always said: 'Never be embarrassed about a 0-0 draw'. So we went for weeks with them. I remember he once dropped me after bringing me back in for one game. He was so apologetic, which I found strange – you're the boss, you're entitled to drop me. Why are you apologising to me? And then Megson came in and…well, I know he did a great job for the club, but I didn't take to him or his methods. He was too personal with some of the players. There's a way of treating people and he took it too far like the way he treated Bob Taylor. He always went on about 'fucking self-indulgent footballers – they make me sick', like it was our fault that we earned decent money back then, albeit nowhere near what they get now. He had his favourites too, like Jordao and Foxy (Ruel Fox), which never works in a dressing room. To his credit, he gave the club the kick up the backside that it needed…but he wasn't for me."

Perhaps Burgess's most mixed memories remain from that 1992-93 season under Ardiles. An injury to his back, followed by a hernia problem, forced him out for much of the campaign before he was recalled for the final throes. Just when it looked like he might have the consolation of a Wembley appearance, he suffered another setback. "There was a real buzz about the town – the football was brilliant and those barcode kits just seem so iconic now," he said. "Yes, we took some dickings but it was a brilliant time to be playing. Personally, though, it was very bitter-sweet. I didn't properly play until March. I even played in a weight-lifting belt to stop me from extending my back too much. It just wouldn't heal. I went to Harley Street with our physio, Danny Thomas. They did an oblique x-ray where they effectively scanned diagonally and showed up a fractured disc. When I rested, it would fuse ok but then when I played, it would reoccur. In the end, they dissolved the disc with some procedure and it was fixed. The worst thing is that I had no pre-season. And that really does mess you up. You can never catch up. It's impossible."

It was Burgess who threw Albion a lifeline in their play-off semi-final at Swansea, scoring a somewhat fortuitous goal to reduce the deficit to 2-1. But a collision with heavyweight goalkeeper Roger Freestone left him facing a race to be fit for Wembley. The prognosis in the final days was that he might just make the bench but wasn't fit enough to start. With teams restricted to just two substitutes, Burgess felt he had no option but to sit it out. "I was naïve – back then, I thought about the team, not myself!" he added. "Had I been older, I'd have thought: 'Fuck that, I'm not missing Wembley'. But, basically, because of my back, I'd suffered a hernia and my body was struggling to recover from knocks. And as I scored, I went into Roger Freestone and went over, having stopped dead. I played on but was in absolute agony. I missed the home leg, which was absolutely devastating. Ossie, to be fair, gave me until the Friday to make the final on the Sunday but it wasn't to be. I didn't want to start and let the team down after 15 minutes. It was more important we won. Now, with seven on the bench, I'd have been a substitute. But managers were always more likely to go with midfielders and strikers on the bench then.

"Wembley was tough. I'll never forget Gary Strodder's parents coming over to mine and saying: 'I just want to thank your Daryl so much – he's given Gary this chance'. That was a nice touch. I was fine in a way because I'd accepted I wasn't playing. On the Saturday, we stayed in the bar and got pissed but when I walked out in my suit and saw the crowd, it really hit me. I saw my family and friends and realised I was missing out. You're missing out on Wembley, missing out on something special, missing out on that team photo that everyone has on their wall. When we did the bus tour around West Bromwich, I ended up downstairs. I was delighted for the lads but didn't feel part of it. I remember when Roy Keane refused to have a winners' medal – I totally understand that. Mind you, I enjoyed everything after the game. We all went out…that was a great night. And at least I knew we'd be back in a higher division."

The euphoria of promotion didn't last long following Ardiles's departure. First-team coach Dennis Mortimer shuffled along as Keith Burkinshaw's no 2. The Ardiles-Burkinshaw axis was built on a push-and-pull chemistry – two men, so different in character, preaching their own mantra to produce brilliant results and even better football. Burgess feels Burkinshaw and Mortimer simply lacked the gravitas in the dressing room. Burkinshaw's reign, which lasted a little over 16 months, collapsed in embarrassment at Tranmere when Trevor Summers, who had just been succeeded as chairman by Tony Hale, left his seat in the directors' box, marched down to the touchline and began berating the players while his manager looked on, ironically from a seat in the stand. It was to be Burkinshaw's final hurrah.

"We were devastated when Ossie left and it just wasn't the same under Keith," said Burgess. "I know Dennis is a Scouser but he really isn't one of the funny ones. Both men were dour. I remember one session, we'd play in a square and every time he (Mortimer) blew the whistle, we would have to do this, or that. We'd be split into groups and if he wasn't watching, the group would just stop. It was so boring, horrendous. Keith was a great bloke, he'd had a good reputation as boss of Spurs but I think he had the wrong no 2 at Albion. That side should have done much better. We had some good players and didn't achieve what we should have.

"Again, much like the Woking game, I missed the drama at Tranmere. I was injured but went to the match with Andy Thompson, my pal from Virgin, who had managed to get me and Hunty tickets for the second anniversary of Cream. John Aldridge had scored a couple and I'm thinking: 'We're getting a pasting here'. The next thing I see is Trev walking down the stand and taking his place in the dug-out. We're sat there wondering: 'What the fuck is he doing?' When a chairman or director does that, you know the manager is finished. Trev was ok. He was a bubbly bloke who clearly loved the club but he didn't have anywhere near the money we needed. He was outspoken and loved being the big man but he overstepped the mark that day."

Yet little compares to the fun and games of the Gould regime. Burgess, like so many of his peers, saw all aspects of his spell in charge – the good, the bad and the downright barmy. "After Brian Talbot left, we thought Pancho (Stuart Pearson) might get it. He'd done ok and the lads enjoyed playing for him but the board wanted a clean break. We knew they wanted a new direction but Bobby was up against it from the start. He wasn't a popular appointment. I know lads who had played for him who didn't like him. I also knew former Albion players who hadn't got on with him when he was a player, so he was a very hit-and-miss type of bloke.

"But those were different times. We went through a period without a physio. We had a guy called Derek who'd come in and put strappings on during the week and then for games we'd hire one. It was ridiculous. These days, you get a couple running on with the full medical equipment, yet we didn't even have a full-time physio. The one thing Bobby did do was bring a sports psychologist into the club. That was unheard of at the time. But here was this bloke, at ten to three, asking us to close our eyes and wonder what we might do during the game. Can you imagine Graham Roberts and Colin West doing that? I was like: 'Fuck this, I just want to get out there'. 2.50pm wasn't the time to be doing that. You're full of adrenalin. Nobody wants to hear some psychologist going on at them just before kick-off.

"The other thing Bobby would do is injure other players. Not intentionally – just with his mad ideas. He liked playing 'pile on'. He'd nominate somebody and you had to pile on when he said it. Poor Winston White ended up with fractured cheeks at one point. Another time, after we went down, we got absolutely rat-arsed – we needed it – then came into training on the Monday. He quoted the law to us, saying that by our contracts, we were only entitled to have four weeks off a year, so we had only June off. It was only the middle of May, so we were training every day, even the players being released.

"From Monday to Friday, we trained on the pitch, played keep-ball, played 15-a-side and nobody was allowed to call for the ball or speak. Then we had to run from the stadium to the motorway island, turn left down Kenrick Way, down some back streets and back to The Hawthorns. We did that every day when we felt we should have been on the beach. And Bobby was doing it with us. But then, the one day, he said he was going to be off for a few days, so the chief scout Norman Bodell would be doing it with us as he didn't trust us. We knew Norm was never going to do the run. We also knew it took about 20 minutes, so the first day, Gary Robson said: 'Fuck this, I know a short cut'. So we ran through some short cuts and jumped on to what was then the disused train line. We came up the side of Halfords Lane, rounded everyone up and got the lads who would normally come first to go first on 18 minutes. Then the next batch would be sent, then the next…and so on. That was what happened after we went down. We'd had a horrible season and Bobby was determined to punish us."

Gould wasn't averse to acts of spontaneity. Burgess recalls one particularly memorable game against Auxerre. The French club were due to play Liverpool in the second round of the UEFA Cup, having beaten the Reds 2-0 in France two weeks earlier. A week before their Anfield second leg, the side were sent to England for a reconnaissance trip. Bobby Gould decided to treat the French guests to a taste of Black Country football. "We finished training on the Monday and Bobby came in and told us to 'have a good breakfast' before reporting in for 11am the next day," Burgess added. "We assumed we must be on a jolly and having a few beers, so some of the lads had a full English. We turned up at the ground and got changed. Bobby walked in and announced we were playing a friendly against Auxerre on the training pitch across the road.

"They must have had a culture shock when they saw that shit hole of a pitch. It was like a cabbage patch. We're all full of bacon and eggs and they're popping the ball around with great technique. They were playing us off the park but what they didn't expect was the physicality of our football. Once they got a few reducers, it slowed them down a bit and it ended 2-2. That was just typical of Gouldy. He'd just drop a game on us with no warning. At least we got the Wednesday off." Auxerre lost 3-0 at Anfield.

On February 3, 2001, Burgess played his final Albion game – a 2-2 draw against Crystal Palace. His debut was a 2-1 defeat against Port Vale in 1989. He made 332 appearances, scoring ten goals. He saw out his career with Northampton, Rochdale, Kidderminster, Nuneaton and Bromsgrove before retiring in 2008. Asked to name his best Albion side of the Buzaglo-to-Balis era, he struggles over most but gives definite call-ups to Alan Miller, 'a brilliant goalkeeper and bloke', Enzo Maresca, Richard Sneekes, Kevin Kilbane – 'such an underrated player' – Taylor and Hunt, with Don Goodman also mentioned. The rest he spends a while dwelling on.

"That's a lot of games, a lot of players and quite a few managers," reflects Burgess, now an active member of the club's Former Players' Association. "West Bromwich Albion was a massive part of my life. I had so many good times, a few bad times and some memorable times. It was a great time in my life. Playing football was all I wanted to do as a kid. And I did it."

Enzo Maresca

"...I was sat with Van Nistelrooy when I was at Malaga and he asked why I had so many letters and cards. I explained they were from West Bromwich. They are always so good to me..."

Enzo Maresca walks past the Mercedes. And the BMW. And the Audi. Nothing against German cars, you understand. And it's got nothing to do with your Vorsprung durch Technik, you know. Italians are fussy about their cars but not usually this fussy. He walks towards the corner of the showroom and immediately falls in love with a Fiat Panda; bland, ordinary, functional. Not an Alfa Romeo, nor a Lancia. A Fiat Panda. An Italian Fiat Panda. And it's his. It's what he intends showing off to his mates at West Bromwich Albion.

May, 2019. Maresca bounds into the players' lounge at the London Stadium. Behind us is a sketch outline of Sir Geoff Hurst's third goal in the 1966 World Cup final, with the accompanying famous quote paying tribute to Kenneth Wolstenholme's commentary. The walls are decorated with iconography of West Ham's past, with TV screens showing Sky Sports News on continuous loop. Further on is a pristine buffet-style counter, where present-day Hammers players are being treated to the finest cuisine two days before their home game against Southampton.

In front of us, Tony Cottee wanders in. This star of the mid-1980s team is looking for company, possibly wondering where he can find Paul Goddard, Alan Devonshire or Frank McAvennie. Manuel Pellegrini will shortly follow. As will members of the Hammers squad. A vicar then walks in. No idea why. Perhaps he's here to bless the lunch. Or he simply wants to absolve folks of their sins. Who knows? The trappings of aspiration and prosperity couldn't be more obvious. If West Ham United aren't a top-six club on the pitch, they certainly are off it. There is a magnificence and pomp about our meeting venue.

Maresca is the joint assistant head coach to Pellegrini at West Ham. But today, it's all about the past. Dressed all in black, with white trainers, he isn't interested in the food. He is here to discuss West Bromwich Albion in the 1990s. And he is delighted to. He thanks me for my time at the beginning and end. He thinks I'm doing him a favour. How wrong can he be?

Summer, 1998. On this particular Monday morning, Maresca reported for a trial with Denis Smith's squad. The pursuit of him certainly hadn't been conventional. Born in Pontecagnano, he started his career with AC Milan schoolboys before joining Cagliari on the island of Sardinia. He was to be capped at under-15, under-16, under-17, under-18, under-20 and under-21 levels and named in Dino Zoff's initial 40-man squad for Euro 2000.

The Bosman ruling prompted Maresca to move overseas in 1998. At the time, it was beneficial for him to leave Italy. His club were powerless to keep him. This was the first time Albion had made advantageous use of the Bosman ruling since its controversial entry into the fabric of football. The situation was thus: Maresca was represented by agents Gianni Paladini and Mel Eves. Both were based in the West Midlands. This was a key detail. Their location meant Maresca ideally needed to be ring-fenced within Greater Birmingham. Neither particularly fancied travelling up and down the motorways looking after a lad who was too young to be married and no longer living with parents. He simply had to remain in the Midlands. But where?

Wolves were out of the question. Their manager Mark McGhee had an almost stoic, stubborn loyalty to his own agent friends and their players. He was not interested in those belonging to other agents. Birmingham? Maybe. But what about Albion and Villa? And so a carve-up was initiated. Maresca was to spend one week with Albion, then one with Villa. Supposedly. For context, Villa's squad during that campaign included England internationals Gareth Southgate, Ugo Ehiogu, Paul Merson, Stan Collymore, Darius Vassell and Dion Dublin. Albion hadn't had an England international since 1985. Maresca never did make it across the patch.

He flops back into his seat in the London Stadium as he begins the story..."I was speaking with an Italian agent and with another agent (Gianni Paladini and Mel Eves) – also in Italy. They spoke about the chance to move to England and join a club, most likely in the Midlands," he said. "I was only 18 but I wasn't worried about moving countries. I gave them the responsibility of finding me a new club in England and left them to it. There were a few clubs who showed an interest. Aston Villa was one and West Bromwich Albion was the other. I was to spend a week with West Bromwich and the second would be with Villa. But, in the morning, I did my first training....and by the afternoon, there was a contract waiting for me. It was so quick. I had no time to think about it.

"Denis and (assistant manager) Malcolm Crosby were there. Cyrille Regis was a coach but he played that day. Fucking hell, Cyrille Regis... fucking hell! He was a very good player, he was the best out there and he was a coach. He was about 40 but in training he was the best striker I'd seen. The best player by far. Denis saw me train and decided he wanted to sign me. Just one training session and I was called into an office to talk about the contract. That's all it took."

The London Stadium couldn't be further from the 1990s West Bromwich Albion, where there was no training ground and a stadium that wasn't fit for top-flight football. Quaint doesn't cut it in the English top flight. And Albion were some way from being contenders for the Premier League in 1998, although they weren't as far away as they maybe thought at the time. They were in a state of flux, struggling to survive in the second tier while retaining aspirations to join the elite of the Premier League. The glory years of the late 1960s and opposite ends of the 1970s were throttling them with an increasing, pronounced grip as each year passed.

The boardroom had all the stability and directional sense of a three-wheeled shopping trolley. On the field, Albion were labouring. Managers came and went. Those who did well left to go elsewhere. Those who didn't were kept too long and, in some cases, given new deals. Albion had finished tenth in 1997-98, having been top during the first weekend of September. Ray Harford quit in the December, to be replaced by Denis Smith, and Albion won only two of their final 16 games, claiming 12 points from a possible 48.

In Maresca's only full season, 1998-99, they finished 12th. The Premier League seemed some time away from an Albion perspective. And, when it did finally arrive, it would not involve Enzo Maresca. Not directly anyway. But he was to play a part in promotion. More of that later after we have returned to that first training session. In it, Smith watched the player closely but rushed off before it ended.

Mel Eves recalled the morning his phone rang: "I left Enzo on the Monday morning with Cyrille, who I knew well. I knew he'd look after Enzo, so he was in good hands. I then got a call into my Cannock office from someone at Albion – 'Mel, get yourself down here'. The squad were having a game between themselves at what was then their training ground, which was basically the Aston Uni grounds. It wasn't a training ground. It was a field, with changing rooms. Students used it when Albion didn't. It was embarrassing, looking back.

"The game was still going when I arrived – first team v reserves. Denis had been watching. John Wile was chief executive and had been told to come down, too. He turned to me and said: 'Mel, we have got to sign this lad'. Denis was also adamant. He'd seen enough and couldn't get to the phone quick enough. Because Enzo couldn't speak English, he was just going round the pitch yelling: 'Enzo…ball'. They couldn't get it off him. At one point, there was a free-kick on the edge of the area. Bob Taylor, who was God from an Albion perspective, was just about to take it when Enzo shoved him out of the way. Bob just shrugged and watched Enzo curl this beauty into the top corner. The goalkeeper had no chance. Everyone just stood there open-mouthed. Ten minutes later, there was a free-kick on the other side. Bob stepped aside again for Enzo, who stuck it into the other top corner."

Maresca, speaking 21 years on, laughs when reminded of the story. "Yes, West Bromwich acted very quickly," he said. "It was basically after one training game. When I left Italy, the idea was that they started me with West Bromwich because perhaps they didn't trust me and wanted to see if I was ready for them, let alone Aston Villa. But even when I was young, I tried to be grateful at all times and here they were offering me a contract after one day. I wasn't thinking about a chance at Villa. I was just happy to be on a training pitch. And then I was told West Bromwich wanted me, so I never went to Villa."

Eves believed it was the right move. He said: "I was working with the agents in Italy, where the main guy, Gianni Paladini, worked between England and Italy. He contacted me to say he had the Italian under-18 captain. There had been a disagreement with the owner at Cagliari and Enzo wasn't happy. He couldn't go to another Italian club without a fee of around £1m but could go for free if he went abroad. Gianni asked where I would suggest. We wanted him to join a club who would put him in their side as quickly as possible. We had a discussion about Villa but they were doing well in the Premier League, so we didn't think that would be possible. Wolves wasn't an option because we couldn't talk to them but West Brom and Blues were also second tier.

"We needed him to be local as his English wasn't great. The clubs back then didn't have the infrastructure they have now, so he was very much going to be looked after by us and we weren't a big agency. It was just me and Gianni looking after him. Richie Barker was at Albion as a scout and had been my Wolves no 2 when we won the League Cup under John Barnwell. And of course there was Cyrille, so I already had connections there. The process was straightforward. Richie was a bit sceptical at first, saying: 'We've seen this kind of player before'... but there was no cost to Albion. It was a no-brainer for them to look at him and they did."

The Bosman free transfer was completed in summer, 1998, so why Albion, Enzo? He explained to me his reasons for the transition from Cagliari to the Black Country, where a dictionary was never far away and where the local dialect was a challenge. "You know what... I was only 17 when I had to start thinking about leaving Cagliari," he recalls. "I was impressed with West Bromwich. They were playing in front of 15,000, a good atmosphere and the club for me was good, especially for where I was. I was young. I wasn't worried about the things you worry about when you're older. I was happy to sign and knew I had a chance of playing first-team football more quickly.

"I had been away from my family since I was 11, so living alone wasn't new when I came here. I was living away from them to play football, so I had no problems. But England was a different culture, a different language. I had studied French, so it was a big move for me. English was...well, I didn't actually speak English. I lived in Solihull, which was lovely. I always carried a small dictionary in my pocket. You can laugh, but I did. I had to have some way of speaking to others. People would talk to me and I would quickly go for my dictionary and see what I could reply with. It was the only way. At the beginning, the club gave me an English teacher but this wasn't a great help because I was learning 'school English' and hearing it in a different accent. The local accent was very strange and very complex at times. To help me settle, I spent a lot of time in Italian restaurants – one in Solihull, but also San Carlo in Birmingham. I just wanted to speak to other Italian people."

Maresca's agents made sure he was given the best. They took him to a car dealership in Great Bridge to select an appropriate mode of transport. Solihull to Sandwell can be an arduous journey in rush hour but the youngster wasn't interested in luxury. While Eves and Paladini pored over top-of-the-range BMWs and high-end Mercedes models, Maresca was gravitating towards something more subtle. "I was a new driver and had only just passed my test," he smiles. "I didn't want a big car. I wasn't a racing driver. I was new to the club, so my first car could not be big. That would not be appropriate. I bought a Fiat Panda because it was me. What kind of 18-year-old turns up in a BMW or Mercedes before he has played a first-team game? I didn't want to show off as a new player in a new country. I wanted people to recognise I was Enzo Maresca the footballer, not Enzo Maresca, who owns a BMW."

Panda or otherwise, Maresca eased into life at Albion, who had played seven First Division games by the time the Italian was given his League bow. The side had won four, drawn once and lost two when he went on as a 68th minute substitute for Sean Flynn in the 2-0 defeat to Bradford, before playing the second half of the 3-0 loss against Smith's former club Oxford a few days later. His first start came in the mid-December game at Huddersfield. An excellent away performance saw the visitors win 3-0 thanks to two James Quinn goals and one from Lee Hughes during the final throes.

Albion's history books might suggest otherwise but there is every possibility Maresca holds the 'distinction' of being the first Baggies player to be booked without playing. He was yellow-carded in a 2-2 draw against Stockport on October 24, 1998 despite being an unused substitute. All part of the English dressing-room humour, it would seem. "In one of my first games on the bench, the lads said they wanted me to celebrate a goal even if I was substitute. They said it was to make me feel part of the team. So I said whoever scores must run over to me and we celebrate together. Lee Hughes scored and, yes, he ran to the bench and got me on to the pitch. We were there celebrating and the referee (Rob Styles) came over. I thought he'd laugh at me but, no, he gave me a yellow card. I didn't understand. The players were joking with me afterwards. They knew this would happen. They were: 'Come on Enzo, come on to the pitch'. I won't forget that. And then I'm getting told off for being booked. I did hope the referee would be sensible, but...no."

Hughes was a big figure in the Albion dressing room. Others, too. Not least

Mario Bortolazzi. The then 33-year-old had been part of the great AC Milan side of the late 1980s and also played more than 250 games for Genoa as well as featuring for seven other Italian sides. He made 35 appearances for Albion in 1998-99 but his influence off the field was even more crucial. The Venetian, be it by design or by accident, had become a mentor, a chaperone to his young compatriot.

"Ah, Mario, he was a big help," recalls Maresca. "He was a very important person for me. I could learn from him. He'd played for Milan and Genoa and knew so much about the game. We spent a lot of time together in the city centre, walking around, studying the city and he was a steady person around me. I always felt like I needed to behave well when I was with him. And, on the pitch, I would watch him. He was in my position and I tried to see what he did because he always wanted to help me. When I've seen him since – in fact I saw him just a month ago (March, 2019) – we always discuss our time in West Bromwich. It is our bond. As a coach, he has had a great time with Roberto Donadoni and I hope he can continue to do so. He was an important person to me in England."

Maresca produces a glorious grin when talk moves elsewhere in Albion's dressing room. For a man who scored twice in a UEFA Cup final (a 4-0 win for Sevilla against Middlesbrough in 2006) and enjoyed a playing career spanning two decades, he feels an attachment to his first overseas club and team-mates. And he shed some insight on Fabian De Freitas's no-show for an Easter Monday game in 1999, when the striker was asleep, thinking it was an evening kick-off rather than 3pm. Maresca hinted that perhaps it hadn't been the first time, adding: "That was a happy time. I have good memories of my time with those players. Lee Hughes was a little bit crazy. He ate a lot of curry and I wasn't keen to try that. I stuck to San Carlo and Italian food. Then there was Kevin Kilbane, who had many games in the Premier League and was a very good player. Richard Sneekes, Fabian, Mario – they helped me a lot, which was a big thing for me.

"I remember when Fabian didn't turn up. He had fallen asleep before that at other times. It wasn't the first time but everyone remembered this one because we lost so badly (5-1 at home to Crewe). Alan Miller, Graham Potter were good men. Potter lived next door to me in Solihull and most days we would travel in together. Good memories. I am so happy to see him as a coach now. We used to have some good chats about football. James Quinn – he was a funny guy, always joking.

"I played for two coaches, Denis Smith and Brian Little. Both were good men but different. Denis wanted us to attack, to express ourselves. But Brian preferred us to be more defensive. It was enjoyable playing in both systems and I learned a lot from those times." Smith, for his part, spoke about Maresca in an interview with The Guardian in March, 1999. "I took a look at him in only one training session," he said. "I said: 'Yes, I'll take him.' His attitude and his ability were outstanding. He's a winner. As soon as he got into the first team, he was demanding the ball from senior players and knocking it about...the better the standard of football, the more he shines. He has had some outstanding games for us and he believes he is a real good player, which helps. The fans love him to death, so much so that when I first brought him off in a tactical reshuffle, I got slaughtered by the crowd."

Maresca's departure from Albion was for financial reasons but he was to remain at the highest levels before announcing his retirement in January, 2017 after some 20 years as a player. A fee of £4.3m was agreed with Juventus when he was barely 20 and he moved on after 52 Albion games and five goals. A beautifully executed long-range strike at Crystal Palace was his finest contribution.

His exit in January, 2000 was pivotal during a period of transition for the club. It came shortly after Paul Thompson's appointment as chairman, at a point when losses were reaching more than £30,000 a week. Maresca was the sacrifice that had to be made. He became Albion's most expensive sale, with the windfall going some way to restabilising them. Gary Megson arrived in March, 2000. The ball was already rolling...

Despite media speculation during the late-2000s, Maresca was never close to a return. Yet the Albion legacy remains engrained, as regaled by then Hawthorns secretary Dr John Evans. The long-standing administrator spent the entire 1990s as the club's main transfer facilitator, unplugging his fax machine for the final time in 2007. He recalled a conversation with referee Howard Webb following a Sevilla game in the UEFA Cup. The Sheffield official was preparing for the match when he was interrupted by a knock on the door. Over to you, Dr John: "Howard told me Enzo marched into his room, stuck out his hand and introduced himself, before asking where in England he was from. 'I'm from South Yorkshire,' came the reply. Enzo then pretended to know exactly where South Yorkshire was and played along with this, making small talk, making out that he knew all about the place. He then turned to Howard and said, with some assurance, 'Mr Webb...I spent 18 months in West Bromwich, I know England...any problems with my players, you speak to me and I will sort it'. And with that, he turned and left."

While Maresca's knowledge of the seven hills of Sheffield remains somewhat slap-dash, his recollections of the Black Country are more vivid. "I arrived as a boy and left as a man," he concludes. "I always said it was one of the best experiences of my life. I still receive cards from West Bromwich fans. I remember once being sat with (Ruud) Van Nistelrooy when I was at Malaga and he asked why I had so many letters and cards. I explained they were from West Bromwich. The fans there....they were always good to me. It was amazing they still thought of me.

"It was my one regret that I didn't get back to see the stadium or get to play against them. Sevilla played a friendly with Albion (in 2005) but I was injured. That was sad – I would have loved to play that game. It will always be a special club for me. It gave me a move to Juventus. I will never forget that. That agreement helped me. They told me they needed money. The situation wasn't good. And then there was the chance to join Juventus. I couldn't say no to them. And West Bromwich couldn't say no." The English second tier is no Serie A, nor La Liga.

As a coach, Maresca has studied the differences. As a player, he lived those differences. West Bromwich Albion was a privilege he enjoyed. "The leagues are totally different in character," he said. The Premier League is different to La Liga, different to Serie A. And the Championship is totally different to Serie B and Segunda División. It's all about the rhythm of the football. The intensity is so different, too. In Italy, they teach you how to be compact, to prevent conceding a goal. In Spain, you are told how to create and score. Italy is about defence. Spain is about attack. England is about intensity. Bang, bang, bang...everything is quick and has to happen now.

"Football is the same sport but a different game. And without this move to West Bromwich, I wouldn't have become the player I did. It was a new experience for me that changed and shaped my outlook. My character changed and improved a lot. I was in a different culture. It wasn't easy but a great experience. It gave me a lot of things. Football now is completely different to 20 years ago and you cannot compare. We are more aware of tactics and analyse those more."

No interview with Maresca could conclude without asking about THAT Superman t-shirt – the one he displayed after scoring against Portsmouth and Oxford in 1999. He no longer has it, disappointingly. "I remember the shirt idea but have no memory of where it came from," he added. "I wore it and I showed my t-shirt after scoring. When you are young, you do that. Now, I'd be booked. But it does sum up what I feel about the club. I have good feelings about West Bromwich. I look back and enjoy my memories. It was a wonderful time in my career that I will always look back on with fondness."

Alan Miller

"...There was blood everywhere, with punches being thrown left, right and centre. The police came in, wouldn't let us leave, the Ipswich staff wanted to press charges against me and after an hour, we got marched to the boardroom to explain ourselves..."

May, 1998. Alan Miller doesn't know if he's in a weird dream or the throes of an out-of-body experience. It might even be the morphine. He is bed-ridden. His employers, West Bromwich Albion, have seemingly forgotten about him and don't even know he's in hospital. His horse was due to run in a race but was a non-starter. Miller missed it anyway and his hero, Frank Sinatra, has died today – May 14, 1998. Is all this happening? Yes, it is. It really is. It feels like the worst of times for Miller but also the best of times because Alan Miller is still alive. He is lucky. The flow of bacteria from a ruptured bowel, following a routine operation, hasn't entered his bloodstream. See, it hasn't been a bad day after all.

Alan Miller is something of a Lord of the Manor these days. He resides near to, and works on, the beautiful Holkham estate, employed as a business development manager with the events team. He has been there for nearly a decade at Holkham Hall, an elegant 18th century Palladian-style country house close to the Norfolk coastline. It is a different world to the hustle and bustle of the Black Country. Miller's appearance has changed, too. The dark short hair is now a touch longer, swept back and a lighter shade. He is clean-shaven no more. A beard has spread across the lower third of his face.

As a player, Miller spent six years at Arsenal as deputy for John Lukic and David Seaman before spending several building his profile with various loan moves. He was part of Bryan Robson's Middlesbrough revolution and ended up at Albion – first on loan, then permanently. For two hours in these stunning surrounds, he is being taken back to the late 1990s, when he was the custodian of an Albion side that all-too-briefly looked to be heading on to better things.

Yet it's often forgotten that his 1997 move from Boro was his second spell at the club. He spent time here earlier and says: "I'd been there in 1991 when Bobby Gould was manager. There seemed to be a real split in the camp between the older players and the younger ones who were coming through. It wasn't a great time for the club. When I came back a few years later under Ray (Harford), I was a lot older, had done more and found it a different, happier place. My Middlesbrough time was coming to an end, so I was just desperate to play. I played with Ray's son at Arsenal, so I knew a bit about him already and we hit it off straightaway. Paul Crichton wasn't having a good time, so it fell into place for me. It was a bad time for 'Crotch'. To say he didn't have the best relationship with Albion fans would be putting it mildly. But he was a good, honest lad.

"I knew I needed to get away from Middlesbrough. It was a big revolution up there. Bryan Robson was manager. He already had Gary Walsh, then Mark Schwarzer came in, so I knew I wouldn't be first-choice. West Brom was a great move for me and knowing Ray was in charge suited me. It went well. There was a real buzz about the club and I couldn't wait to play from week to week. It is exactly what I wanted. I felt I would be reaching my peak and I needed football."

Ray Harford took over from Alan Buckley in February, 1997, a few weeks before Miller's arrival. Harford, who appointed Cyrille Regis and John Trewick as his assistants, had had an undulating coaching and managerial career. Following the relegation of financially-crippled Fulham, he led Luton Town to successive League Cup finals in 1988 and 1989 (winning the first) before taking Wimbledon to seventh place after succeeding Gould.

Yet it was as a coach that he excelled. In 1992, he joined Second Division Blackburn as Kenny Dalglish's right-hand man and they won promotion that season before claiming the Premier League title in 1994-95. When Dalglish moved 'upstairs' to take a more executive role, Harford was thrust back into management. Following an unsuccessful spell, he left in October, 1996 and was replaced by future Albion boss Roy Hodgson.

Regardless of Harford's record as a manager, Albion had appointed a man of pedigree. And Miller feels extremely strongly about the suggestion that Harford was a better coach than he was a manager. There was also a misconception that Harford was a dour, down-beat man. Miller believes that could not be further from the truth – a sentiment shared by many team-mates from the time. Indeed, everyone who played under Harford and was interviewed for this book, cites him as the best coach they played for. Miller is arguably his most impassioned cheerleader. He paints the picture of a man who enjoyed playing a dry poker-faced persona for the media and public but opened up to his players.

"I thought there were some very unfair comments made by people who didn't know him" he added. "They were saying he was miserable. Absolute rubbish! He was nothing of the sort. Ask any of the lads….he was one of the funniest blokes around. Hilarious. He, John Trewick and Cyrille got on so well and the chemistry between them was brilliant. Ray loved being on the training field, he loved coaching. He wasn't a fan of press conferences or dealing with people outside the football bubble. Maybe that's why there was such a misconception about him. He was once asked at Blackburn about signing a big-name player and replied: 'I'll sign Englebert Humperdinck to keep you lot happy, shall I?' His humour was great but very dry and some people didn't get it. But I found him hilarious. People outside the club didn't realise how wonderful he was as a personality."

Harford was regarded as a supreme coach, with a flair for innovation. His Albion sides were well-drilled, with a focus on ball retention, defending in packs and a midfield often supporting one or two strikers. That he had Bob Taylor, Paul Peschisolido, Andy Hunt and later Lee Hughes to choose from was a blessing. Miller cites a match at Middlesbrough where Harford's passion for football came to the fore. He offered an insight into his manager's versatility and influences by continuing: "The thing with Ray is that he just loved everything to do with football but especially about learning new things.

"At Boro, he clocked me loitering around the hotel foyer, so he asked me to stay behind. With him was Malcolm Allison, who was Ray's big hero. Malcolm had been renowned as a tactician, a coach who wasn't afraid to try different things. We sat there and I just listened to them talking football, talking tactics. It was wonderful. Malcolm told us this idea about starting a game with two banks of five to totally confuse the opposition. He always said he wanted to try it to confuse the full-backs and then have the players splitting, so the opposition would be caught unawares.

"Ray had his own views. He loved the concept of exploiting space but in the opening few minutes of games, he wanted to stretch opposing full-backs, put the ball over them because he knew that would unsettle them and they would hate it. He knew they'd get deeper, which meant the centre-backs would get deeper. Although Ray loved playing it on the floor, he knew he could unsettle sides and create space. If he could do that early in games, he knew it would trouble defenders. It worked. It was so simple. He was ahead of his time totally and was always wanting to know why this worked, or that worked or why something else might not work. He'd be fantastic in today's game. He had so much more to offer. He was engaging, great company. If the manager believes in you, you play well and it was my favourite time as a player. The other thing with Ray is that he made better players out of the ones he inherited. You'll struggle to find anyone with a bad word about him."

Albion started 1997-98 in eye-catching form. This was new territory for supporters following several years of mediocrity under Buckley and Keith Burkinshaw. An opening-day victory against Tranmere came courtesy of a strike by Andy Hunt and a goal by debutant Kevin Kilbane. The following week, Albion were 2-1 behind at Crewe, only for Lee Hughes to be pitched into the fray. It was a gamble. Hughes had signed from Kidderminster that summer and was extremely raw – with his enthusiasm frequently overriding common-sense. Yet, on a sunny afternoon at Gresty Road, the abandonment of conformity was exactly what Albion needed. They needed an off-the-cuff option and Hughes provided it. The gamble paid off. Hughes scored twice in the closing minutes to give Albion victory.

Miller speaks fondly of the young striker. "Hughesie was this raw talent, with such an infectious personality. He reminded me of Ian Wright when he came through at Palace from non-League. He was just glad to be there and, certainly at that point, it wasn't about money. He was there for the love of the game. He couldn't stop scoring and came at a perfect time for us. He would just score goals and the game at Crewe catapulted him into the limelight. Ray just gave him licence to do what he liked. He played on instinct. He was just phenomenal."

There was also plenty to keep Albion players entertained off the field when Hughes was around. His naivety, boyish charm and want to impress his seniors left him vulnerable to more experienced, savvy colleagues. Miller added: "He loved horses. We went to Cheltenham and he said: 'Bloody hell, Alan, have a look at this horse's form. He's been first, first, seventh.'. That didn't seem right, so I checked and replied: 'Hughesie, what are you talking about? That's his weight, you idiot: 11.7.' It was too late. He'd only gone and put a load of money on at 25/1. I think the horse is still running. My worry with Lee was that if he didn't have someone advising him, he might fall into the wrong company. Whether that happened, I don't know but it was a big shame how his career panned out. When I was there, he was a breath of fresh air. He was a good kid."

Better was to come the following week when Wolves came to town. Albion won 1-0 courtesy of a Keith Curle own goal. Two years later, Curle was to miss a penalty in the derby at Molineux. Not for a while had a Wolves player endeared himself so much to Albion supporters. The Baggies were flying without even needing to score goals for themselves. Fans were starting to believe this was more than just a lucky streak.

Miller kept a diary of that particular season. His notes remain unpublished and the draft was handed to me for further background. The entry for August 24 reads: "Well, it's actually happened: West Bromwich Albion 1 Wolves 0. It was the biggest and most enjoyable game since I started with Albion. The scenes afterwards were amazing, the atmosphere was incredible and now I understand what it (the derby) is all about. I got a taxi in the evening to go out somewhere and the cab driver who picked me up said he'd earlier picked up an 85-year-old woman from her house. As she got into the car, she turned to him with her fist in the air and said: 'We've done it. We've beaten them.'"

That was the game Miller wore his 'Boing Boing' t-shirt and pulled up his jersey during the celebrations to reveal it. It remains one of the most endearing Albion images of that era. Unfortunately, it was used on the front page of the Express & Star. Miller, clearly in need of a social event planner, was already looking forward to a night out…at Wolverhampton Racecourse.

"At Middlesbrough, Fabrizio Ravanelli had this thing where he pulled his t-shirt over his head," added Miller. "I hadn't played in an Albion-Wolves derby and didn't realise how big it was. I just loved the build-up, the phone-ins and all the media attention. I thought: 'I know what I'll do…I'll get a t-shirt with Boing Boing on the front'. I didn't tell anyone but the fans were so, so up for the game. I couldn't wait for it and, as the whistle went, I turned round to the

Wolves fans, showed it to them and ran down the other end. I didn't think any more of it until leaving the game. I had a horse running at Wolverhampton. I called a cab and the driver said: 'Where are you going?' I told him and he just said: 'You've got no chance…I'm not taking you. I've just been listening to the phone-ins and they want to kill you'. He then showed me the paper with the photo on the front. Some years later, I was in Spain and was accosted by a group of Wolves fans – they were ready to lynch me. It must have cost me two hours, loads of flannel about how big Wolves were and about 200 Euros for beer before I finally calmed them down. I put it on Twitter some time ago and it went mental. There was no social media then in 1997. Had it happened now, I probably would have been lynched!"

Albion claimed a draw at Ipswich to finish August unbeaten and topped the table with ten points from 12.

On August 31, the nation woke up to the most brutal and grave news. Diana, the Princess of Wales, had been killed in a car crash in Paris. Her partner Dodi Fayed also perished. The country became suspended in shock and grief. It was the UK's equivalent of the 'JFK moment'. Anyone old enough to recall that Sunday morning will have their own vivid memories of where they were, or what they were doing when they heard. Days of recriminations, reflection, anger, upset and so much more dominated the agenda. Football seemed a long way from people's minds. News bulletins were dominated by one story – much like 9/11 four years later.

The funeral was arranged for the following Saturday, which meant the entire sporting schedule was scrapped. It would be a national day of mourning. Albion's game against Reading was switched to the Sunday as the week was set against a backdrop of unprecedented grief and remembrance. This might seem small fry now compared with the blanket coverage of 9/11 and the coronavirus pandemic but, in 1997, it was new territory for us all. A country that wore dignity and stoicism with national pride suddenly found itself crumbling in collective sadness. Flowers were stacked several metres deep outside Buckingham Palace. To underline the contradiction and paradox of human behaviour, an angry populace turned on the media. This was while they were lapping up round-the-clock coverage, hanging on every word broadcast on the BBC's news networks and boosting sales of every newspaper. You simply couldn't buy a paper after 10am that week. Yet any journalist was fair game for public abuse. It was a strange time.

While this outpouring might seem bizarre now, Miller's diary offers a fascinating insight into how Diana's death impacted on him. He was unhappy with the 'business as usual' approach of the football authorities who insisted games would go ahead on the Sunday. His entry for September 2, when the funeral date was announced, reads: "I think it is wrong. I don't think there should be any games over the weekend. We've got a game on Wednesday (against Stoke), which is fair enough. That will be played and obviously we will be wearing the armbands and have a minute's silence. But with the game on Sunday, it means we're going to have to train on the Saturday, which will be difficult. I just think the whole weekend should be left clear as a mark of respect. The whole country is still in shock. Everywhere you go, there seems to be a sombre mood. I just feel it's going to be a long and awful week with a lot of attention. Sometimes, you don't know what you've got until you lose it and this is definitely the case for everyone in this country now."

On the day of the funeral, a clearly emotional Miller noted his feelings. Reading them now, some 23 years later, it seems remarkable that a nation could grieve for one person in such a way. Yet this was a very real reflection and Miller wrote: "It's a very emotional day. It has been a very long, upsetting week. I couldn't really concentrate at training. I just wanted to get it out of the way to watch the service. Sport comes as secondary on days like this…I'm not afraid to say, I cried a few times during the service and after watching the telly in the evening. These last few days have brought everyone together. Everybody seems to be united on this, which I've never seen before."

The following day, Albion returned to the top of the second tier thanks to a 1-0 victory over struggling Reading. It was all starting to look promising for Ray Harford and his side.

But promise often remains unfulfilled and so began a chain of events that was to see Albion's season unravel, including the departure of the popular Harford. The initial issue was, inevitably, about ambition – or, rather, Albion's perceived lack of it. And the matter revolved around one of their hottest properties, Paul Peschisolido. He had been a surprise signing from Birmingham – the deal seemed so sudden that many Albion fans on the Isle of Man for a pre-season tournament were shocked to see him rock up at a bar on the day he signed, looking like a little boy lost. He hadn't even met his new team-mates properly and those supporters who spoke to him found him somewhat shocked to be at the club.

Peschisolido signed a three-year deal but took a £30,000-a-year pay drop. So it was always on the cards that he would be looking for a better deal at some point. According to reports at the time, he had been promised a review in the summer of 1997. By then, he was playing some of the best football of his career, so, not surprisingly, his agent Eric Hall began agitating for a new contract. The then chief executive John Wile gives his account of those discussions elsewhere but Miller's diary offers an interesting version of events.

He wrote: "Eric Hall isn't everyone's favourite but he is good at his job. Pesch said to me: 'They've broken their promise and they've offered me a contract which we both felt was unsatisfactory'. It was embarrassing and he felt and said that the best thing for him to do would be to put in a transfer request. Pesch added: 'I've had two or three meetings where we would speak and I would tell them what I wanted and they'd say 'ok we will get back to you on that' and got my hopes up. Then, each time, they would come back and refuse to budge, so we cannot even meet half-way. Not even an inch. If they are going to rate me at £2m, why wouldn't they give me a contract worthy of a £2m player? They said I wanted big sums here and there, it's not true really. I know what other players are on and I'm on the lower end of the scale as far as salaries are concerned. What I'm asking for isn't a Premiership (sic) wage. What I'm asking for wouldn't even put me in the top three earners at the club. I just want to be paid what I feel I should be paid and what they promised to pay me. I'm not being ridiculous. I want to stay at this club. I am enjoying it and I just want a long-term contract in line with what other players are earning. If offered that, I will sign it and be settled. I do not want to leave.'"

Miller, who was good friends with Peschisolido, was unimpressed with Albion's stance on the protracted contract tug o' war. "The whole Pesch thing was badly handled," he added. "He didn't want a lot of money, there was no communication and the frustrating thing was that he was loving his football. It was a very strange situation. I remember calling him once and he was distraught. It was being portrayed in the press that he was trying to leave. That wasn't the case at all."

Peschisolido's views fell on deaf ears. Albion weren't about to budge. And, in their defence, they most probably lacked the financial muscle to budge. On October 24, the Canadian international joined Fulham for a fee that would eventually exceed £1.25m. Financially, it was understandable, although the player was taking a drop in standards, with Kevin Keegan's big-spending side in the third tier. Inevitably, they won promotion, overtook Albion and reached the Premier League in 2001, by then under the management of Jean Tigana.

Back in autumn, 1997, Albion's problems were about to gather pace. By the end of October, Ray Harford was being linked with other clubs, notably Sheffield Wednesday and Queens Park Rangers. Wednesday turned to their former manager Ron Atkinson but, on December 3, a concerned Miller noted: "Hearing very strong rumours about QPR trying to get Ray Harford as manager. The way people are talking, I think this is a real possibility now. It's going to be a nightmare for us and the club if he leaves…it would be the worst thing that could happen to us." The following morning, Harford resigned.

Miller was himself being linked with big-money moves to Liverpool and Chelsea, such was his form. He feels Albion's momentum started disintegrating following Harford's exit. Albion were fourth but the sparkle was fading. Where they had played with a strident streak earlier in the season, now they were beginning to toil. Too many of the better results were down to Miller producing match-winning performances.

Harford had known the money was running out. In Albion's defence, the board perhaps had every right to be reticent. For while Harford had signed Kilbane and Miller, he had also spent the best part of £1m on Graham Potter and Mickey Evans from Southampton. Neither player justified such an outlay. Even so, Miller's mind was made up. He added: "In the end, a lack of ambition was the reason Ray left. Later in my career, I went to Blackburn and could see what was in place. He had experienced this and wanted to bring elements of it to West Brom. It just didn't happen and it got frustrating for him. He was used to higher standards and the club weren't willing to aspire to those standards.

"When I was at Middlesbrough, we had players like Bryan Robson, Juninho, Ravanelli. Before that, I'd been at Arsenal, where we'd had Adams – people who were big characters or leaders. We had good players at Albion but had no leaders. I tried to use my experience, to try and bring some of that to the dressing room without taking over. It worked. People got a lift. They were buying into the way Ray wanted to do things, how we trained, the plans he had and the club was showing signs of coming out of this slump. We finished that first season under him and thought we would have a really successful time under him."

Albion were linked with Celtic's Paul McStay during summer, 1997 – a fanciful pursuit that simply came to nothing. McStay retired instead. Aston Villa's Graham Fenton rejected the same move. Harford was finding Albion's lack of financial clout a struggle against his own ambitions. "I know he was very close to leaving that summer," Miller said. "We had no training facilities. We were told on the morning where we would be training. He'd been promised things that didn't come to fruition. Had he had a club to join that summer, he would have moved on earlier. We felt we had been going somewhere. The younger lads I knew from 1991 like Raves and Burge were more experienced and we had players like Bob, Andy Hunt, Richard Sneekes, too. And we had this manager with a refreshing way of playing and approaching things. It was an exciting time for us. And then it was over."

Harford's time at Loftus Road was unsuccessful. He went on to work as a coach for Millwall before falling ill in the early 2000s. Sadly, he died from cancer on August 9, 2003.

Denis Smith took over from Harford but the chemistry between players and manager was completely different. Perhaps Smith was unfortunate to be the 'next guy in'. Successors frequently struggle when replacing successful or popular managers. Miller believes Smith's approach repelled many of Albion's senior players. Instead of bringing the more experienced campaigners onside, Smith felt inclined to push them away. In the same way Miller had observed a split in Bobby Gould's squad in 1991, it appeared the same issue was arising on Smith's watch some seven years later.

The keeper was still coming to terms with Harford's exit, continuing: "I was devastated. We lost someone who was taking us in the right direction. It ripped the soul out of the club. He joined QPR and the commute was probably an hour less but we really, really missed him. I didn't know Denis at the time. He was methodical, set in his ways and structured. He was obsessed with practice games. I felt we went backwards under him. We disagreed on a lot of things. Under Ray, I knew what he wanted between myself and the defence.

We had confidence in each other. Under Denis, that line of communication became blurred. I didn't know what he wanted and, because of that, my relationship with the defenders became confused and it impacted on our performances and confidence."

Of particular annoyance to Miller was Smith's interference in goalkeeping matters. Smith explains in his own chapter that he preferred Phil Whitehead's ability to play out from the back with his feet. Miller feels his own strength was the ability to boss his area. Smith stifled that by instructing him to absolve himself of the responsibility of being the dominant unit at set-pieces. The new boss made it clear Miller was to cede his dominance to the defenders in front of him. This in itself illustrates the challenges a change of manager can have, with one coach allowing his keeper to be the alpha force at the back while another wants the defenders in charge. Miller's role was reduced to merely rubber-necking his defenders' contributions and being alert to any efforts on goal they failed to deal with. Crucially, Smith's favoured system of set-piece defending was contradicting Miller's strengths. Whether or not that had anything to do with Smith being a dominant centre-half himself, and with a history of having strong centre-halves at his previous clubs, such as Matty Elliott and Darren Purse, is up for debate. But Miller wasn't pleased.

"During one practice game, he had a go, telling me I had the wrong starting position for crosses. I totally disagreed with him, especially with free-kicks – he wanted me to stand in a place which would have left me exposed and looking embarrassed had I conceded. There was a game against Port Vale where I made a mistake. I'd made some good saves in the game but in the final seconds, I misjudged a corner. They scored and I felt absolutely awful. I was devastated. The gaffer came in fuming and absolutely slaughtered me in front of the other lads saying I should have caught the corner. I told him that had I been able to catch it, I would have done – and reminded him it was he who told me to stop going out for crosses and leave them to the defenders. It got very heated and fortunately a couple of the lads held me back, otherwise it would have got nasty. It got to the stage where I could have done something I would have regretted. The way I was criticised, the manner of it, I felt was out of order. Some of the lads felt he was wrong, too. The next day, I'd calmed down, only to read he had absolutely slaughtered me in the press."

Things deteriorated further. With the transfer deadline approaching, Smith's desire to rid the club of its stronger characters was bearing fruit. He was prepared to sacrifice three of Albion's 1993 promotion heroes, all of whom were strong, vocal forces in the dressing room. Ian Hamilton and Bob Taylor left and Andy Hunt's departure collapsed late on, although he would exit in the summer. Miller shakes his head when reminded of that period.

"I couldn't believe what was happening," he added. "We sold Ian Hamilton to Sheffield United, Bob Taylor went to Bolton and Andy Hunt almost left for Manchester City. All big characters. Had Hunty gone, it would at least have earned Albion £1m. He ended up leaving for Charlton on a Bosman free transfer a month or so later. Andy was not only highly-rated but very astute. He thought about things, he was switched on and a bit like Pesch actually – both were educated. He'd become aware of this rule, read into it and he was right – why should a club have ownership of a player if that contract runs out? It worked out for him as he ended up moving to Charlton and doing well in the Premier League. To lose Bob and then Andy was a big thing. They were two big names and a strike-force. They scored goals and were figureheads. That set alarm bells ringing. The place was becoming unstable. They just let Bob go. He was another who engaged with the fans, which wasn't something Denis liked particularly. When I left for Blackburn, it kind of happened. I found myself gone, wondering how it had happened."

Miller felt his manager could have done more to overcome his own insecurities around dealing with the senior players; those who clearly had presence in the dressing room. "Some managers welcome players like that but he obviously regarded them as a threat," he said. "He didn't like people like that. He suppressed us, he stopped us functioning. I would stop coming out for balls and my confidence took a knock. It was long-ball in training. It was just boring. Bob was another big personality. He didn't take to Denis either. I have nothing against him at all now. Denis later told me that he'd probably read me wrong. We should have talked. The mutual respect was there. I could have helped him rather than be perceived as a threat. He was wrong to think I would cause trouble. I could have given him background, some intel…he was wrong but I admired him for being honest. It's all water under the bridge but it was very difficult at the time."

Albion's form dropped alarmingly on Smith's watch. Behind the scenes, it was clear the Smith-Trewick dynamic was not working. Malcolm Crosby would be appointed no 2 by the end of February. Around the same time, Albion lost 3-0 at home to bottom club Portsmouth and, for the first time, supporters turned on Smith, calling for his dismissal and chanting: 'Are you Buckley in disguise?'

It was after that Pompey game that defender Shane Nicholson failed to provide a drugs test – his second such misdemeanour. He had previously been warned about his behaviour after claiming his drink had been spiked by a friend. Once was bad enough. Miller said: "Shane had his obvious problems and I felt he let himself down quite badly, which is a shame because he was a good player. He got caught with a substance and, sadly, there was no way back. Deep down, he was a good lad but he had a colourful social life. I remember one of the incidents well. He drove in to where we were training – I was behind him – and he must have recognised the testers' car and just drove straight out again. I presume he thought he'd get into trouble."

On the pitch, Smith had already decided Miller wasn't the keeper for him. As well as the issue of who commanded the penalty area, the manager believed Miller wasn't adept enough with his feet. He returned to Oxford to bring in Phil Whitehead. Albion fans were already fearing the worst. Alan Buckley persistently returned to Grimsby to sign players. Now, their current manager was replacing their hero with a goalkeeper from his old club. It wasn't going to end well.

In the summer of 1998, Smith stated that Whitehead would be his no 1. Once the season kicked off, though, Miller kept his position. It wasn't an ideal situation for Whitehead to be thrust into. Despite Albion struggling for form, Miller remained a popular figure among supporters. Whitehead, a completely different character to his rival, never enjoyed a particularly fruitful relationship with Albion fans. At times, it appeared he was disliked for simply not being Alan Miller.

"The gaffer had said a few weeks before that Phil was going to be his no 1, even though I had a decent pre-season," Miller recalled. "But then the fans started to turn on Phil. They were chanting my name and I guess that would have crushed him. I can understand that totally. I think Phil always had a problem with the affinity I had with the fans and I felt sorry for him in that respect. It really hit home in a friendly against Coventry. Phil and I got on great and I always felt his battle was with the supporters, rather than with me. But I do remember cringing a bit at the fans chanting my name when he was playing. It can't have helped Phil, although I appreciated the support they were showing me."

At the end of 1997-98, Miller needed surgery. He had a double hernia and the operation was the kind footballers put on hold until a season ends. All routine stuff. With luck, Miller was going to be out for six weeks, catch up with his pre-season training and be back in time for the new campaign. And, indeed, he was. But not without dramas. The surgery meant Miller would have to make do without an end-of-season jolly with some of his team-mates. However, he did not account for the complications that followed. Major complications.

Miller takes a moment to compose himself as he describes how an error during the procedure led to one of his major organs becoming punctured and to an infection that could easily have claimed his life. Incredibly, because of the timing, nobody at Albion fully realised the gravity of his ordeal. They knew he had gone under the knife but were not aware of the complications and there was little contact. Miller said: "The lads went off to Magaluf but I stayed behind for the operation and it just didn't feel right. Something was wrong. The doctors said: 'You'll be fine, it's just the operation'. I remember going home and falling very, very ill. I was rushed back in and they examined me again. I had to have another anaesthetic, which wasn't ideal as I'd had one so recently. The next thing I know, I'm waking up with loads of tubes and pipes coming out of me. The physio had gone on holiday, the gaffer was on his jollies, the chairman was away, the players were away. Nobody from the club knew I was in there still. They'd assumed I was getting on with rehab. I ended up being in hospital for a month. I developed a massive abscess and it was then they discovered they'd ruptured my bowel. My temperature went up to 40c. They told me that had the infection entered my bloodstream, I'd probably be dead. Game over."

To ensure he returned to his usual body weight, Miller took himself off on holiday, with club colleagues still unaware of his traumatic few weeks. He does end the tale with a smile, though, fully aware that the gravity of his immobilisation requires a slightly jauntier conclusion. He added: "I just decided to take off to Vegas to catch up on my body fat. I went straight back into it in the new season but I wasn't right. It ruined me. My body shut down. I couldn't run, I couldn't function. Because I'd put the weight back on in Vegas and had a sun tan, nobody realised how ill I'd been. All I got during that time was a box of fruit from John Wile. That was it. But had that bowel burst the wrong way or the infection spread, I would have been gone. There were days I was high on morphine and didn't know where I was. But I did have one memory. I was sitting one day and my horse 'Sydney Safehands' was meant to run. I thought: 'Brilliant….it'll be on TV'. Then it came up as a non-runner. The next thing I heard was that my big hero Frank Sinatra had died. "If it comes in threes, I thought, bloody hell, what's going to happen to me? I didn't know what the hell was going on. Thankfully, I came through it…but it was scary."

Miller's Albion career petered out on a low-key note. His final League game for them came in their last match of the 20th century – a 1-1 draw with Bolton. He did play once more for the club, in the 2-0 defeat to Blackburn in the FA Cup, and moved to Ewood Park shortly afterwards. Rather than allow him to see out his contract, the Baggies cashed in despite it being little more than a nominal fee. Such was Albion's desperation for money that the deal made financial sense.

By then, Albion were in the final throes of the Brian Little era, weeks away from appointing Gary Megson. Miller felt sorry for Little, not least as a power struggle between Tony Hale and Paul Thompson was impacting on all aspects of day-to-day business. It was also around then that they sold Kevin Kilbane to clear urgent debt. Miller believes all control of the dressing room was lost over Christmas – a period in which the Albion boss was also in the teeth of dealing with personal problems. The keeper says it was all too much.

"It didn't work for Brian," he added. "The Kevin Kilbane fiasco really hit him hard. Kevin was sold and he wasn't aware of it. That's when he realised the club was a mess. That was the end for him really. Paul Thompson was posturing to be chairman and there was an under-current that things weren't right. It does impact on the dressing room. We went to Ipswich and on the way there, we found out the chairman was leaving. Brian didn't know what was going on – none of us did. The club was totally imploding." And then came the defeat at Portman Road.

Larus Sigurdsson was dismissed in the 29th minute and Matt Carbon followed him five minutes into the second half. Tensions escalated after the game, with Miller at the centre of a bust-up that ended with him having to explain himself in the boardroom and almost ending up facing criminal charges. He added: "I played that game and had a shocker. Brian had lost control. We were 3-1 down and down to nine men. We were dropping down the table and, in the dressing-down afterwards, I remember Jason Van Blerk was sat to my left. He was usually opinionated and I got on well with him. After a win, you enjoy it and ride with it. After a defeat, you have to react the right way, too. He had a towel over his head and was going on but wouldn't look anyone in the eye. I just thought: If you can't look someone in the eye after a game like that, it's not right. Brian was distant and never once looked up. That got me wound up, too. I was fuming. It was falling apart and a dark time.

"I just lost it. I confronted Jason and told him not to give us crap. I went down the tunnel and he comes running after me. I turn around fully loaded ready to hit him. As I do that, Raves jumps on top of me and unfortunately his elbow swings round and hits this steward right in the nose. There was blood everywhere, with punches being thrown left, right and centre. It quickly died down and I walked back into the dressing room and said to Brian, who was still sat in the corner: "I might have caused some trouble". The police came in, wouldn't let us leave and the Ipswich staff wanted to press charges against me. After an hour, we were marched to the boardroom to explain ourselves. Eventually, we left about 7pm and I was fined two weeks wages. A few weeks later, I was gone. It happened very quickly and that was me done with West Bromwich Albion. A sad way to end, really. My contract was running out, Paul Thompson had taken over and they realised they would be getting nothing, so they let me go for £50,000. It wasn't a great way to end my time there."

Albion were about to undergo their biggest transformation and, within two years, would be in the Premier League, having also constructed a new main stand and a purpose-built training ground. "Our facilities were awful," Miller added. "We had nothing. It wasn't so much the showers, or other things, but the actual playing surfaces were shocking. When you've been at places likes Arsenal and Middlesbrough, and later Blackburn, you realise what we didn't have. It was uninspiring. And it would get to you. Come January, you're training in mud and it's no good for you. We were professional footballers. Another thing – when you're trying to sign players, it's the training ground they're most interested in. Yes, a nice stadium is lovely. But if you're slumming it on some rugby pitch or mudheap, you're going to struggle to bring that player in.

"Look at the money now and what happened at my former club, Arsenal. When Arsene Wenger took over, the first thing he did was change the whole set-up. He signed Nicolas Anelka for £500,000, then sold him for more than £20m. That paid for the training ground. Before that, they trained at a university. Your training ground is your place of work. It's where you go to earn your place in the team. You go to a stadium once a week and Saturday is the bit the fans see, but the work towards that game is Monday to Friday. We simply didn't have the facilities. We had to check in every day to find out where we would be training. That was crap for a club like West Brom."

Despite his back-door exit, Miller remains very fond of his time in West Bromwich. What's more, he frequently removed his goalkeeping gloves to act out dramatic soap scenes. For a while after he arrived, he lived in the town, in a cul-de-sac near Dartmouth Park. By a quirk of coincidence, his rented bungalow – next door to my family home – stood on the site of the Four Acres ground, which Albion had occupied more than a century earlier.

It was during this time that his profile soared beyond the back pages of the local press into the celebrity gossip columns as he dated Brookside star Claire Sweeney. The Liverpudlian actress played gun-waving bi-sexual gangster Lindsey Corkhill in the Merseyside-based soap. [Miller wasn't the only Albion player during that period to step out with a TV celebrity: Shane Nicholson was also in a relationship with Coronation Street actress Tracey Shaw]. Sweeney became a regular at Albion games and accompanied her other half to club events. They split up following Miller's move to Blackburn, although they seemingly remain on good terms and he has fond memories of living among Albion fans. With these assurances comes a further revelation.

While Miller was a goalkeeper by day, at night he frequently became Jimmy Corkhill – Lindsey's maverick father! In fact, Miller would frequently act out parts, although his other half did draw the line with certain scenes, much to his disappointment. For the sake of any junior Baggies reading this, we shall say no more…

"I actually met Claire through another actor," recalled Miller. "He set me up on a blind date with Claire, who was on Brookside at the time. We got on well and met up again after that. She was doing well in the soap and it worked for us. I used to help her rehearse. I would play Jimmy Corkhill one week, then somebody else…the only thing she wouldn't let me play was her lesbian lover, which was a big shame! About four weeks later, I'd see Jimmy Corkhill deliver the lines I had done. I must say 'she' went off the rails a bit: lesbian lovers, shot a few people, gangster stuff… thankfully, real life wasn't like that. It was a good time. West Bromwich people embraced us and were very friendly. We could go to the Five Ways pub or the Crown & Cushion and not have any fuss. We could have a laugh and chat with the locals. These people were working Monday to Friday, then stood on the terraces when I was playing for their club. I had the utmost respect for the supporters. That probably couldn't happen now.

"Claire was very down-to-earth. We broke up when I was at Blackburn but we're still friends. She's doing very well for herself and our lives have changed, moved on. I'm not sure we could do now what we did then – live in the town of the club I played for, me a footballer, her a famous actress. You could stay under the radar then."

Miller's profile among Albion fans has seen a renaissance thanks to his presence on social media and willingness to engage. The 'Boing Boing' t-shirt remains fresh in the mind of many who were at The Hawthorns for a game that heralded the start of a ten-game unbeaten Hawthorns run against Wolves – a sequence that extends to the time of writing. Miller is happy with life away from football, at Holkham. "I'm at a stage where this suits me fine, working on a big country estate and looking after corporate events and concerts," he says. "It's a good life and I work with a great team. I enjoyed most of my time with Albion – 75 per cent of it was unbelievable. That period under Ray, the relationship with the fans, working with coaches like big Cyrille and John (Trewick) behind the scenes and some great friendships that remain to this day. I was lucky to be part of it all."

Denis Smith

"...He trained one morning and I couldn't get him signed quickly enough.
'Give him what he wants'. He was 18 and the best player on the pitch.
From the first morning I met him, I thanked my lucky stars – he was
an absolute winner, a leader..."

The view over the Staffordshire countryside is somewhat bleak right now. Extremely scenic but nevertheless bleak. Rain pours, winter is drawing in. Denis Smith reflects on his West Bromwich Albion career in much the same way. It was bleak. His words, not mine. Smith admires the view from his living room and admits: "I thought West Brom would be a great job...but it was a job I shouldn't have taken." These days, he can smile about it. Back then, less so.

Denis Smith arrived at The Hawthorns in December, 1998 as a Christmas surprise following Ray Harford's departure to Queens Park Rangers. But, first, a bit about Smith the player.....born in the Meir area of Stoke-on-Trent, he hasn't ventured far – his current home is a few miles north of Stone. Various artefacts and mementoes point to his career up the road at the Victoria Ground, Stoke's long-time home before moving to the Britannia Stadium.

More than 400 League appearances followed for the Potters between 1968 and 1982 but Smith made the call to steer clear of taking over his home-town club. "My wife banned me from ever becoming Stoke manager...and she was absolutely right," he says. Instead, he earned his managerial stripes elsewhere, first at York, who he guided to the Fourth Division title, then Sunderland. At Roker Park, he oversaw the winning of the Third Division title in 1988 and the climb to the top flight two years later. He was sacked in 1991, leaving his assistant Malcolm Crosby to lead the club to the FA Cup Final in 1992. After a brief period at Bristol City, he guided Oxford from the third tier in 1996. So, three promotions elsewhere mean Smith was a better fit for Albion than many give him credit for.

When he was approached, he had a dilemma. He was happy at Oxford but mindful the tills were beginning to run empty. "Ray (Harford) had left and one of the directors got in touch – I'm pretty sure it was John Wile actually," said Smith. "He was a good man. We'd been playing contemporaries and I thought it might be a good opportunity. The problem was that I was doing well at Oxford. We were top six [in the second tier] but had run out of money building the new ground. In fact, I was on the board, having invested some of my own money – money I never saw again, by the way. I had no more players to sell, so it was a decision that made sense to Oxford. I was the only one left they could get money for. We had massive cash flow problems. Robin Herd was involved. He was an amazing bloke, a genius in the aircraft and motor racing world. He'd worked on Concorde, he was a brilliant engineer and was a big name in Formula One but wasn't much of a businessman. We'd sold Matty Elliott and I was the last one standing of any collateral worth to the club."

At the time, Albion were hardly the epitome of harmony. Chairman Tony Hale was coming under increasing scrutiny. A failure to satisfy Harford and key players – Paul Peschisolido had left for Fulham following lengthy but fruitless negotiations – gave the club a stench of stagnation. The promise of the Harford spell was beginning to flounder. Albion's successful Stock Market flotation was championed as a bright new period for the club, yet, behind the scenes, Rotherham businessman Paul Thompson was loitering with intent. Smith recalled: "West Brom were in a poor run of form around the time Ray left but were a massive club compared with Oxford. I knew the board weren't happy with themselves. I said to them: 'I know you lot aren't getting on…' but they looked at each other awkwardly and said: 'No, we're ok'. So, 'ok' it was. And I went there. I should have taken the hint from the looks they gave each other."

Smith arrived without an assistant. He was made to wait for right-hand man Malcolm Crosby. Smith was not a natural coach – he was a man-manager, a pointer, a shouter, a motivator. But he was no technician when it came to the tactical element of the game. And it showed. Albion didn't win under him until taking on Wolves six League games into his reign, although they knocked Stoke out of the FA Cup in the days when beating the Potters was unusual. "That period wasn't easy," he said. "Malcolm and I had worked well together for a while. I had all my coaching qualifications but that doesn't make you a good coach. You need different dynamics. I felt I was a better man-manager, who worked well with a good coach. And that's what Malcolm was. Results weren't going well but thankfully there were a couple of things I did – one was to beat Wolves, which will always help. The other was beat Stoke, who West Brom very rarely beat back then."

The perception of Smith from others within these pages isn't one of charm, nor warmth. There are suggestions that he tried to change the dynamic of the dressing room too quickly. His mistrust of Albion's senior players bordered on acrimony at times, with seasoned men noting a deterioration in their relationship with him. Yet, at the same time, non-footballing staff react with surprise when such observations are put to them. What was clearly evident is the manager-player relationship was more fraught than the counter perception of Smith as the thoroughly kind and decent man he so clearly is. Two and a bit decades on, he admits Albion were an aberration rather than a constant. He doesn't so much invite criticism as show a willingness to dive into the pool of blame. He reckons he pretty much got everything wrong that he could have got wrong.

Smith's want to make Albion a better football side – they were somewhat pragmatic, if effective under Harford – fell at the first major call. Sensing that they needed a keeper with greater ball-playing abilities, Smith opted to replace the popular Alan Miller. From that point, it was all downhill for him, with many never accepting his replacement. That Phil Whitehead came from Smith's former club Oxford after 200-odd appearances there, had some fans writing him off quicker than it takes to say: "It's Buckley and Grimsby all over again". That was never the case. But Miller's diminished status wasn't taken particularly well by the punters, making Whitehead's position almost untenable before it had begun. Some inconsistent performances and a tendency to let in long-range shots didn't help his cause. "I wasn't particularly happy with any of the signings I made – apart from one," said Smith. "That was Phil Whitehead.

"I was happy with him but even that backfired on me. The fans absolutely adored Alan Miller. He was a great lad, very popular in the dressing room and a good shot-stopper but I liked my goalkeepers to come off the line for crosses, pushing out and squeezing the space behind the back four and able to deliver balls from there. That wasn't Alan. And the fans didn't like that change. Phil Whitehead joked he'd never forgiven me for signing him – he said he'd never felt so hated. You want to do things differently when you're a new manager. At Oxford, we were attacking, we squeezed up, spread the play and passed it around. Ray had Albion playing down one side, they were compact and solid. I tried to change things too quickly. I had that whole shift to deal with. I think back and I should have stuck with that."

Smith might not have been the most popular among players but, off the pitch, he was considered a more stable option than Alan Buckley and had a conviction towards playing better football than Harford. His decision to live locally – in the heartland of Birmingham's nightlife – was unexpected but he enjoyed the experience. It wasn't unusual to see him wandering along Broad Street, close to his Brindley Place flat. Albion finished 10th and 12th in the second tier on his watch. It was not the progress many wanted but things were certainly stable and there was no danger of relegation. In January, 1999, Albion won at high-flying Watford, courtesy of goals by Richard Sneekes and Mark Angel, and looked a good prospect for a promotion push. It wasn't to last. They won just three of their final 17 games and a play-off pursuit had descended into relegation form. They finished 12th but were nearer the bottom three than the top six in terms of points.

"I actually got on better with the fans than the board, which isn't always good from a job point of view," he added. "If anyone had told me I'd have enjoyed living in Birmingham, I'd have said they were crackers. I bought a flat in Brindley Place near restaurants, bars, theatres. It was wonderful. West Brom had been out of the top flight for the best part of 15 years and I had people telling me what great players I had but nobody was coming in for them. It seemed to me we had a lot of players who were comfortable sitting on decent contracts; players with reputations but not a lot else."

Smith did not manage Bob Taylor at Bristol City but was now prepared to let him go despite the heroic status the striker had in West Bromwich. Others, identified as the senior cartel of players, were perhaps doing little to help matters. While Smith has openly admitted making mistakes, he hints at being let down by certain experienced figures. In many respects, the narrative isn't dissimilar to the one pursued by Gary Megson. Yet where Megson succeeded,

Smith couldn't oversee the change he felt was desperately needed in the dressing room. Baggies players will no doubt point to the inconsistency of results that did little for Smith's reputation.

"I sold Bob and that wasn't a popular move either," admitted Smith. "But I thought Lee Hughes was what we needed. He was already at the club and was not playing when I thought he should be. Bob was a great player – his record spoke for itself – but he was past his sell-by date in my view. Players can get you the sack. You will never please everybody. I 'died' by my signings at Albion. You will never find a manager entirely happy with all his signings. Sadly, I got pretty much all of mine wrong. When you're a manager, you're trying to recreate a family environment but equally that can be your biggest challenge. You move in with people hoping it'll work. Richard Sneekes, for instance, had a free role. But he had barely created anything and scored only two or three goals, so I was asking myself what the end result was. Richard wasn't happy with me questioning that or being critical of him. You have to manage such issues. And West Brom had, for too long, been used to such a culture. Which is why they were in the second tier and even lower for so long. I tried to change things too quickly. I was fearing resistance and did too much way too quickly."

These days, it isn't uncommon for managers to moan about fixture congestion, refereeing calamities and VAR. Such quibbles are small fry compared with the surreal managerial experiences Smith endured. Never mind hamstring strains and want-away players, how do an emergency landing and a 5-1 home defeat against Crewe grab you, not least when your main striker has literally slept through the latter?

In the early summer of 1985, Smith was flying home with his York side from a post-season trip to Majorca. As the British Airtours Tristar Flight KT01Y landed at Leeds Bradford on May 27, the pilot was unable to prevent it overshooting the damp runway 14 and it eventually came to a halt on a grass slope, with the nose pitched into the ground. None of the 416 passengers were seriously hurt, although eight suffered slight injuries during the escape and required hospital treatment. One suffered a broken leg and Smith, in his typically understated way, described it as 'not the best day I've ever had.' That so little is known about the incident underlines the football-media relationship of the mid-1980s. The drama came barely two weeks after the Bradford fire killed 56 and the day on which a schoolboy died at St Andrew's following the collapse of a wall after fans rioted at the Birmingham v Leeds game. York's flight back from Palma was also two days before 39 Juventus supporters were killed at Heysel. Football, in England especially, was in a dark place, with bad news prevalent and happier stories going unreported.

This tale is worthy of a wider audience because players from two clubs were on the flight and came together to assist crew in the hour of need. The other squad on board were from Lincoln, who had been the visitors at Valley Parade on the day of the Bradford fire just over two weeks before. The scene ended with Smith sliding down a chute after he and his York players had helped others evacuate the stricken aircraft. "I remember being sat next to Keith Houchen, who later won the FA Cup with Coventry," he said. "He was a super player but a nervous flyer and I said to him: 'Don't worry…..flying is the safest way to travel.' It had been a lovely flight, without any problems. And then it happened. Something didn't seem right as we hit the runway and seemed to speed up. It sounded like we were struggling to stop. We kept going and going and the next thing I know is we've overshot and come to a sudden stop on the grass. As you can imagine, there was some panic. Apparently, pilots throw the nose of the plane into the ground when that happens, so the whole plane shuddered forward. It wasn't the nicest experience.

"Thankfully, nobody was killed and I'm pretty sure nobody was seriously hurt. I was so proud of my lads. They were brilliant. They handled it wonderfully and were doing what they could to help and reassure other passengers. They were mature and behaved themselves impeccably, as did the flight crew, who were just brilliant. Me? I did what any football manager would do – I took control of the situation. I tried to help others, waited for them to escape and then slid down the chute. I was the last passenger off. It could have been a lot worse. It didn't stop me from flying but I'm pretty sure Keith Houchen never listened to my travel advice again."

So it's unlikely anything could surprise or faze Smith in football management. Until, maybe, Easter Monday of 1999. This was another surreal drama – albeit a fraught-free incident, bordering more towards farce and misfortune than panic or potential suffering, although fans might disagree about the 'suffering' bit. Albion had lost their three previous matches, without scoring so much as a single goal while managing to concede eight. On that Bank Holiday, they welcomed Crewe. Dario Gradi's over-achieving side were seen as a lower-division team batting above their average in the second tier – savvy, adept in style and not averse to occasional brilliance. But they were to finish 1998-99 down in a very unremarkable 18th place, their survival no doubt owing much to their performance at The Hawthorns on April 5. In what was a horror story for Albion, Alex won 5-1.

Sneekes scored Albion's goal in front of a crowd of just over 12,000. It is hard to envisage that, three and a half years on, the club would be playing in the Premier League. In this nightmare, they looked more like third-tier fodder. Worse, it was to emerge later why Fabian De Freitas had missed the game. Not because of illness or injury but because he hadn't realised it was starting at 3pm. Albion staff had desperately tried to locate the Dutchman but it soon became clear he was asleep at home. His landline phone was engaged because his girlfriend was chatting to family while her partner snored away in another room before heading to The Hawthorns for what he thought was a 7.45pm kick-off.

While Smith wasn't to lose his job as a result of the defeat, there is little doubt it was to become a huge factor in his fate. "When you get beaten 5-1 by Crewe… " he added with a sigh. "I don't care how well Dario was doing up there, West Brom shouldn't be losing to them like that. We'd done all of our planning and the lad didn't turn up. Where was he? Asleep….? Unbelievable. Regardless, we lost 5-1. Whatever I did that afternoon wasn't acceptable either and I can't just blame one player for that. It was a ridiculous, stupid thing to do. I remember we'd had people trying to find him but nobody could get hold of him. Some days later, I sat down with him and we had it out but, daft as it sounds for something so stupid, after a 5-1 defeat, you're wondering what you did wrong to lose by five goals at home to Crewe. That was concerning me more than anything else. Would Fabian have made a big difference to that scoreline? I suspect not. So we can't use that as an excuse. Yes, his story was hugely embarrassing. But I found a 5-1 defeat at home to Crewe even more embarrassing.

"My daughter brought the two grandchildren to a game for the first time that day. She wasn't used to hearing me being slaughtered, so she was in a bit of a mess. The youngsters had to see their mother cry, which was extremely unpleasant for them. But that's what the job is sometimes like. I was living the dream, being a football manager and doing a job I really enjoy. The down side was that when it was bad, it could be horrible. And Crewe was bloody horrible."

Smith had been an accomplished centre-half. Yet the axis of his Albion defence would be a weakness. Daryl Burgess was out of favour for much of his time and Paul Mardon struggled for fitness. Neither Shaun Murphy nor Matt Carbon particularly impressed, with Paul Raven the only constant. Carbon, a relatively high-profile signing from Derby, initially showed promise and potential before his form tailed off considerably. Smith believes a lack of desire and ambition was a big reason progress wasn't made. He also made plans to bolster Albion's back-line during a crucial period, when the club were in prime position for a play-off push.

"Matt was the biggest one that disappointed me," he went on. "For the first couple of months, I thought it was a great decision, then something changed. I always felt Matt didn't want to drive himself. He had huge ability; pace, strength, height. He could pass it, he could tackle. And then it stopped going for him. I'd brought through Matty Elliott at Oxford, Phil Gilchrist and Darren Purse also – all had careers with Premier League clubs. Gary Bennett at Sunderland as well. He became a legend up there. All of those were tremendous. And I thought Matt Carbon would be good for us in the same way. I'd generally done well with centre-halves but it just didn't happen for him. I'm not sure he believed in himself. Had he done, there is no doubt we'd have ended up one day selling him for a lot of money because he had everything but that belief.

"I'd tried to bring in Colin Calderwood, who was at Spurs at the time. We were going well (January, 1999) and I knew he would improve us. We'd had references from David Pleat and George Graham. Tottenham were happy to let him go and I knew Mario (Bortolazzi) would be gone in the summer, so we could balance the two wages by losing Mario's salary. I thought he would strengthen our defence and bring out the best of players who needed that little push. It might have even made a difference. The club blocked it, despite the fact Villa ended up paying less for him. What really annoyed me is that I hadn't been greedy and I'd always been respectful of the club's decisions over recruitment. But that one really annoyed me because we were close to it happening, only for the club to pull it late on. It made us look stupid. Likewise Keith Curle. He'd have improved us, too, and was on a Bosman free transfer. I thought we could get him done. Again, the club wouldn't allow it. That was a big disappointment."

Two players certainly not short of belief and confidence were Italian duo Bortolazzi and Enzo Maresca. The latter's path to The Hawthorns has already been dissected but what of the 33-year-old ex-Milan midfielder, who moved to Albion from Genoa? He cut a stylish figure, with team-mates and staff describing his standard every-day wear as beige Gucci trousers, quality loafers and an expensive sweater draped around his shoulders. He would also be in a perfectly pressed shirt. Unfortunately, his English wasn't the best, prompting good-natured merriment among his team-mates. Lee Hughes took it upon himself to give advice about the formal and appropriate way to address the manager following an instruction. Smith was therefore no doubt surprised to hear the otherwise polite Italian responding to him with a thumbs-up and 'Dogshit, si signor… dogshit, okay, Signor Denis' as he was issued with final instructions before matches.

"Mario could play, make no mistake about that," added Smith. "He was my type of player. Sadly, my Italian wasn't great and his English wasn't much better. He was struggling with injuries by then but what a player he was. I wish we'd had him before his injuries, because there is no doubt he'd have been a hugely influential player in our squad. But I think he found the transition to the Championship a little tough. And then there was Enzo. He trained one morning and I couldn't get him signed quickly enough. I just said: 'Give him what he wants'. He was 18 and the best player on the pitch. From the first morning I met him, I thanked my lucky stars. He hated losing, he was a diamond. I just wish Mario had been a few years younger, and definitely with younger knees!"

Smith doesn't remember the crash course in English delivered to Bortolazzi but isn't surprised to hear of it. "He (Hughes) was a joy to be around. Infectious, enthusiastic and right up my street as a striker. I would have hated playing against him because he was one of those forwards who just wanted to play off the shoulder. He reminded me of Andy Cole, who I took to Bristol City, and Marco Gabbiadini (at Sunderland). Just play that ball for him to run on to and he will score. And more often than not, he did. But it wasn't just about the goals – he had a bit of devil about him that made us a better side when he played. He was a joy to have at the club. I was asked about him so much at the Player of the Year night (at the Tower Ballroom in Birmingham) at the end of that season (1998-99) when there was speculation about him leaving. I remember announcing back then: 'I will be here next season and so will Lee, and I mean that'…"

For Smith, the Albion assignment was to be one of frustration. Right-hand man Malcolm Crosby left to join Jim Smith at Derby in 1998-99 and, having tossed away a chance of reaching the play-offs and failed to bring in Colin Calderwood, with strikers not knowing kick-off times and with Smith needing to find new staff, it wasn't a particularly enjoyable time for the manager. Behind the scenes, there was mutiny. Shareholder Paul Thompson, who had quit the board in February, 1999, called for an Extraordinary General Meeting so 'shareholders have the opportunity to decide whether they wish Tony Hale to continue as chairman.' Hale was long-serving, an Albion man through and through. Thompson was a supreme businessman with a ruthless but savvy streak. Crucially, he was also very wealthy, having made his millions through South Yorkshire-based computer software business Sanderson Group. Directors Barry Hurst, in February, and Clive Stapleton, in May, resigned from the board to support Thompson's call for change. The remaining directors were keen for Hale to remain in office. They pointed to huge advances during his first years at the helm – the Tom Silk Building (now the site of the club's academy headquarters) had opened in 1995 and fund-raising which had generated £13m. Thompson, however, was critical of the final League positions on Hale's watch – between tenth and 19th in the second tier – and also pointed to expected losses in June, 1999 of around £2.5m and a recruitment policy he felt wasn't fit for purpose. Having also announced plans to redevelop the Rainbow Stand and raise £10m, he expressed alarm about a balance sheet that showed just £6,000 in the bank in December, 1998 compared with about £1.6m a year earlier.

Hale then announced his plans – to appoint to the board the former QPR owner Richard Thompson and Jim Driscoll, the creator of the children's TV show The Shoe People. With Hale backed by carpet millionaire Graham

Waldron, he gained an overall majority – winning by 42,829 votes to 37,826. It was a power struggle that Smith neither needed, nor welcomed. "They couldn't agree on anything. They kept falling out with each other," he recalled. "A club of that size should have been aiming for the Premier League but they were too busy bickering through the media. That's not healthy. A lot of stuff behind the scenes wasn't right. There were factions taking each other to EGMs, votes, hammering with each other, we had no training ground and they were all too busy arguing. Malcolm saw what was going on, had a good offer from Derby and left. I couldn't blame him."

The summer of 1999 wasn't without drama elsewhere. Albion unveiled a stylish, new change shirt for the coming campaign – a Patrick-manufactured 'Homer Simpson yellow' in an interesting design that featured a blue horizontal band across the chest. The jersey also displayed the West Bromwich Building Society logo. It was an attractive item and one the club were keen to promote to a wider public. A photo opportunity was swiftly arranged by Albion's commercial manager and director Tom Cardall, who invited local media to the old sponsors' lounge on the corner of the Smethwick End and Halfords Lane Stand. Next door, in another suite, Lee Hughes, Matt Carbon and Enzo Maresca had been summoned as models and it was while the players changed into the new kit that Carbon and Maresca started exchanging playful comments. The harmless barbs swiftly became more opinionated, to the point that the initially friendly exchange descended into a joust of nasty, acerbic comments, with finger-pointing and shirt-pulling. A highly amused Hughes, having stoked up the banter, left them to it.

It was at the height of the heated dialogue that Cardall emerged at the door to beckon the players in the next room, only to be greeted by the unexpected sight of Carbon and Maresca being held apart by a flustered member of staff, desperately trying to keep the peace, with a bemused Hughes looking on. All three were swiftly called into the sponsors' lounge – Hughes a grinning picture of joy in his new, neatly ironed Albion kit, followed by Carbon and Maresca, both with faces of thunder, forced smiles, wearing shirts that were dishevelled, pulled and stretched around the neckline – with the waiting media totally oblivious to the stand-up row. They never did find out.

Despite this backdrop of political upheaval and warring footballers, Smith was looking forward to a fruitful 1999-2000 season alongside new assistant

John Gorman. But it wasn't to be. On July 27, 1999, Albion released a statement on their somewhat rudimentary website about a change in catering arrangements for the forthcoming campaign. It wasn't exactly headline news, nor was it as exciting as the signing of a new player – but nevertheless, news is news. But there was more. Buried some way down the same statement about culinary arrangements was the revelation that Denis Smith had left Albion with immediate effect. He was dismissed ten days before the start of the season, having completed most of the summer schedule, including a pre-season trip to Denmark. That very week, it had emerged that Smith had tried to sign Simon Grayson and Calderwood from Villa.

Worse still, the bombshell coincided with what was to become a farcical pre-season photo-call. Albion had no manager, Gorman was on a day off and Matt Carbon, arriving late, was unable to access the stadium as it had been locked while the team photo (without him) was being taken! Regardless of results and whether he was the right man, Albion's delivery of Smith's sacking was desperately poor and a crass way to treat a senior member of staff, further highlighting the club's increasingly poor public reputation.

Brian Little was swiftly appointed as successor, with Gorman also leaving. The ex-Villa and Leicester boss had seemingly been parked up while the formalities of Smith's removal were completed. Smith remains philosophical, almost bemused, by the whole saga. "Maybe Brian had already been tapped up," he said. "He told me he got the job thanks to an impressive slide show… and I'm there thinking: 'Christ, they wouldn't even give me a computer when I was the manager as they saw no need for me to have one.' John Gorman was an excellent coach and a super guy. That suited me. He allowed me to do my job and I could leave him to coach. Next thing I know, I'm sacked, just a few days before the season was starting. It didn't surprise me in some respects. The club was a complete mess. Was I surprised by how they announced it? Probably not. Nothing surprised me about the club back then.

"I shouldn't have gone to West Brom in the first place. Oxford got some money out of it but it was a bad move for me. I tried to work through the problems but it wasn't to be. The place wasn't up to standard – it was scandalous. That's also why I tried to buy Colin Calderwood in January, 1999. I thought he would help us hugely and help the other players but I wasn't allowed to sign him. He'd have made a difference, I'm sure of it. West Brom is a great club on the face of it. A big club. But I was fighting people above me and I was fighting people below me. There were exceptions, of course. John Wile was always sound and first-class. He was a football man. He knew where I was coming from, I expect. In any job, especially in a senior role, you need buy-in from all areas and I was struggling with it.

"The one outstanding thing were the fans. The supporters club they had back then was huge, even bigger than Sunderland's network of supporters clubs. It was great to see. But there was no training ground. On the first day, I thought they were taking the Mickey when they took me to this place and I was shown a pitch. We got there on Monday and some clubs had played on it on Saturday and Sunday. 'Here you go Denis, that should be fine…' It was a complete mud-heap. It was just assumed we would be fine. It was horrific. And we were a club with Premier League ambitions. It was silly little things like that.

"I'd worked with sports scientists at Oxford – mainly guys from the university. They were brilliant in knowing how players should refuel. There was barely anybody doing that in football back then. I brought one in at West Brom and that didn't go down well either. Their view was that players would still go drinking after games, so what was the point? And when I told them I wanted a computer, they thought I was crackers. The feeling was: 'You're the football manager…what do you need a computer for?' As for the scouting, I just cannot recall us having anything. Our training facilities were just shocking. Embarrassing really. At least at Oxford, we were building a new stadium and had access to brilliant facilities at the university. We couldn't even find proper pitches at Albion."

Some two decades on, Smith looks on his Albion career as an inglorious 20-month spell of bickering and, at times, fire-fighting. His story feels like one long mea culpa, albeit against the combustive backdrop of boardroom politicking. "I had faith in my own ability," he said. "Money has never bothered me because football was something I enjoyed. I've done over 1,000 games as a manager, so I must have done okay to get anywhere near that figure and I'm proud of my achievements – mainly because I was at clubs where there was buy-in from all. But not at West Brom. It was a constant battle. I used to tell Malcolm Crosby to look after coaching because I had to keep 'that lot' off my back. Sometimes, a club is just a bad fit for you. And that's how it felt at West Brom. It's funny....my wife had always stopped me from managing Stoke because she knew how well liked I'd been there as a player and that it might ruin everything if I became their manager. She was right about that. Maybe she should have stopped me from going to West Brom as well."

Paul Thompson/John Wile

"…Had I stayed and Gary Megson worked with me, I think we would have become a top-eight Premier League side eventually. He was a good enough manager to have managed in the top eight…" (Paul Thompson)

It's December, 1999. The world prepares for a global meltdown of computer and technological systems. We're told a new Millennium is due to bring us major problems. Of greater concern to John Wile is the influenza he is struggling to shake off. He also has other things on his mind. He is considering ending all ties with West Bromwich Albion.

As it happens, all turned out well. Y2k, as the so-called 'Millennium Bug' was named, was a false alarm. Planes did not fall from the sky on New Year's Day, ATMs continued to spew out paper £10 notes to drunken revellers and there was no synchronised meltdown of PCs. The nuclear New Year didn't happen. A relief to all. The dial-up you were using for your Internet access was working just fine. Wile's flu subsided and a pep talk from elsewhere convinced him to hold fire on his Albion future. For now at least.

March, 2019. John Wile is in familiar territory. We are at the Park Inn Hotel in West Bromwich. It was once called the Moat House and the person sat before me can remember even further back, when it was named the Europa Lodge. It was here that Albion players would congregate after matches, led by their captain Wile and manager Ron Atkinson. That was then, in the late 1970s. This is now.

Albion fans start trickling in for drinks before joining the coach at The Hawthorns for tonight's game at Queens Park Rangers. Darren Moore's men are to win that game. Supporters idly carry on their business, failing to notice they are stood a few feet from an Albion legend. Centre-forwards, tricky wingers, World Cup winners, hell, even a toothless Joe Jordan were of little worry for Wile during his 619 games for Albion as a masonry centre-half. Only two men have made more appearances for their club. He rightly takes his place alongside Tony Brown and Ally Robertson as a club legend. Wile is a man of granite. As a player, he had the presence of someone quarried from igneous rock. He remains a man of significant presence – one you wouldn't mess with. The County Durham accent is still there as well. With leadership skills that ensured he was the custodian of the Albion captain's armband for many years, he became an icon of one of the great sides in the club's history. Formidable and driven, he became chief executive of West Bromwich Albion in the late 1990s and part of a backroom team that was to propel the club into new territory. He is here with me now to tell the story.

Wile was with his wife on an overseas festive trip in 1999 when he took a phone call that was to define Albion's step into the new Millennium and all that came with it. The East Stand at The Hawthorns, the training ground just across the Walsall border, the flex from a second-tier crawl to a journey through the gears, destination Premier League – Albion were unrecognisable within ten years. Y2K with blue and white stripes running through it, if you prefer. And John Wile was at the heart of Albion's evolution. It was all thanks to this chat. On the other end of the phone was Paul Thompson. More about him shortly.

In summer, 1997, Wile was asked to attend an Albion board meeting. He had no idea why. "I was happy doing what I was doing at GEC Avery," he said. "I'd been to some games but not many, although a year or so before I'd been invited to the opening of the Captain's Suite in the Halfords Lane Stand. There was nobody there to greet me and nobody knew anything about what we were doing there even after I said who I was. I had to buy my own drink and eventually somebody from the commercial department came. It was a shambles."

Wile's north-east dialect, as it is occasionally prone to do, slipped into the conversation as he continued: "I wasn't impressed with how I was tret (sic) and wrote a letter to the chairman Tony Hale to say how proud I was to accept the invite but how disappointing it was to see the club operating in this shoddy way. I assumed they wanted to talk to me about that." Wile was wrong. He was about to go through the throes of being re-recruited by the club he'd served so brilliantly, this time as chief executive. Not everyone was impressed.

"My wife wasn't keen at all," he recalls. "She could see what might happen down the line if things didn't go right and we didn't need that. But the opportunity of going back in that position was one I couldn't refuse. I'd had a call from Clive Stapleton asking if I would like to attend a board meeting and then they asked me. It was apparent they wanted a chief executive with business knowledge. We chatted about various things, how I saw the club running and that was it. I was asked to wait outside, which I thought was a courteous way of being asked to wait while they decided I wasn't what they were looking for. But I went back in and was offered the job. Paul Thompson had come in as a director, invested some money and he especially was pushing for somebody to take over as chief executive."

And so, all those years after Albion had mooted bringing in a former player to take over as chief executive, they finally did something about it. Where Graham Waldron failed in 1993, Paul Thompson succeeded four years later. Where Brendon Batson had been mentioned in 1993, it would now be John Wile stepping up, although, ironically, Batson ended up replacing Wile years later in a rebranded role. After speaking with manager Ray Harford to seek reassurance, Wile accepted the challenge. And with it came the stark realisation that the Albion of the late 1990s were a different proposition to the successful club he'd been part of two decades earlier.

"I had a long chat with Ray," he continued. "I'd met him before, we'd played against each other, were a similar age and had that mutual respect. If Ray hadn't been comfortable with it, I wouldn't have gone in. But he was really pleased – he felt it would help him do his job and I was very comfortable with that. But the club was an eye-opener. It was a learning curve. There didn't seem to be any kind of strategy in how we move forward. It went from issue to issue. There was no plan at all. It was obvious there was a disconnect on the board as to how the club should operate. Paul wanted a structured operation, Tony Hale wanted to deal with things as and when and be seen as popular. It seemed to all be off-the-cuff. There were difficulties on the board between members (Paul and Tony). Tony didn't want to relinquish what he was doing. Others wanted change but Tony held the sway with the shareholders and was very popular. It just wasn't a comfortable business landscape.

"We'd have board meetings, then I'd get into my car and what we'd been discussing was being reported by Tom Ross on the radio. There were leaks everywhere. It was disgraceful. It just wasn't a good environment. We wanted to develop and build a new stand but it was determined on what happened with the team and the manager. That impacted on everything. I had strong views on football but I didn't want to be seen to be interfering with the manager. I didn't want to go to the training ground and be that person where people say: 'John Wile said this, or John Wile said that'. But maybe I should have done that more. I didn't want managers to think I was a threat to them."

March, 2019. Paul Thompson is bang on time. He said midday and arrives with a minute to spare. We meet at an Italian restaurant deep in the bowels of Sheffield's Meadowhall shopping centre. The one-time Albion chairman has barely changed since we last met, with one exception. Gone is the moustache. He is in good spirits, keen to know the latest about his one-time club. Who is playing well? How is Darren Moore doing? What are the prospects of promotion? His enthusiasm for a club he had no links to before 1996, when he was already 44, underlines the mark Albion left on him.

Thompson made his fortune with his successful leadership of Sheffield-based software firm Sanderson. But by the mid-1990s, he was seeking new pursuits. Football appealed. Sanderson were sponsoring Sheffield Wednesday and Southampton – both established Premier League clubs at that point – and Thompson was keen to do some heavy lifting elsewhere. He was looking for a club with potential and growth, but also a club of significance. So why Albion? He said: "It goes back to the fact that Sanderson were sponsors of Sheffield Wednesday. I learned a fair bit about how football worked, how it was run and how it ought to be run. And I learned that most clubs were run badly. I felt that if you apply good football principles to a club, you would make progress. I knew my time at Sanderson was coming to an end. IT is a young man's game and coming up to 50, it was time to look at other things. I put an advert in the Financial Times for a minority stake in a club and received about 30 replies from the 72 League clubs. It was becoming apparent there was potential to grow clubs through Premier League revenue opportunities.

"In my view, there are four things that make a professional football club succeed or are key drivers. The players, the manager, the board of directors and, more importantly, the supporters. The stadium and training facilities are important, too. I looked at each of the replies and felt Albion was the one where

The various outfits and roles in the busy life of Alan Miller. Above left: The one that Albion supporters are most familiar with - the keeper patrols his goalmouth, probably with more on his mind if a certain manager was in charge at the time! Above right, microphone in hand, he regales an audience with tales of his years between the Hawthorns posts. And despite the various jerseys in which he played for the club, one item of clothing probably stands out more than any other; the mischievous top he wore under his keeper's shirt in the victory over Wolves more than two decades ago. That, presumably, is something he gets asked about at all supporter gatherings he attends. Below: Miller links up in his very different present-day life with his former Arsenal colleague Alan Smith and their other halves. At first glance, the setting is a long way from the muck and bullets of a Black Country derby showdown.

They were opponents many times in Stoke v Albion matches in the 1960s and 1970s but Denis Smith and Tony Brown found themselves wanting very much the same thing many years later. The Potteries hero's arrival as manager at The Hawthorns inevitably and regularly brought him into contact with the club's all-time record goalscorer, who has lit up the local airwaves with his thoughts as a radio co-commentator. Right: Smith in more pensive mood as he surveys matters from the touchline. But this photo wasn't taken while he was Albion boss. It is from a Wrexham v Albion pre-season fixture in late July, 2003, by which time Smith had been appointed in charge at the Racecourse Ground. And it was his side who won 2-1 against Gary Megson's Baggies.

John Wile and Denis Smith, both of them titan centre-halves in their day, reunited in Hawthorns corridors of power when the latter was named as Ray Harford's successor in 1997. There was a bond and a mutual respect, alas the link-up did not bring the success they both hoped for. Wile was the chief executive, though, when Albion installed Gary Megson and went on to win a remarkable promotion race with Wolves in the spring of 2002. In earlier decades and as a lion-hearted skipper, Wile went both up and down, with Division One football back on the menu by the time of this home game against Norwich (right) in the late 1970s.

Like John Wile, Paul Thompson played a very full part in the building of a promotion-winning operati
The Hawthorns and then departed before a ball was kicked in the Premier League. The South York
businessman could see the writing on the wall in the top flight if the club were not united off the field, a
as on it, but he has remained a keen supporter and maintains that his relationship with Gary Megson
good one. Two of these photos were from Thompson's Albion time, the other was taken in 2019.

A Chambers puzzle...can you tell the twins apart? Adam is the one above in action in the blue and white stripes they were both so proud to wear. He is also the one with the shorter hair in the posed brotherly photograph at the top of the page. A yellow-shirted James is seen starting to climb back to his feet (above left) in a game away to Wimbledon while mom Maureen makes an appearance (left). The happy group shot is from James's wedding, at which he is in the black tie. We hope that clears things up...

The different guises and faces of a young man with lots to live up to. Jason Roberts in action (left) in the stripes that his uncle Cyrille helped make famous. Right: A top to match the summer setting for a friendly at Chesterfield while (below) following a fast-forward of over a decade and a half, a happy reunion with another of the 2002 promotion winners, Darren Moore.

...ssion time for Gary Megson and his assistant ... Burrows (above) during their fruitful ... at The Hawthorns. Below: The boss on the ...ine - impressed or ready to go off on one? ...s a very competent player as well in his day ...howed this year there's a speaking-tour ... available to him if he wishes when he was ... hit at a sell-out fans' night organised by ...ORT's Nigel Pearson (below right).

Was there ever a scarier Albion penalty than this? Igor Balis prepares at Bradford (left) to do what he had to do. A sweet right-foot strike, a good aim (bottom photo) and promotion became VERY close. The Ice Man, now retired and back in Slovakia, is pictured (right) in his home early in 2020 during a weekend in which he happily welcomed a group of Albion fans, including the author of the book bearing the full-back's name. Below: It will surprise no supporters to be told Balis was a good trainer - as shown by this photo (below) in the gym.

I could have the most success. I wasn't out to make money. I just wanted to improve a club. West Brom were near the bottom of the second tier but had a great history. They had a decent stadium with two good ends, one side adequate (Halfords Lane) and one side very poor. I knew we'd need a new stand. Training facilities weren't adequate and weren't the club's own either. Clearly, they needed a facility that was capable of not only servicing the needs of the current players and staff but also make potential players think: 'Wow, this is a club going places.' We simply didn't have that. Financially, the club weren't in trouble at that point. (Director) Barry Hurst was the key driver. He responded on behalf of the club and came up to see me. We spoke and found we had a lot in common. He made me feel it could work if I got involved. I had no wish to be chairman at that point. I just wanted to bring some expertise."

Thompson immediately set about trying to redirect Albion's course. It was clear a financial injection was needed – both fiscally and, eventually, in terms of progress. By the mid-1990s, mediocrity was setting in. Alan Buckley's reign was fast becoming tired on the pitch and there was apathy off the field. In terms of transfer business, Albion looked hopelessly outdated. Buckley's approach to recruitment at The Hawthorns had been to pursue players of a certain age, preferably those he had previously managed. Of those who became regular Albion first-teamers, the average age was 30, so there was little re-sale value. Also, he had been rude and condescending to fans when questioned about his transfer record at forums. There was no creative thinking to Albion's buying policy. Peter Barnes, who signed from Manchester City in 1979, remained their record signing at £748,000. As the Baggies hurtled towards the 2000s, they seemed 20 years out of date. It wasn't until 1997 that there was a seven-figure signing, Kevin Kilbane from Preston for £1.2m.

Thompson pushed for a share issue to help bring in much-needed funds but first, the club was re-registered as a public limited company, allowing those shares to be offered to fans. On March 29, 1996, an emergency general meeting was held at West Bromwich Gala Swimming Baths and the club's constitution was completely rewritten. The 15 per cent limit on shareholders was lifted, allowing others to invest. It was also proposed that a new Premier Share would be on offer, incorporating an 11-year season ticket at 1996 prices. Thompson was the instigator and financial backer of the changes, injecting an underwritten £2.5m into the club. Of the 6,666 votes cast, 6,515 were in favour with just

143 against (eight votes weren't cast). It was viewed as a major breakthrough.

"Albion was a community club owned by many but there were many shares owned by many," Thompson added. "Each share was worth about £3,000. If somebody else came along to buy shares, the existing shares had to be offered to other shareholders. It gave shareholders the right to buy those shares. I was happy to acquire a minority shareholding of under 50 per cent. They had to vote in favour of that at an EGM, where I explained what I wanted to achieve for the club. They had to approve that. That raised £2-3m, which was a significant amount and gave us funds to improve the team, which didn't really happen. We had a couple of good players, like Kevin Kilbane and Alan Miller, but there were some less successful ones. Unfortunately, prior to that, we had ten or so ex-Grimsby players. That confirmed to me the football club was badly run and I couldn't influence what had happened as a director.

"Before all of that, one of the things we did was a Premier Share issue. Some of the stakeholders had chance to convert their share into a ten-year season ticket and a Premier share. Each one had a photo of The Hawthorns, with the roll call of honours, and was signed by six greats – Ray Barlow, Ronnie Allen, Cyrille Regis, John Wile, Tony Brown and Jeff Astle. We were at the Throstle Club to award these certificates to those who opted for the Premier share. That's when I first met John Wile. What you don't want at a club is someone with too much power. When that happens, you have a problem. For instance, if one in four things I do is a mistake, we increase the probability of success by working together and only one in 16 things we do is then a mistake. This is why it's important two or three people are involved in decisions. Football managers operate on their own and make mistakes. But I was determined to have people around me because it reduces the percentages. My view was that not only did Albion need a good chairman, but also a good chief executive. This is what you also need to operate a recruitment strategy. You need more than one view on signings. Before that, we had a manager (Buckley) who basically signed players who had played for him before. That's no way to run a club.

"Looking back, I can say with confidence that John Wile has done more for West Bromwich Albion than anyone else in their modern history. Not only was he a wonderful player, but as chief executive he got the club from the bottom of the second tier to the Premier League. And it all started that day I first met him. I said to him: 'Do you know anyone who might make a good CEO for Albion?' He expressed an interest, which was exactly why I phrased it that way. I didn't want to put pressure on him but he gave me the answer I wanted."

Thompson's biggest gripe following his appointment as director was the lack of strategic direction over transfers. More so, he felt contracts were so poorly structured that the club was paying players over the odds. Notably, he felt Albion were struggling to offload under-achieving players because of hideously bloated contracts. Very soon, it was Thompson's view that autonomy needed to be removed from the recruitment process – any pursuits were based around analysis and intelligence delivered by a committee of individuals, rather than the instinct of a manager. It was an issue that would come back to bite him after he became chairman in 2000. Then, he was determined to see through a revolution of player recruitment and, to help him do so, he enlisted the help of other chairmen.

"Player contracts were the big issue for me," he added. "You cannot afford to pay a player more than he is worth. If you do, you'll be stuck with him. The manager is not the best person to determine this. Agents talk to each other and share information. One of the first things I did as chairman was to write to the chairman of each League club to ask what their fifth highest-paid and 11th highest-paid players were earning. I then said I would put together a summary of the information with averages for each division and distribute that to each chairman willing to share information. About 40 of the 72 replied. I put the info together and shared it. Knowing the highest earner was of no interest because you might get a rogue player on so much more than others. This helped me learn a lot about what footballers could earn at our club – or expect to earn. In any business, you need information. I knew from that point that if I gave a player a contract and he only ended up being a League One player, I knew what he could move to a League One club for. That's something we weren't doing. Our valuations were so wrong. I knew our approach to contracts had to change. And I knew that from a very early stage, before I became chairman."

One of Thompson's biggest, but lesser-known, legacies at The Hawthorns was the restructuring of how players were remunerated. It was to become a staple of his time as chairman between 1999 and 2002. He added: "I always asked what a selling club were paying their outgoing player and got a copy of the player's contract before they signed here, including some we didn't sign. I picked out the best clauses from those contracts to create a standard contract for players, which was then agreed by myself and John Wile. We would always have a one-year option in the club's favour, for instance. We also developed a way of negotiating with agents. We would send a fax to the agent, telling him what we would be willing to offer. If the agent thought it wasn't in the ball park, we told him not to even bother getting in his car. It was important we set the parameters. Any agent will want to negotiate but you need to show him some latitude. You developed an approach for negotiation and we, when I was chairman, made about 15 signings. If you look at those, 12 were very good. The average hit rate for most clubs of our size was much lower."

Thompson wasn't shy in seeking advice. He claims one such exercise ended with Albion signing Jason Roberts, the Bristol Rovers striker becoming the club's record buy in 2000. He felt that courting information from elsewhere could only strengthen his own intelligence and knowledge, although some mocked him for this approach. "When Brian Little was manager, I sent a letter to all 72 clubs," he said. "I said West Brom wanted to progress, we wanted to make our squad better and were looking for better players, who wanted to develop their career. I made it clear we had money to spend and said: 'If you have any young players you think could benefit us, for a fair fee, please let me know'. Jan Molby was Kidderminster manager and gave my letter to the Express & Star. They had a field day and I was mocked by the press. He thought it was wrong a chairman would do this.

"But sometime later that year, we had a call from Bristol Rovers – would you be interested in Jason Roberts? It was a direct result of that letter. I asked Gary Megson if he would like him and he said he would. A proper scouting system would have known about Jason. But we would have known about others, too. The moral of the story is that you can never have enough intelligence or knowledge. Never assume you know everything. We are always learning."

Alan Buckley was sacked in early 1997 and replaced by Ray Harford. But perhaps it should have been Chris Waddle. The former England winger was then with Bradford City, still as a player but looking for a way into management. He had already impressed Albion's board during an initial interview. On February 1, after manager-less Albion drew 2-2 at Port Vale and the players were filing past the media towards the team bus, Sunday Mercury journalist Graham Hill was called over by Paul Raven and told that Waddle was due to be appointed as player-manager. The player's source for the information was a director.

Hill continues the story: "Paul said: 'Joe (Brandrick) has just told us that Chris Waddle is getting the job'. He wasn't a player to make things up or play pranks, so I knew it was cast-iron and from a credible source. I drove back at high speed and was even flagged down for speeding on the M6 in a Vauxhall Astra that was barely road-worthy. I got back to our office in Colmore Row to find my colleague Ian Johnson on the phone to Joe Brandrick. He confirmed that Chris Waddle was getting the job. He didn't say who would be his assistant but suggested it might be Glenn Roeder. So that was our back page. It was big news and an exclusive. Back then, before the Internet, regional stories would get picked up by agencies, who would circulate them to national media. Sure enough, the Waddle story landed with national newspapers, radio stations, the BBC and such like.

"Later that day, Gary Lineker was hosting a show on Radio 5 Live. He was a former team-mate of Waddle's and called him to verify the story. It transpired that Waddle did meet Albion directors for talks, which is when he found out about our story. He decided to turn down the job, claiming he didn't want to work for a club where such a leak of information was possible. That was that. A lot of fans blamed me for writing that story, claiming it wasn't true. But it was true. Had I not written it, I'm convinced Waddle, not Ray Harford, would have been appointed. And when a director tells you something like that, you take it seriously."

As it turns out, Albion probably owed the Sunday Mercury a debt of gratitude. Waddle eventually became player-manager of Burnley but his flirtation with the dug-out was short-lived and forgettable. More so, his decision to turn down Albion opened the door for Harford, under whom Albion's form flourished. But it was a union with flaws. Harford was underwhelmed by the lack of investment from Tony Hale despite the arrival of Kilbane and Alan Miller. Mickey Evans and Graham Potter also joined for significant sums but were unsuccessful. Yet it was the departure of Paul Peschisolido – the proceeds of which went towards the signing of Evans – that cut deep with Harford.

There was also the small matter of the manager living in Surrey and effectively spending only three days a week at the club. When Queens Park Rangers came calling in December, 1997, Albion knew they might struggle to keep him. John Wile, by then installed as chief executive, admitted the club had little hope of retaining Harford's services. Hale did all he could to keep him but Wile adds: "Ray was living near Ascot – it was a canny drive. We knew he was close to taking the QPR job and I remember sitting with Tony Hale in the boardroom. Tony wanted to give him a massive rise plus only working two days. I liked Ray but it can't be right that we were offering somebody more money to work fewer days. That was Tony – he wanted to look good with the fans. Sadly, we lost Ray and had to replace him. That was symptomatic of the club. It was all done without structure."

The Harford saga ended up in the High Court and Albion received £180,000 from QPR, including costs. Wile was learning quickly about the quirks of football administration, not least when it came to Peschisolido's exit. The striker was represented by Eric Hall, one of the better-known agents of the time, and married to Birmingham City's managing director Karren Brady. Albion had signed Peschisolido in the summer of 1996 following Trevor Francis's controversial decision to sell him. Francis has since revealed in his autobiography 'One in a Million' that the now-ennobled Brady was not at all pleased to see her other half sold – especially to a local rival – and told the manager: "I wouldn't have brought you here if I knew you were going to sell my husband." Quite.

Albion had already offered 'Pesch' a contract but he was not in the mood for renewing. Indeed, Fulham, then in the third tier but bankrolled by Harrods owner Mohamed Al-Fayed, were ready to give Albion a healthy profit on their £600,000 outlay. In the meantime, Wile was going to have his work cut out dealing with Hall and Brady. "Crikey, he had Eric Hall and his wife, who was then high up at Birmingham – what a combination!" recalled Wile. "He had no intention of signing that contract. He was playing it all through the papers. He wanted to get a better deal elsewhere. The fans were saying 'give him what he wants' but the club was in trouble. We couldn't afford to give him the money. Not only that but there were so many differences in contracts in terms of signing-on fees, bonuses etc that it was causing problems between players.

"Paul (Thompson) and I decided later on that when it came to renewing contracts, we would offer three elements: a basic wage, win bonuses and appearance money. There would be no cars, no insurances, no add-ons, no houses…that was hard to swallow for some players. But that's what they were used to. Peschisolido at one point came to see me, saying he wanted a chat. Karren came with him and he asked if she could come in. I refused. Surely he could see that including the chief executive from the club down the road was going to be a conflict of interest for everyone? So I told him no. Karren had to stay in the reception area. He wasn't best pleased and nor was she. Whatever conversation Eric Hall and this club had was in the press the following day. Nothing stayed private. In the end, Paul left for Fulham but we did what we could and, well, Paul and his representatives got what they wanted. Paul said at the time he wasn't happy with the way he was tret (sic) but he did ok out of us."

Denis Smith lasted 18 months as Harford's successor before the club took the nuclear option of dismissing him just before the start of the 1999-2000 campaign. He was replaced almost immediately by another figure who had graced Midlands pitches throughout the 1970s, Brian Little. The question must be asked of Wile, as chief executive at the time, how he allowed such a decision to be made with less than a fortnight to go until the new season started. "We needed a change because it hadn't worked with Denis," he admits. "There was an opportunity to bring somebody else in and Brian should have been a safe appointment. He did well at Villa and Leicester. I was away at the time but know he presented himself well. He gave a PowerPoint presentation that impressed some of the elderly members of the board. That certainly helped him.

"I wouldn't take myself out of the responsibility – I'm a firm believer in corporate responsibility – but it was a decision taken very quickly and I'm not happy with the way we handled it. It wasn't handled well. But certain people at the club wanted that change. Brian was available and the change came. I felt for Denis. He was experienced and he'd done well at Oxford. He had a good reputation. We thought he'd be ideal for us but you can never be sure. And Ray was a hard act to follow. Ray was very clever, he knew how to mix with the players – they liked him, they enjoyed his methods. He was a coach but he had that ideal chemistry with our players at that time. I often wonder how we would have got on had he stayed a bit longer. He had them playing well and Denis was, in some respects, a different animal. Results started to go badly and some players made their minds up."

By 1998-99, Thompson was growing increasingly weary of Albion politics. His efforts and desire to bring a new approach to the club were floundering. Old-school values predominated – there was little time for Thompson's promotion of new, business-led ideas. Albion remained the parochial corner shop, led by community men of modest wealth who were shaped by a lack of ambition but clung to power for all it was worth. Thompson admits it wasn't an easy period for him before he became chairman.

"I was finding out transfers were being referred to the board after the event," he added. "I might get a call while the agent and club were talking to each other. That was too late. What was the point in that? I was concerned there was no research into the players we were pursuing. How do you do that research? Easy, you look at his playing record. That's a scouting report in itself. If a guy has played 60 games in the Championship over a two-year period, you know he's probably a decent Championship player. I also analysed the ages of players. If a player was 23 or under, I knew he might get better. If he was in the 24-28 bracket, he was probably at his peak. Over 29 and he would probably get worse. I wanted to hit the middle level or the younger level. But I couldn't influence this at the time and that was frustrating."

Where Thompson lacked gravitas over player recruitment, he gained momentum in pushing for off-field improvement. But even that venture fell short and Thompson saw little other option but to relinquish his position as director. "Initially, I felt I could influence the building of a new stand," he said. "Clive Stapleton was excellent in his contribution. He had a lot of knowledge in that respect as he had been involved in the building of the Birmingham Road and Smethwick End stands. But we needed a £5m loan from the bank and that was a problem. The negotiations between us and the bank were by the chairman and they wouldn't lend us it. They had no confidence in us. At that point, I felt there was little more I could achieve. I asked Tony how long he wanted to be chairman and he made it clear he wanted to continue and wasn't happy to relinquish that. I resigned and sat behind the goal for the best part of a season. Tony was a guy I liked. And he always did the best for the club as he saw it but I just felt I couldn't continue with the way things were."

The nadir for the Hale administration – and indeed chief executive Wile – came in December, 1999. Little's men headed to Grimsby for their third successive away game, having lost their previous two at Norwich and Crewe. But, somewhere en route, the decision was made to withdraw Kevin Kilbane without Little being informed, Albion having accepted a £2.5m bid from Sunderland. Wile, struggling with the aforementioned flu, was absolutely seething as the news filtered through. The year before, he felt he had been ignored during the negotiations over Fabian De Freitas. The Kilbane departure was one too many for him. At this point, Wile wasn't a popular figure. The local media were gunning for him, despite him frequently being no more than a bystander to deals done behind his back. His mind was made up.

Then came that phone call. As the clock ticked towards the end of 1999, Wile was to make a decision that was to transform Albion into the 2000s. Before that, though, the Kilbane saga played out. "The club were desperate for money but I had no idea what was going on that day," he added. "We had an offer for him and he was gone. Just like that. I didn't know until I walked into the car park that he'd been sold. We had that game at Grimsby and all hell broke loose. When I'd left the previous game at Crewe, I was told Kevin would be staying. The next thing I know, Brian is telling me that Kilbane has gone. 'No he hasn't, Brian,' I said. But he had. Nobody told me. With Fabian De Freitas's signing, I had a few meetings with his agent. Nothing came of those and I wished him all the best. The next thing I know, Fabian has signed. Again, I knew nothing about it.

"This was bubbling up to me leaving. We're selling players, signing players, I'm trying to negotiate contracts where I give somebody a bottom line and the chairman (Tony Hale) is going behind my back and agreeing other things. Paul Thompson had distanced himself and I was ready to leave. People were giving me stick. Fans on the phone-ins, at the stadium, journalists were hammering me yet I didn't have much to do with what they were unhappy about. Paul Thompson had grown disillusioned and things came to a head for me with that Kilbane deal. I was really laden with flu. I'm at Grimsby and getting absolute pelters from all quarters, especially the press and supporters. Over Christmas and New Year, I had arranged to go away with my wife. We often did for a few days. I was fully intending to jack it in because I was sick of getting all the flak. Anyway, Paul rang to see how I was. I told him I was thinking things over and had pretty much had enough. 'I've had it…I'm packing it in. Paul, this isn't working any more, the club isn't being run the right way and I'm done'. He had stepped away from the boardroom but said: 'If you stay, I'll come back. But it's important you stay. If you don't, I'll also stay away for good."

Thompson's final salvo was key. Without Wile, there would be no return. Without Thompson, Wile wouldn't stay. That phone call set in motion a change of the guard. Hale would leave and step aside for Thompson. Wile would stay after all. Thompson had been trying to wrestle control for a while. In July, 1999, he attempted to convince hundreds of Hale loyalists to switch their vote at the extraordinary general meeting at West Bromwich's Gala Baths. In the power struggle that followed, Hale clinched the victory. But only just. His power was slipping. Thompson was defiant in defeat, knowing Hale's victory had come through Graham Waldron's backing. Waldron attached his massive proxy of 10,230 votes to a cross and put it beside the chairman's name. Had Waldron gone with Thompson, the result would have seen a swing of 15,000 against Hale.

Yet within a few days of Kilbane leaving, Hale was finished. Thompson returned and was immediately appointed chairman. Wile saw the benefit of the change immediately. As the 20th century drew to a close, Albion were finally catching up. "From that moment, it was a different club and a different working environment," added Wile. "The first meeting we had, Paul said: 'Right, go and get the training ground sorted out.' We discussed St Margaret's (in Great Barr), then the site at Aston University in Walsall, which is where the training ground is now. We agreed to buy 90 acres. We also put plans in place for a new stand. Paul helped to bring extra finance in. He invested his own money.

"That whole period was a whirlwind. It felt like West Bromwich Albion was finally returning. I know the fans couldn't see all of that but it felt like we were right back on track. It was the first time I had felt that as chief executive. The structure was finally in place. I'm not underestimating that phone call. Had Paul not called me when he did, there is little chance I'd have stayed on. I felt like I was finished with Albion. But Paul made that call and everything changed."

Barry Hurst and Clive Stapleton also ended their boardroom exile. The band was back for one more gig and Albion's financial course was to change dramatically. Kilbane's departure created some financial respite yet the situation remained perilous. It was around this time that stories emerged about Thompson getting ready to bring in Ron Atkinson as a technical director. Those were played down by the newly-installed Albion chairman. There were also remarkable back-page claims in a Sunday tabloid that Albion were considering merging with troubled Premier League club Wimbledon in a move that would effectively pitch a newly-formed West Bromwich Dons mongrel straight into the top flight. Thompson and Wile insisted there were no such plans. Tabloid speculation also linked Wimbledon with a move to Dublin and further investigations suggested Albion were merely the chosen target for agents acting for Wimbledon. Albion, with their boardroom issues and their long-time absence from the top flight, were easy and convenient rumour fodder.

Thompson had enough pressing issues in the Black Country. Within a month of Kilbane leaving, he rubber-stamped Enzo Maresca's exit to Juventus – a move greeted with a nod of acceptance by Baggies fans. Losing someone to Sunderland was one thing. Selling a player to an Italian powerhouse was easier to take. The Baggies received £4.3m for the midfielder – their highest sale for some time. There was another windfall and the playing of Albion's ace card. In summer, 1991, while Albion had been busy preparing for their first season in the Third Division, Ron Atkinson was settling in as Aston Villa's new manager. He moved for young defender Ugochuku Ehiogu, with Albion vulnerable as the player had yet to sign professional terms. Their resistance was meek against a top-flight club and Ehiogu, having made just two senior appearances, moved for £40,000. Crucially, though, Hawthorns chairman John Silk included a clause that meant Albion would receive 50 per cent of any future fee.

It was barely given another thought, until nearly a decade later. By 2000, Ehiogu had played almost 250 games in a strong Villa side and was an England international. He was also courting interest from elsewhere. Albion were in a strong position, with Manchester City and Bryan Robson's Middlesbrough keen. He was rated in the region of £7m. Knowing Albion were vulnerable under Hale, Villa owner Doug Ellis had tried to broker a deal and offered £250,000 to settle the clause. There was also discussion of Villa throwing in utility man Simon Grayson and veteran defender Colin Calderwood. Due to their wage demands, though, both players were non-starters.

Thompson's eyes light up at the mention of Ehiogu in our conversation. He was pitted into a battle of wits and negotiations with Ellis and clearly enjoyed the joust. "Doug phoned and said he had talked to Tony a while back about the 50 per cent sell-on clause," said Thompson. "He had offered us £250,000 but Tony wanted £500,000. Bear in mind that, by this point, Ugo is being talked about as a £6m or £7m player. Doug continued: 'I've been thinking about it – I would pay the £500,000 if it's ok with you'. I thanked him and declined his offer. I took a call from Manchester City chairman David Bernstein, who said they were interested in buying Ugo but the sell-on clause was threatening to thwart it. A while later, I was at a dinner when I saw Bryan Robson. He said exactly the same. I had about ten calls between myself, Doug and the Villa secretary Steve Stride and conceded it wasn't right we should get 50 per cent but I wasn't going to leave us short either. And I certainly wasn't willing to accept a one-off payment to waive the clause. I was determined to get the best deal I could for West Bromwich Albion. So after toing and froing, we finally got there. I said they could have the first £500,000 of what he goes for and we would have 50 per cent of the rest. So we received a good £3m for Ugo when he joined Middlesbrough for £6.5m."

Thompson continued: "John Wile asked me to come back. So we met. And I would only go back if Barry Hurst and Clive Stapleton came back and we had a happy board. But there is no doubt the sales of Enzo and Kevin and the payment we received from Villa for Ugo went a long way to putting us back on the right road. It wasn't ideal but we had to start somewhere. When I became chairman, the club was losing £1.5m a year on £10m turnover, which is a huge amount. The transfer policy wasn't in a good place because we were paying too much for players who weren't worth what they were paid. The bank said they would not extend any further loans unless a player was sold. They also wanted to call in the overdraft agreement. For that reason, Kevin Kilbane was sold. Tony didn't want him to leave but the bank had said they would cease to provide overdraft facilities if a player wasn't sold. Tony sold Kevin and the fans were up in arms. After that, he couldn't stay, so he resigned.

"One of my first tasks was to sort out the contracts, so we knew what we would be doing. The next significant act was the sale of Enzo Maresca. I knew there were major financial problems. The sale of Kevin only plugged the hole. It shoved the day of reckoning forward. It didn't provide any money to do anything, merely covered the losses. But there were only two players worth money – Lee Hughes and Enzo. I would have preferred not to sell either but, if we had to, they could be sold."

On the pitch, Albion were struggling. Between November 23 and February 12, they played 12, drew six and lost six. The increasingly beleaguered Brian Little was going through marital issues that became so pressing that he was forced to miss a game during the festive period and Albion told the media he was absent with flu. A 1-0 victory over Crewe gave Little a lifeline but not for long. A 6-0 defeat at Sheffield United was followed by a defeat at Blackburn. On March 4, Albion were beaten 3-0 at home by Trevor Francis's Birmingham and fans turned on Little in no uncertain terms. They chanted obscenities at him, egged on by away supporters no doubt enjoying the plight of the former Villa boss. Little effectively triggered his own P45 by accusing people of 'poking their noses in'. He said: "Everyone is talking about me behind my back and saying what the team should be. The only person who should get on with team affairs is the manager." He was also scathing about the supporters. By the Monday, he was gone and Albion began the search for his successor. Thompson said: "I liked Brian but things weren't going well for him. He more or less resigned on the radio during his interview. He could have been very successful at the club but he had a bad start, which didn't help. We got together on Monday and basically agreed things weren't working. He was a gentleman and it's a shame but you have to make those decisions."

Thompson explained the procedure that led to the appointment of Gary Megson in his place. Several names were linked with the role, including Joe Royle, Colin Todd and Steve Cotterill. So why did Albion opt against the experience of Royle and Todd? "We set seven criteria," explained Thompson. "We wanted a manager with at least five years' experience. But we also wanted one in the 35-45 age bracket so he would be out training with players. And we wanted our job to be the best job he'd had. Gary fulfilled most of those criteria. The fans were deflated – they wanted a big name. And we could have done that but it would not have been the best job that person had had. Managers don't want to be interviewed and not get the job, so we didn't actually speak to many.

"But what I did do was phone other chairmen who knew Gary like Peter Coates at Stoke. He told me how well he had done there and how he had only lost his job as Icelandic owners came in. I also phoned Derek Dooley as he wanted Gary for Sheffield United but didn't appoint him because of Gary's Sheffield Wednesday connection. In my view, we got the best man for the job. I still think that."

Megson was to transform the club. Thompson and his board backed him with the money for five players on transfer deadline day in March, 2000. One of the five was Bob Taylor, who arrived back following two years at Bolton, Sam Allardyce having signed him on the back of two successful loan periods in 1998. Taylor became an instant hero at the end of his first spell when he scored in Wanderers' 1-1 draw at Manchester United. The goal prompted misfortune for John Wile, who had already come under fire for allowing the club hero to leave at a time when Albion were struggling under Denis Smith. "By 1998, Bob wasn't the player he had been," he claimed. "He lost a bit towards the end of his first period here, whether it was focus or sparkle. Denis had made that observation, too, and we couldn't agree a contract with Bob. It was unfortunate one of the press lads phoned me up when he returned to us after that first loan period and I said: 'Denis and I both think his better days are behind him'. I added that if you'd seen the last game in his first spell for Bolton (against United), you'd have been amazed it was the same player. That wasn't meant as a criticism, more a case that Bob had rediscovered his touch. But the press used it to create a negative story. It was a football decision only. And, let's not forget, we did bring him back a couple of years later."

Taylor was not the only hero whose future Wile had to deal with on his watch. Lee Hughes's rise to prominence brought with it almost persistent speculation that he would move to bigger and better things. Middlesbrough, Villa, Manchester City and Derby were among the top-flight clubs linked with him and he finally earned his move in 2001 when leaving for newly-relegated Coventry, with no Premier League club willing to take a gamble on Albion's goalscorer. Wile believes Hughes was too easily guided by middle-men, as well as the promises of head-turning riches.

"Lee didn't want to leave," added Wile. "He was happy to stay but his agent was determined to get him out. He didn't advise Lee well. We offered him a fantastic contract but we knew it wasn't going to happen because people were forever in his ear about him earning more. I didn't think it (Coventry) was a good move for him but his agent pushed for it. We went out to lunch with his agents to San Carlo in Birmingham and agreed everything. We came back and the figures went up again, so that was the end of that. We simply couldn't offer any more and no matter what we were offering, there was clearly a want to get him out. It was all about money. And there comes a time where you have to say: 'Enough'."

Albion progressed superbly under Megson. A play-off finish in 2000-01 was followed by automatic promotion in 2002. Yet all wasn't well between manager and chairman. It was during the spring of 2002 that Thompson made his well-publicised comments about the need to introduce a more structured scouting system. Thompson thought any scouting or recruitment must fit under the club's umbrella rather than be shifted from manager to manager but his comments caused ructions, especially given Megson's popularity. It seemed the chairman was causing trouble at a time when the club was motoring towards promotion. Yet, removed from the context of a highly-charged period of the season, his views made sense – and still do.

Megson's style was completely different to that of Smith and Little. Likewise, his two successors, Bryan Robson and especially Tony Mowbray, advocated different principles again. It seems prudent for the club to have control over player recruitment, albeit with the manager having an integral say. And, likewise, that recruitment should probably be extended to managers, to ensure the transition from one to another is seamless. If that sounds familiar, it's because it is – it was exactly the policy introduced by sporting and technical director Dan Ashworth in the late 2000s. Paul Thompson wanted to implement such a strategy a decade earlier.

The fall-out from Thompson's comments were seismic, with the media kept busy in the run-up to promotion and beyond. What should have been a celebratory period, ended up somewhat flat. Yet Thompson has no regrets. Despite the apparent animosity from Megson towards him, he has no such feelings towards his one-time employee. Any differences were purely about professional matters, rather than personal disapproval – certainly from Thompson's point of view. "Gary and I got on superbly well all of that time," he adds. "But it's very difficult when what is appearing in the press is either not correct or not consistent with what you want to achieve. The other difficulty is that we put in place many good things, which perhaps remain now, but in order to succeed in the Premier League – which is what we were striving for –

we needed to overhaul our scouting system. This caused tension between Gary and myself but had we not had a good relationship, we would never have been promoted to the Premier League in the first place. Managers like to put pressure on clubs via the media. They always want more, it's what they do. Gary and I did speak about this. Changing the scouting system was the thing I was unable to achieve during my time with Albion. That was why I left as chairman. If we couldn't improve our scouting and we went up, I knew we'd come down. And we did. But I wasn't going to be the chairman when that happened."

Matters came to a head following promotion and it appeared Megson might be the one to leave. That's how it generally works when employees fall out with employers – there is only ever one outcome, surely? Not this time. Thompson was to spring one final surprise. On April 30, nine days after the famous victory over Crystal Palace, he announced his departure. He was to leave on May 20, the day after Albion officially became Premier League stakeholders.

Sacking Megson was not an option, although not everyone agreed with that stance. It emerged some time later that after Albion's 1-0 FA Cup win over Leicester in the February, one board member spoke openly about replacing him. That director was Jeremy Peace. At no other point, on Thompson's watch as chairman, did Albion consider dismissing the dissenting manager. "I knew Gary didn't want the revised scouting system, so therefore I could not bring any more to West Bromwich Albion," Thompson continued. "I couldn't preside over failure. The only way we could bring it in was by Gary not being manager. And at no point did I consider sacking him. In all of that period, there was only one person who wanted him sacked. That came after our FA Cup game with Leicester."

Thompson added: "Bobby Hope was chief scout at the time. I said I'd like to chat with him. Gary said: 'That's ok'. I arranged a meeting but Bobby never came. He wouldn't meet me without Gary. That showed how much influence Gary had. The chief scout wouldn't come to a meeting with me. Bobby's loyalty, as he saw it, was to Gary. You can only put in a proper scouting system if the manager is not against it. He doesn't have to be for it but if he's against it, it won't work. A manager might want several 35-year-olds to get promoted but what happens when they stop playing, or he leaves? It was very clear we needed to develop a strategy to ensure the club prospered. Gary was totally against it. He wouldn't let us talk to the scouts. He wouldn't let us talk to other coaches. It was ridiculous, especially as we wanted Gary very much involved in the process. When I look at how so many clubs are run now, it is exactly what John Wile and I wanted to implement then.

"Gary and I didn't have a wrong word until after we were promoted and then it was a case of either Gary went, or I went. We needed a different approach to scouting and Gary didn't want that. Gary can say what he likes but I never fell out with him. I had always said I would be chairman for three years but I didn't think I would be chairman for that long given the money going around. People like Mike Ashley can tough situations out. I couldn't do that. The club belonged to the fans. I answered every letter personally and there was no way I wanted to be chairman and preside over failure. Without my plans being implemented, I knew that would happen. So I resigned the day after Albion officially became stakeholders of the Premier League. I wasn't going to resign without them being a Premier League club."

Thompson remains adamant that he chose the only option available – to take one for the club, effectively. "I was a consensus person. All I did at West Bromwich Albion was via consensus. I wasn't a dictator. Had I stayed – this might sound conceited – and Gary had worked with me, I think we would have become a top-eight Premier League side eventually. He was good enough to have managed in the top eight. We had a very strong set-up and my ambition was for a top-eight finish in the top flight. We were making very good progress."

Thompson's resignation left Clive Stapleton as acting chairman. But while Stapleton looked after the nuclear briefcase, one director was ready to challenge for the chair and was politicking behind the scenes. That was Jeremy Peace. He played the most significant card of the power struggle by publicly throwing his support behind Megson, the very man he had called to be dismissed a few months earlier. It was in early June that Peace made his move. After trying to force through an EGM, he, despite not having the backing of directors Hurst, Stapleton and Bob McGing, motored on with support from rogue director Joe Brandrick. He effectively claimed control and appointed himself as executive chairman. In doing so, Stapleton and Hurst were moved on immediately. Crucially, so was John Wile – even though he wasn't even there to fight his corner.

Wile remains angry with how his time as chief executive came to such a brutal end. "We were aware Jeremy wanted to be chairman," he said. "I wasn't in favour of that and told him so. He didn't have the experience to be in charge. Even on the board, we had better qualified people. I think Paul would have stayed had it been a different set-up. But Jeremy could see the treasures that lay ahead. I went on holiday when it was all happening. There was a lot going on. I came back, Jeremy called me in. Mike O'Leary was with him – I knew Mike, we'd spoken before and he was a nice bloke. Jeremy said: 'This is Mike…he's going to be the next chief executive. We are making you redundant.' I said: 'You cannot do that'. But he did. I asked if I could say cheerio to people and he refused. He wouldn't let me go to the training ground, the offices, I had to leave there and then. From there on, it was all done between lawyers. And then Brendon (Batson) came in as managing director. That's football. It was symptomatic of the way the club was going. No value was given to people who cared for the club. I wasn't the only one treated with disdain. It was a big thing. I'd given my career to West Bromwich Albion, I had been a captain, a good captain, returned as CEO and thought we'd achieved something fantastic. It was a team effort. And I was proud of that."

Wile believes Albion could have prospered had Megson and Thompson called a truce and found a way of working together. He continued: "We were portrayed as trying to make life difficult for the manager – that was totally and utterly wrong. Given the circumstances, I think the board did a fantastic job. We turned the club from a loss-making one to a profit-making one, we built a new stand, we were building a new training ground. Paul and I were robbed of the Premier League. Had we stayed – certainly with Paul as chairman – we'd have prospered. I told Gary: 'You will never work for a better chairman than Paul Thompson'. I'm sure Gary would still be working at the highest level in football had things worked themselves out. It's a shame Paul and Gary fell out. And I think it ended up serving Gary badly in the long term. I've not spoken to him since but, in his heart of hearts, perhaps he might have handled it differently. He would certainly have had a better career had Paul Thompson stayed. And what happened in the end? He ended falling out even worse with Jeremy… so it didn't exactly work out well for him anyway."

These days, Wile reflects on his second time at the club with serenity and even fondness. It was not always the case. For a long time, a man who made the third highest number of appearances for the club, stayed away, ravaged by bitterness and disdain for the manner of his enforced exit. It was almost as if anything pre-June, 2002 had been airbrushed from history by the new regime. Wile's stance has softened in recent times, not least following the change of ownership in 2016, when Peace sold his 87.8 per cent majority shareholding for £200m to the Chinese consortium led by Guochuan Lai.

"It was hard – for me and my family," Wile added. "I had no control over my exit. As a player, you can do something about it. But as a chief executive, you can't. It's why when I left Peterborough as manager, I didn't want to be a manager again. There were people I thought were friends, people in the press who I thought were friends… all of a sudden it suited their agenda to be negative against me. It marked your card. I haven't forgotten. When I was chief executive, I didn't want to be associated with going to the training ground, I purposely kept away from the dressing room. I didn't want to be that ex-player who hangs around making unwelcome comments. That wasn't me. I didn't want to interfere. Maybe I should have done more of that. Maybe I should have shown my face down the training ground once a week. Maybe I should have gone into the dressing room after wins and said: 'Well done, lads'. People at least then could have made up their own mind whether they liked me. Yes, I regretted going back. I think it sullied my reputation. I was there during a difficult period, certainly initially. But I learned a lot about football, business, negotiation…and that has helped me since. I think there was a certain innocence and naivety that people might be fair and have no agenda. In fact there were some bastards out there, as I was to find out."

Yet Wile's admiration for Thompson is strong. The two remain in touch. He also revealed that immediately after Thompson's departure, the remaining board members discussed whether a change of manager might prompt him to return. There was even talk of pursuing Bryan Robson, who eventually replaced Megson some two and a half years later. "Paul was a massive influence," continued Wile. "Even now in business, I will stop and ask myself: 'What would Paul do?' I've rung him a couple of times to ask him. I think it's tragic he was pretty much chased out of town. It could have been so different. Not many chairmen leave themselves rather than sack the manager. That sums Paul up. But, then, Gary could only win after promotion. Paul and I had strengths that complemented each other and, more so, fitted the club well. But if you'd asked supporters to choose, they would have gone for Gary. Paul never got the credit and certainly not the joy he deserved. He had a saying: 'A reasonable man and a reasonable man will always find an arrangement' and he was right. Clive Stapleton, Albion through and through – an emotional but great man. He got kicked in the bollocks when he was acting chairman. Barry Hurst, too. Good men, treated like crap.

"When Clive was acting chairman, we had that conversation about bringing in Bryan Robson if Gary had gone. It never happened and those discussions with Bryan never came to fruition. But we had that conversation between us and I wonder what would have been the reaction had we done so. I really hope history is kind to Paul Thompson. That day when we went to Grimsby and sold Kilbane, that was me done with Albion. I'd had this public shellacking and I wanted out. I really did. But Paul made me stay. And it seems I made him stay. I hope people recognise some of the good we did for the club, but especially what Paul Thompson did. West Brom became a Premier League club because of his hard work and decision-making."

There was to be one final hand grenade launched in Paul Thompson's direction. Before his exit, the former chairman had included a Premier League bonus clause, so every player would receive £5,000 for a first-team appearance, £7,500 per game if the team drew and £15,000 for a victory. Thompson felt it was a fair incentive for top-flight newcomers. Yet, within weeks of taking over as executive chairman, Peace had scrapped the scheme, prompting uproar from the players during their pre-season camp in Devon. Such was the fall-out from his action that there was talk of a players' strike. Thompson maintains that his scheme was economically viable and dismissed Peace's claims that it would have created a financial catastrophe for Albion in the event of relegation, which duly followed.

"No, no…it isn't true that we would have been in trouble," insisted Thompson. "The bonus system we had for the Premier League was incorporated in contracts that if we went down, it would revert to Championship levels. Basically, and speaking broadly, the money in the Premier League was four times what it was in the Championship then. Those bonuses in the Championship added up to £40,000 a year. For instance, when we signed a player, we didn't give him £250,000 a year but signed him on

£210,000 plus £40,000 in bonuses. The agents complained it wasn't guaranteed but we said it was because if those players didn't think they'd get that bonus, they weren't the kind of player we wanted anyway. It was designed to protect the club and offer incentive to the player."

Thompson was to end all ties with Albion when he sold his stake to Peace some years later. He clearly maintains affinity for a club to which he had no emotional attachment before 1996. He added: "Believe it or not, I enjoyed so much about being involved with the club. As a chairman, I went to every single supporters club, including Australia. We had a fantastic fanbase. More than 30 branches and I was determined to go to each one. The fans were key and it was quickly apparent the appetite for supporting the team was full of potential.

"Enzo gave us the funds to survive and prevent the losses. It was a big turning point and we ended up getting Jason Roberts in the summer. That signing gave us the belief we could do something. There was a very honest board of directors when I arrived. Tony (Hale) was chairman and clearly had a big passion for the club. Joe Brandrick, Barry Hurst and Clive Stapleton were all good businessmen, all West Bromwich Albion through and through. And Gary was a great manager. He did two things. He instilled a fantastic work ethic in players and also played a 5-3-2 system [which could flex into a 3-5-2 system when attacking]. It still bemuses me that more clubs in the Championship didn't play that way and don't play that way today.

"Jeremy Peace had always said he would support me – he didn't want to be chairman. But as soon as we got into the Premier League, he wanted to be chairman. Once the club went into the Premier League and he saw I wasn't for continuing, he changed. Had Gary left, I might have come back. When I resigned, I didn't think it would be forever. There was always the possibility I might return but by then Jeremy wanted to be chairman and that became the new scenario. My only regret was not taking West Bromwich Albion where I thought we could – top eight of the Premier League. I thought we could achieve that. It's absolute rubbish to suggest Albion should be mid-table in the Championship (a comment subsequently made by Jeremy Peace, in 2013, when asked about Albion's rightful place in the pecking order).

"I've been part of some very exciting things. Three years at West Bromwich Albion, with a fantastic club, fantastic supporters – which other club has achieved in three years what we did? We survived on the last day against

Charlton, got to the play-offs, got promoted, built a new stand when everyone said we should be spending it on players and invested in a new training ground. We did some good deals. After that play-off defeat (in 2001) at Bolton, I was in tears. Not just because of the defeat, but the emotion and sense of occasion. I think that's when I realised this club had got under my skin. And that was a special, special feeling."

James/Adam Chambers

"Megson was quite amusing...he'd pull us both over about something – you could tell he only wanted to speak to one of us – so he'd give us a broad comment or criticism. In the end, he just told us to stop hanging around together. That was a problem because we lived together, we drove in together..." (Adam Chambers)

Adam is wearing red. James is in white. Or is it the other way around? Okay, let's try this again: James is on the right, Adam on the left. I think that's correct. James tells me that Adam has a slightly thinner face. In the absence of a ruler, tape measure or any perspective, we carry on but, unhelpfully, they have the same haircut. It is 20-odd years since James and Adam Chambers started confusing coaches, team-mates, fans, media and opponents. And here we are in 2020, in highly unusual circumstances, with me looking at a mobile phone screen and seeing two near-identical 30-somethings. All three of us sit in our respective lounges. James in Edgbaston, Adam in Sutton Coldfield.

It would be wrong to identify the Chambers lads as twins only. It would be insulting to insinuate they were anything but talented players in their own right. Yet the fact they are identical siblings has enabled them to create niche, keynote moments in football. Whether they like it or not, it has been a cachet to their respective careers. And, as you'll find out, their brotherly relationship and rivalry, call it what you will, was instrumental in their careers, certainly early on. They were the first twins to represent England in competitive games at any level – and remain the only ones. They are also the only offspring from one pregnancy to wear the navy blue and white stripes of West Bromwich Albion at senior level. We are meeting via FaceTime in mid-April to talk about those times. The lockdown makes any other kind of meeting off limits. Let us all raise a glass to modern technology.

James, the elder of the two by 29 minutes, has recently become a father to Solomon. The youngest member of the Chambers family is a little over a month old. James made 75 appearances for Albion, Adam played 70 times for the club. So, 1-0 to James. But Adam scored once for the club whereas James did not. Let's call it 1-1. James made his debut before Adam but Adam was to stay longer. From that point, their paths split. Adam had spells with Sheffield Wednesday, Kidderminster, Leyton Orient and Walsall. James played for Watford, Cardiff, Leicester, Doncaster and Hereford, before a sibling reunion at the Banks's Stadium.

Back in 1999, the duo were the subject of a regular FourFourTwo magazine feature called 'The Boy's A Bit Special', with the title amended to reflect the fact both players were being interviewed. Even then, it was all about the double act. Even then, they were individual talents, defined by their circumstances of birth. Both have played Premier League football, yet you could rake through an entire back catalogue of players before finding two as down-to-earth and humble as the Brothers Chambers. Personality-wise, they were surely model professionals for any manager.

It could only have been down to their upbringing. Living in Great Barr, just a stone's throw from the Scott Arms, the brothers were pupils at the old Dartmouth School, playing for the football team belonging to the local church school, Holy Name. Early interest from Albion was respectfully declined by Bert Chambers, the twins' late father – a man who clearly played a huge part in their development, as footballers but more so as children and adolescents. It is there that Adam takes up the story.

"Myself and James played for the local school team and we'd been scouted by West Brom when we were younger to try out for teams," he said. "But our dad wouldn't let us go. He wanted us to enjoy our football. Then, when we got to 14 or 15, John Trewick and Richard O'Kelly got back in touch. They were involved in the youth set-up at Albion and had been asking. It got to a point where we were that much older and our dad just let us go there." It is at this point that James interjects.

"Actually, Adam, it began before then, remember that competition?" he asks. "When we were at school, we went into a national six-a-side tournament that ended up with us playing at Wembley." We encourage him to continue. "At the final stage, we had to represent our local club and that was West Brom. We wore Albion's kit and some of the coaches came down. We won the competition, so maybe we were already known to some of the coaches. On the back of that, they wanted us to go to the under-11s but Dad felt we were too young. There were two big teams in the area, Holy Name and Bustleholme. And then we were allowed to go for trials. There was a mish-mash of games held over a few days and there were the likes of Adam Oliver, Justin Richards and Adam Davies, who didn't quite get a professional contract. There were a few of us. Dean Joynson, from Castle Vale, also joined us. On the back of that trial game, some of the lads from Holy Name and Bustleholme made it. The lads who came through successfully went on to sign for the club. We had some decent players. Daniel Gabbidon and Lloyd Dyer were at Albion then, too. It was a good time to be coming through the ranks."

But first came a calling from their country in 1999 and the Chambers siblings became the first twins to play for England before representing their club. Joining them in the 18-man under-20 squad to go to Nigeria for the FIFA World Youth Championships were Adam Oliver, Peter Crouch and Ashley Cole. Only Arsenal had more representatives in the squad than Albion. England played Cameroon, USA and Japan, the latter including in their squad future Albion man Junichi Inamoto. England failed to qualify from the group but the trip provided fond memories for both.

"It's only in later years that you realise the players who were there in that tournament," James said. "Cambiasso, Ronaldinho, Xavi and Iker Casillas were representing their countries. We had Cole, Crouch and Andrew Johnson but some like Michael Owen, who was already in the Liverpool and England sides, didn't go. Before the tournament, they sat us down and said there was a threat of kidnapping. Some of the lads, like Luke Chadwick of Manchester United, pulled out but we decided to go. It wasn't the best for us results-wise but, as an experience, it was amazing."

Back to Albion. James was first to make his debut. On the 15th day of the new Millennium, he was thrown into the deep end of a second-tier relegation fight. Albion were scrapping, as were their opponents, Port Vale. This was in the teeth of the Brian Little era and when, frankly, it looked only a matter of time before Albion would be looking for a new manager, or preparing for relegation – quite possibly both. James merely wanted a good night's sleep but after his family learned from him of his big Hawthorns day, his mother insisted on spreading the good news. James can laugh about it now, perhaps less so then. "The team were struggling," he continued. "We'd been performing well in the reserves and some fans were pushing for us on radio phone-ins. The day before the game, I was pulled over and it was made clear to me I was in the team. That's a strange feeling, to be honest. All of a sudden, you realise you're going to be playing in front of a big crowd. I went home and told my mom and dad. Mom was on the phone all night telling people I was playing – I was there trying to get an early night and all I could hear was the phone downstairs.

"As for the game, the nerves were going and it didn't seem like I had a kick for ages. I didn't feel part of it at all. Then I went in with one tackle, which was what I needed. It produced a cheer from the crowd and got me into the game. We got a clean sheet [it ended 0-0] and it ended up going well for me. Looking back, there was an expectation some of us would be playing. Daniel Gabbidon, Adam Oliver, myself and Adam… there was a feeling we all had a chance of playing back then."

Adam's first-team introduction was more stark and even brutal. Having already made his debut as a substitute at Stockport in early 2000-01, he was summoned by Gary Megson for a League Cup tie and asked to man-mark Georgi Kinkladze, Derby's brilliant Georgian play-maker. It was an unenviable task for a full debutant yet Adam clearly made an impact as Albion won 2-1 at Pride Park. Sadly, they lost the home leg 4-2 against the Premier League club and went out on aggregate. His full League debut came against Crewe yet he wasn't aware he would be playing until very late. On the morning of the game, Adam threw himself into some weight training, then went off to play pool in the afternoon with some of his other uninvolved team-mates. Unbeknown to him, Megson had been presented with an injury problem in the morning when Des Lyttle was ruled out. Despite having trained with considerable gusto, Adam came through his first League start unscathed, although he suffered a little earache courtesy of Megson's enthusiastic touchline encouragement. Over to you, Adam…..

"We drew 2-2 against Crewe and I wasn't supposed to be playing," he said, smiling away. "I wasn't involved in the squad at all. Normally, those not involved trained in the morning and just reported for the game in the evening. We did some leg weights and body weights in the morning, along with some fitness work, so it was quite significant. We then played pool locally to pass some time and someone was trying to get hold of me. Chris Adamson had a call asking if he was with me and, if he was, to tell me to report to the stadium because the team was doing a light session in the afternoon. So I went assuming I was going to make up numbers on the bench, only to find Des was injured and I was starting. There was me thinking: 'I've done an unbelievable session in the gym and now I'm making my full League debut'. Crewe had a winger called Rodney Jack and I was told to look after him – he was quick as lightning. So, I'm there, absolutely knackered from my morning session, having to keep up with him. I was hoping Megson might extend some leeway but, no chance, he was on at me from the first five minutes. He was on my side of the ground, too, so I got it all half, in my ear."

Adam continued: "I was very proud of James making his debut. When you're a player, you don't always watch with the same nervousness as I would have done as a non-player. The big thing for me was seeing one of my peers, who happened to be my brother, paving a way for me. I went on against Stockport away early in the following season but the day you look forward to most is when you start for the first time. That came for me against Derby in the cup. I was brought in to do a marking job on Georgi Kinkladze – no pressure there, then!"

Despite growing up together and the obvious overlap of their playing careers, the twins were to play just eight times in the same League side for Albion and a further three times in cups. Not once did they start in the same League or cup match for the club. They featured in a little under 150 games in total but spent only 174 minutes on the pitch at the same time. Their first time together was Adam's League debut, at Stockport, where he went on in the 73rd minute of a game his brother started. Their final match together was a mere two-minute overlap in the Boxing Day home defeat by Arsenal in 2002-03, when James went on as a late sub two minutes before his brother went off. And that was that.

They were only the second pair of twins to play in the Premier League – Ray and Rod Wallace at Leeds being the first. Since the Chambers made their mark, there have been four more sets: Fabio and Rafael Da Silva, Martin and Marcus Olsson, Will and Michael Keane, and Josh and Jacob Murphy. And how did coaches, team-mates and even opponents deal with identical twins playing for the same club, occasionally together? Adam is first to pipe up. "When James and I were there, we didn't see it as a big deal. The reaction of people could be funny but we ended up with a joint nickname of 'Chambo', so if someone called that out, we'd both look round and still nobody knew who was who. Managers and coaches found it difficult. There were team-talks where a manager or coach would turn to one of us and take a chance he was talking to the right one – you shouldn't have done this, or done that. It was difficult for some of them and mistaken identity did happen. At one point, we started wearing different coloured boots and I grew my hair a bit longer but it still didn't work."

James is smiling and dying to have his say. I sense we're fast approaching a recollection of mischief. "Once, only one of us had played, but they recorded it incorrectly that the other had played. So the wrong one got the bonus. Adam played but I got the bonus... I probably still owe him!" Adam tries to interject but James hasn't finished, picking out one particular opponent who simply couldn't get his head round the psychology of facing identical twins. This was a time when the two were occupying central defensive roles before hitting the senior squad. After that, Adam became more a shielding midfielder while James tended to play as centre-half or right-back – on one occasion expertly marking Norwich's Darren Huckerby out of a game at Carrow Road.

But that came later, some time after Andrew Johnson, a future nuisance for Premier League defenders, found himself flummoxed by Albion's likely duo. "Andy Johnson, the one who played for Birmingham and Crystal Palace, was about our age so we came up against him a few times," added James. "He used to hate it. He said he found it difficult psychologically because he would go past one of us and then run into the other. So especially when Adam and I played as centre-halves, it was quite a surreal experience for strikers thinking they'd beaten me, only to think they'd run into me again. It must have been difficult. But I don't see myself as a twin. Even when we're out together, we're out as individuals."

Adam returns to the conversation with a further recollection. "Megson, in particular was quite amusing," he added. "A few times, he'd pull us both over about something – you could tell he only wanted to speak to one of us – so he'd give us a broad comment or criticism. Once, we got pulled up over running. It was quite clear that the point he was making is that one of us did something we shouldn't have. In the end, he just told us to stop hanging around together. Well, that was a problem because we lived together, we drove in together… but somehow he wanted us to stay apart! I think he got used to us in the end but I can still see him now wondering if he's speaking to the right one."

The notion that twins have a mutual sixth sense has been popularised by others. The feeling of synchronised pain is another theory projected. If such a thing exists, perhaps Albion missed a trick by not partnering the duo in more matches. Adam isn't so sure. "The only thing I shared with James was pain. When we were little and I punched him, I would feel the pain in my fist as he felt it wherever I hit him! Maybe now we're getting older, we will see that more. But, as kids, we did things together. We often would say the same thing, have the same answers, know what the other was about to say, but that was because we spent time together growing up. I'm not sure that is different to other brothers and sisters." James shares the scepticism. "I've got a bad back but I haven't heard any complaints from Adam – he seems ok to me. I'm also the 'older' one, so I'm the more responsible one…obviously."

All of their joint appearances for Albion came with Gary Megson in charge, all but eight of James's outings for Albion coming under the same firebrand manager. Both were already part of the first-team squad under Brian Little and it was the ex-Villa manager who handed James his debut before giving him further opportunities during his ill-fated spell. James is the first to offer his observations about his two Albion managers – while revealing that he owes his progress to Cyrille Regis, who had been coach under Little and briefly occupied the same role under his successor. His take on his different bosses is somewhat philosophical.

"Little and Megson were very different characters," he continued. "Brian was calm and more relaxed about how he spoke to you. He could pick up his voice if things weren't going right but he would try to encourage you. I only had him for a short period but I appreciate him putting his faith in me. Gary Megson was totally different. His way was the opposite. He liked to have control over everyone on the pitch. He had expectations. There would also be a particular way of playing that he demanded when reacting to particular phases during a game. You had a choice – you had option A or B, with no flexibility or discussion. Option A was to do what you were expected to do. Option B was that you'd be out of the team because you hadn't gone with option A.

"I have to give Cyrille a shout-out. When Megson first took over, he was still getting to know the players. Some years later, Cyrille relayed to me that Gary wanted to revert to Matt Carbon in place of me because Gary wanted somebody bigger and more experienced. But Cyrille backed me and said he would be better off sticking with me. So he ended up going with me and because I had the backing of Cyrille, I probably had a chance where Gary might have gone elsewhere. Gary couldn't have managed the club any differently. We were in trouble at the bottom of the League. There was no room for discussion. He told us what to do it and we did it.

"You have to give him his due because of what he achieved with us but having played for other managers since, you appreciate there are different ways to get the best out of players – give them licence to play, engage in discussions. The controlling element was a big part for him and it could be difficult playing for him in that respect because he laid down huge expectations with no margin for error. You wouldn't get a second chance and that's the way he was. But it worked for us. It wasn't always an enjoyable way to be managed but that was his way. And what he did and how he managed was totally vindicated by two promotions, not to mention a survival and a play-off. From the moment I made my debut, when the squad was of a certain calibre, to where we were within 18 months was some turnaround. It became harder for myself to get into the team but that's to Gary Megson's credit that he was improving the side all along and results were improving."

Adam offers his own insight into Megson's modus operandi. He admits that younger players often struggled with his methods, with more leeway afforded to more experienced team-mates. Adam cites one memorable occasion when Megson turned a blind eye to a late-night gaming session, simply because one of the party happened to be Ruel Fox, who had been a contemporary of Megson's at Norwich and was seemingly immune when it came to the manager's wrath. Adam smiles about it now and you detect a streak of respect from both players for their one-time manager. Both James and Adam are way too civil to speak ill, although you sense both might be biting their tongues now and again. Time has clearly also been a great healer.

Adam's insight offers an interesting perspective on a manager who, while revered by fans, perhaps finds praise harder to come by among the many players who turned out for him. Yet, by the time he finishes, Adam still manages to see the good in his one-time boss. "I can't speak for his dealings with every player but you did get the feeling it was a one-way line of communication. As a youngster, that can be difficult to deal with. Other players who had longer careers didn't always respond to that style as well and felt pushed back, almost a bit restrained in what they were allowed to do on the pitch. I didn't have that problem when I was developing. Looking back, had I been as I am now, would I have spoken up more? Yeah, probably.

"But you have to remember that to get that team promotion was a massive feat. He gave me my debut and I'll always be grateful for that. He also instilled a work ethic, resilience and fitness that served me well. He was very intense, sometimes aggressive and that was the culture. He got the best out of so many players over a period. How sustainable that is over a longer period of time, I'm not so sure. But there were times he could be funny, too. Before the Bradford game (THAT Bradford game), we went to one of the rooms to play on the play station. We were up until late and some of the lads were coming in and out of the room all the time. It was getting a bit loud and, about 10.30, we had a knock on the door. We opened it and Gary was stood there, looking like he was about to kick off. Thankfully, Ruel Fox was in the room and Gary clocked him. They were more like mates than manager and footballer. Gary just said: 'Ok lads… maybe time to go to bed'. Ruel being there totally defused it. And thankfully we won the next day.

"Gary liked a laugh and a joke. There were times we thought he would blow his top and he didn't. What did impress me is that quite often when people get angry, they lose their train of thought or stumble over their words. Not Gary Megson. He would be going bright red, yelling at you, rolling his sleeves up and delivering the bollocking word-perfectly. It was brilliant multi-tasking and some skill to have. He didn't ever trip up over his words when he was telling us off. He was the only manager I had who was so smooth when he bollocked you." Adam is not quite finished and remembers that Megson did not take too kindly to being addressed informally. Once again, a telling-off was delivered with word-perfect Anglo-Saxon eloquence. "There was one training session where the gaffer lost it," he added. "We had a few London lads in the side, like Lee Marshall, Jason Roberts and Danny Dichio, and they would end every sentence during training with 'mate'. It caught on. We had a session one afternoon and the manager got involved. Someone yelled to him: 'Oi, pass the ball, mate'. And then there was silence. Megson turned round and said: 'I'm not your ****ing mate'. He was old school in that respect. Nobody called him 'mate' again."

No mention of Adam's time at Albion would be complete without discussion of the game at Sheffield United in March, 2002. Others from that era have said their piece, as has Megson in a chapter later in this book. For some time, there was innuendo about potential racist slurs being made from the United dug-out. Adam has no recollection of any but admits there were offensive comments made when he was sat on the bench after being replaced some ten minutes before the fun and games started. "There was a sense of tension," he continued. "The two managers didn't seem to get on. There had also been talk of an issue between Andy Johnson and Georges Santos. I got on really well with Georges when he was at West Brom, so it was really unusual what happened that day – completely out of character with the guy we'd seen during his loan spell (in 2000).

"I just remember it being a really intense game. Both teams were aggressive in the way they played. We were two up when everything kicked off. I started the game and remember being taken off just before things started to escalate. But I do recall Michael Brown doing something strange – we went up for a header and, as we landed, he grabbed my shirt. It felt like six or seven seconds and we were stood there just holding each other around the throat while the game carried on. I went off and things just went crazy with players walking off the pitch after the sending-offs of Suffo and Santos. I don't remember any of their staff saying anything racist but, when I stood up after I'd been taken off, I did hear some racist comments towards me from their fans. That was very sad to hear. It's gone down in history but it wasn't an enjoyable game to be part of. It wasn't something I have fond memories of."

James was at Bramall Lane but very much as a spectator. "It was the only game that had been called off in such a manner, which is astounding," he said. "Watching in the stadium, it was so tense. It reminded me of those Arsenal v Manchester United games a few years later where you could feel so much aggression between players. And I can only echo what Adam said – Georges Santos was a lovely bloke but that challenge was just incredible. These days, I actually think more players would have been sent off. Sheffield went way too far."

Albion's first promotion was a highlight for both players, although Adam starred most of the two by far during the season. "It was a very enjoyable season," he added. "I was playing regularly. I started more than half of the games and went on as sub a fair amount. We were so effective. We had people who could score but people who could defend. We thrashed Man City 4-0, we beat Portsmouth 5-0. So we could dish out big scorelines, too, when we wanted. We didn't always dominate games but we always felt we could win. What more could you want at the time?"

James's memories of the historic campaign centre more around off-the-field activities. From holidays, to top-flight football, to unpaid restaurant bills, the players were as one as a unit. "We went to Marbella, so we celebrated as a team," he said. "Through all the issues that Gary had, what he did do well was knit the players together in the way nobody else did. We all got on so well. And 2001-02 felt like a real achievement. Bear in mind that I'd barely played first-team football and then, just two years later, there I was in the Premier League. That was an amazing feeling. We would hang about after training. Jason Roberts, Ruel Fox, Neil Clement, Danny Dichio – we would go out. We had this thing where you took it in turns to pay for a meal. On this occasion, it was Ruel's turn, so we are all ordering three starters, huge main courses, desserts, all sorts. Everyone is adding extras, too. Ruel just sat there shaking his head. Next thing he just stood up, grabbed his credit card and walked out. So, one by one, we are all trying to get out as quickly as we can. I cannot remember who paid for that, but it wasn't me…"

The Chambers brothers had gone their separate ways by the mid-2000s. James joined Watford in 2004, with his brother following him out of the exit door a year later when he signed for Kidderminster following a loan spell with Sheffield Wednesday. Both are now retired as players – James in 2017, Adam in 2019 – and are involved in a joint property business, mainly restoring buildings for student accommodation. James has another venture on the go; building a 'story-boarding' digital app, that enables people, particularly those with terminal illnesses, to leave farewell messages for loved ones, catalogue life milestones and even provide an alternative to traditional wills.

The memories of their professional careers remain fresh. Both feel they owe debts of gratitude to many influencers, not least their late father Bert and mother Maureen. And, above all else, each other. "There were a few people we owe a lot to," said James. "Our dad and mum were very big influences. We had a massive support network in that respect. I used to see other lads whose parents couldn't be there, so that was a big thing for us. Adam was obviously a big motivation – not just support, but rivalry too. I'm not sure what would have happened had one of us not been interested in football. I really don't think either of us would have had that drive to pursue a career in it.

"And then there were the coaches. John Trewick and Richard O'Kelly put a lot of faith in us and used to egg us on. I remember going into the office one day – I must have been about 16 – and he (Trewick) was telling me I was good enough to be in the first team at the time, which gave me such a lift. When I stepped into my early years in professional football, one of the biggest influences was Cyrille Regis. He was a big presence around the club."

It is a discussion to which Adam adds his own weight by throwing in the names of two other coaches: "I agree with all the names James mentioned, but also Denis Smith and John Gorman were huge. I was around the first-team squad when Denis was sacked about a week before the season started. I had been involved in pre-season and on the night the manager left, a group of us went out to say goodbye to him. He told me he'd been looking to put me in the team and give me some game time. That was a lovely confidence boost but if only he hadn't just been sacked! John Gorman took over briefly and was a brilliant coach. After the senior training session, he would seek out the other sessions and be out there for hours with the junior players – not just tactically, but technically. This was a guy who had not long before been coaching with England at the World Cup, so to have someone who had been at the very top showing so much interest, it was a big thing."

Adam has nothing but glowing memories of his years at Albion and continued: "They were wonderful times. Coming up through the ranks, I had a sense of belonging and feeling for the club….interacting with all of the youth coaches, office staff, local reporters and other people who were around. Being local lads, too, we knew a lot of Albion supporters and therefore had a feel for the club. It gave us a platform to have good careers. The way I see it is that because I experienced so much so young – play-offs, promotion, playing in the Premier League, playing with and against some amazing players – it gave me confidence to take on in my career. Wherever I subsequently went, I had that experience to draw upon. I had the experience of playing against Henry, or playing against Scholes, or Lampard, etc. I will always remember that as one hell of an experience."

Adam ended his career with an eight-year spell at Walsall, with James joining him for three years from 2012. Like his brother, James is reflective of his time at their first club. "What a great upbringing it was," he said. "I got to play next to my brother, played with the likes of Jason Roberts and Jason Koumas and then you look back on some of those big highlights. There were some great people along the way, not just players but the backroom staff and people who worked in the offices. It's a dream you have when you're growing up. To be able to fulfil that is amazing."

And so their place in Albion's history remains, not to mention their unique contribution to England's football set-up. James and Adam Chambers remain an integral part of Albion's transition from Championship dwellers to Premier League stakeholders. At a time when the club were barely spoken about for their youth development system, here were two of just a handful who bucked that trend – with some distinction. And now it's time to leave them to squabble over their mistaken bonus payment…

Jason Robert

"...I was angry and it still rankles that I was trying to do my job and being called all sorts because of my colour...Looking back now, I'd say there was a real anger to my celebrations. I wanted to show them I wasn't going to let them stop me doing my job..."

It is not a mistake, before you ask. Jason Robert is his correct name. It has been with his family for four generations, since his great, great grandfather Robert decided to use his forename as a surname. We shall return to this ambiguity and story later on. For now, we return to the name we all know him by.

Jason Roberts is a man on the move and remains driven, ambitious, but extremely courteous, well-mannered and good-humoured. He is inquisitive of his interviewer. He takes an interest in others. We catch up in Florida. Well, kind of. Roberts is heading out to pick up his children in Miami. It has been his home for some time. I am sat at home in Walsall. It isn't Miami, by any stretch.

Roberts, a one-time Grenada international, is the current director of development for CONCACAF, the Confederation of North, Central American and Caribbean Association Football. They are one of FIFA's six continental governing bodies. I don't get around to asking him but suspect he is one of those who doesn't need to buy a World Cup final ticket. More likely, it's a perk of the job. His role as an international statesman is in stark contrast to his former guise as a centre-forward in the higher echelons of English football. Let's rewind.....

It's the year 2000. West Bromwich Albion survive relegation to the third tier but only just. Manager Gary Megson is in the second phase of transforming their fortunes. The first – ensuring survival – is complete. Now there is an ambition and need to bring about growth. Megson, backed by the enthusiasm and measured ambition of Paul Thompson, is busy rebuilding, re-energising and re-establishing a sorry old club. By the turn of the Millennium, Roberts was scoring freely for Bristol Rovers, having started his career at Hayes. His attributes were swiftly recognised. He pitched up at Wolverhampton Wanderers in a £250,000 move but failed to break into their side and spent time at Torquay on loan. He scored six goals in 14 games and shared a house owned by then Soccer AM presenter Helen Chamberlain before a successful loan spell at Bristol earned him a move up the M5 on a permanent basis. Roberts scored 38 goals in 78 League games for The Gas in the final years of the 20th century.

Kevin Kilbane became Albion's first seven-figure signing when he joined from Preston for £1.2m in 1997. Thompson was determined to make Roberts the club's first £2m player but there was more. The final transfer fee was £2.1m and it was no ordinary acquisition. He also carried the distinction, privilege and potential burden of being the nephew of Hawthorns legend Cyrille Regis. Every high, every low, every breath, every goal, every challenge, every tackle and every individual bead of sweat would be measured against his uncle's career, whether he wanted it to be or not. There would be no hiding place. Or at least that's how it seemed. Albion were not only breaking their transfer fee record but investing in a player who, from his first kick of the ball in blue and white stripes, was inevitably going to be pitched head-first into comparisons with one of the club's all-time greats.

From the moment he was unveiled to the media, Roberts knew he was in new and challenging territory. "First and foremost, I thought: 'Stay away from the no 9 shirt'," he said. "Don't go anywhere near it. I knew I couldn't be the 'next Cyrille'. I went for no 11. It was a lot easier in a way because Bob (Taylor) already had no 9. That helped. And I cannot imagine Bob was going to hand it over even if I had asked, which I didn't. I didn't want it. It wouldn't have been right for me. It was my uncle's shirt, so I stuck with no 11.

"Moving to Albion felt like the right step. I was used to playing regularly. I played for (ex Bristol Rovers coaches) Ian Holloway, Gary Penrice and Garry Thompson …they taught me about football and how to be a striker. Joining the Albion felt right. But the first thing I really took on board was how big the club was and then in just how high regard they held my uncle. I tried to establish my own identity very early on because I knew that was important but it remained very much on the agenda. I was there, in the press conference as the record signing, and yet I was there with my uncle and he was the jewel, not me. At times, I felt like he was the signing! That was a real moment for me to take on board – that was what I would be facing. I had a great relationship with my uncle and that was never going to be a problem. But I knew I would have to do something special to build my own story at West Bromwich Albion, so I could be treated and acknowledged as a footballer in my own right, not as the nephew of a legend. Did it affect me? I think maybe it did at first."

Roberts took five games to find his feet. Going on as a 55th minute substitute for Ruel Fox against Swansea, he opened his account eight minutes later before scoring the decider two minutes from the end of a 2-1 win. Albion were going through a transitional period. Also arriving in the summer of 2000 were Fox, Jordao, Derek McInnes and Neil Clement. Megson's Albion were to eventually become recognised for having a frugal defence built around parsimonious principles and the all-consuming work ethic demanded by their manager. If the opposition were fit, you could guarantee Albion would be that little bit fitter. More enticing for Albion fans was the prospect of Roberts linking up with Lee Hughes or Bob Taylor.

In the early 2000s, there was still a tendency for teams to play with two strikers. The trend for lone strikers, supported by deep-lying forwards, more advanced midfielders or wingers, was still evolving. Roberts was already familiar with the necessity to gel with fellow forwards. At Bristol, he had formed a brilliant partnership with Jamie Cureton and, in 1999-2000, they had scored 22 goals each. Albion's interest was prompted.

Hughes, like Cureton, was still playing non-League football in 2020, with both men well into their 40s. Back in 2000, Hughes was in the teeth of his career. It was never to get better. His 2000-01 form alongside Roberts was to earn him a move from The Hawthorns, with Albion reaching the play-offs, only to fall against Bolton. Roberts, meanwhile, speaks of the adjustment from being a young player at Bristol to being a record signing at a club with such an emotional hook to his family. There was more to it than merely being related to a club great. This was also about Brendon Batson and Laurie Cunningham. Roberts explained the influence Albion brought to his north London community – the mere significance of employing three black footballers in the late 1970s had left an imprint on Afro-Caribbean communities. He might have grown up in the shadows of Wembley but Roberts felt a pull to West Bromwich long before he pitched up in the Black Country.

"I knew I was coming into a historical club. It was historical because my uncle was such a legend but you also had Lee Hughes, a local boy, who had come from Kidderminster – I'd played against him when I was at Hayes and knew he would make it. Then you had Bob Taylor, who was a playing legend. I was a record transfer with expectations of filling those shoes. I was a young man, positive in my ability and with something to offer. But there was a warm feeling, not only because of the community, but because it had a special place in the heart of people from the diaspora, from the Windrush generation, because of that historic tie of Brendon, Laurie and my uncle. It was a symbol of something special. If I was to describe it best, I would say it felt like a homecoming – it felt a natural move for me. It was meant to happen. I was meant to play for West Bromwich Albion.

"You have to remember I was brought up in north-west London. My parents came over in the mid to late 1960s. Those were the communities that had to cope with the 'no blacks, no Irish, no dogs' slogans and notices. It was concentrated in certain areas and north-west London was very much a diaspora area. It was a Caribbean area. I was from the Stonebridge estate. I could see Wembley Stadium from my bedroom. And because of the impact made by Brendon, Laurie and Cyrille, I knew people who had no connection to West Bromwich who were Albion supporters. We might have been 100 miles away from the club but it represented something iconic in that community. Here were three very visible footballers who had projected this club into the mainstream of lives, blowing away prejudice as they did. This is why West Bromwich Albion brought such a significance to our community."

Hughes and Roberts were to score 40 goals between them in 2000-01. Roberts netted 17 and enjoyed his partnership with his slightly older partner, even though he feels they were far from being a natural fit. He claims both played with a cynical edge brought on from playing in non-League longer than they hoped. Hughes eventually joined Albion in 1997, having previously worked as a roofer. Roberts had been an export clerk for a freight company. Both used the meat and potatoes of grass-roots football to elevate themselves into the professional game. And they brought that raw energy with them. Neither took the conventional academy route afforded to so many in the current age.

"Lee and I had a lot in common," recalled Roberts. "We both had upbringings in fairly tough football environments and definitely both played with a chip on our shoulders. I think we knew we were playing catch-up, especially Lee, who was a bit older. We were enjoying our first experience in the limelight. Yeah, we bonded, but we were single-minded and we learned a lot of lessons together. We were footballers in a big city. At 19, I had been working for a company that exported freight. By 22, I was in professional football with West Bromwich. I was learning quickly. I went from being a record signing from a non-League club to Wolves, to being a record signing at Bristol Rovers to being a record signing for Albion, all in three or four years.

"Lee was so dynamic. It was strange because we never had a chemistry on the pitch as a partnership, but things happened for us as individuals that would cause and create problems for defences. We didn't have that telepathic relationship you expect partners to have but we had individual streaks that enabled us to work well. We scored goals. Lee was such a hard worker. He would work, work, work. I would play just behind him. It suited the manager's style. We were direct. It suited us as a team; it suited us as strikers. Unfortunately, I started slowly. I didn't score for a few games and came out of the side. I was sub against Swansea, then went on a good run. But I didn't analyse my form. I was myself. And we definitely had something special that year. I knew I operated well in partnerships. I'd played well with Jamie Cureton and Barry Hayles at Bristol and knew Lee and myself would score goals.

"I alternated with Bob in that first Albion season, which was good. By the end of it, I was growing and in my best form. I scored a goal and created the penalty against Bolton in the semi-final. But we conceded. I was marking Gudni Bergsson and he scored. I was disappointed with that but I still felt confident we would get something up there. We didn't – we lost 3-0. That was a huge disappointment. And when we lost that night, I was absolutely confident we would go up the next year. I just knew it would be our year."

Sixth place in 2000-01 generally raised hopes, with Roberts expected to be the focal point of Megson's side. He has fond memories of his team-mates and speaks highly of many, less so of others. Off the pitch, he was to enjoy nights that he now files in the '18' Certificate category. Luckily for the class of 2001, including Messrs Roberts and Hughes, the mobile phone remained no more than a device you would make a call on. Camera phones and social media were to arrive a little too late to capture their moments. But Roberts had a desire to be one of the big players in a dressing room of strong characters. He considered Hughes's departure to be one of fresh personal opportunity rather than disappointment.

"I learned very quickly that Hughesie was on another level to me when it came to socialising," laughed Roberts. "We had an incident once where we got into trouble (near Merry Hill) and it created negative press. That marked my card. But we were young lads. We had a good time and we learned about being footballers in a bubble, especially in Birmingham. You learn that you cannot stay out all night and go training. Hughesie's metabolism allowed him to do things I couldn't. He could eat and drink in ways I couldn't, so it wasn't long before he dispensed with me as his going-out partner. I just wasn't at his level in that respect. When he left for Coventry, I was a bit surprised. Coventry? Really? This will sound weird – it's also how I felt when Barry Hayles left Bristol Rovers for Fulham. But I was excited in a way because now it was 'My Team'. As a striker, you have to feel that. I felt: 'Right, it's down to me…it's my turn to shine'."

And what of the others? Roberts continued: "Foxy…what a legend he was. His personality was infectious – one of the funniest guys you could come across. Deech (Dichio) was a great guy and doing very well for himself. I cannot believe Deech is a coach (with Toronto FC) because he was one of the worst trainers I've ever seen. I used to call him Daniele Sloppio because Gary Megson had called him Sloppy. He was a joker, too. One day, I wore this bright pink jumper. It was a cool, zip-up top. But it was very pink. It was a bold and brave item to wear back then but I liked it. I finished training and went into Stratford to do some shopping. As I was walking back to the car, a guy comes over and said: 'Mate, have you seen your back?' I took the jumper off and somebody had taped on 'Hello Boys'. So I'd spent a good couple of hours wandering around Stratford-upon-Avon wearing a bright pink jumper with 'Hello Boys' stuck to my back. That was Deech, a proper Italian guy, despite being from London. He was good for me. He changed the way we played and helped my game. I just wish we'd stayed together for longer.

"Mooro was a leader. He was someone you could easily see going into coaching or management. Everybody loved him. He brought so much to our dressing room. Derek McInnes was somebody I loved but I'm not sure he liked me too much. I was young, hungry and ambitious and I'm not sure Derek knew how to take me. We didn't have huge fall-outs but we had a couple of moments – but, actually, I really liked him. There was only really one team-mate I didn't like and that was Jason van Blerk. As footballers, we can be ultra-competitive and ruthless but there is always an element of respect. It's easy for experienced pros to bully younger pros. I don't like bullies and didn't appreciate Van Blerk's way of dealing with young players. The same could be said of some of the coaching staff. It was very uncomfortable at times and I learned a lot from that.

"Houltie was a top man. So was The Beast, Brian Jensen. I felt bad because there can only be one goalkeeper. And then there was Bob, a club legend. Yet I always felt there was an edge with Bob – mainly because I was brought in to take his place. For someone who was so loved by the fans, as he so clearly was, I guess that it's only natural he should be a little edgy with someone coming in as a replacement. I totally understand that and I probably felt exactly the same ten years later when younger players were being brought to the clubs I was with then. 'What's this new guy doing here? I'm the main man here.' So I can totally sympathise if Bob felt like that."

Summer 2001 brought new challenges. Lee Hughes was gone. Replacing him was Scott Dobie, a little-known striker from Carlisle. Dichio joined in late August. Roberts was looking forward to being the senior striker in Gary Megson's plans. It didn't last. He broke his fifth metatarsal – the outermost metatarsal bone of the foot – three times during the campaign. It was an injury he never fully recovered from in his time with the club, not so much physically, but more so because the fall-out over the best form of treatment went against Megson's wishes and damaged their relationship. The first injury came in a pre-season game against Cheltenham on July 26, the same day Hughes rejected an improved Albion deal, effectively releasing him to the highest bidder (Coventry, £5,000,001). Albion staff returned to The Hawthorns that night and were met by the reserve team who had just played a Bass Charity Vase game. It was then that rookie striker Scott Dobie was informed he was now the club's senior striker, alongside Bob Taylor. Staff members say Dobie went pale at the thought…

Luckily, Dobie adapted quickly and effectively, scoring nine goals in his opening 12 games for Albion. Roberts missed the start of the season but recovered for the home game against Manchester City. Megson's side battered the eventual champions 4-0 with a brilliant, composed display that hinted at better times to come. The only down-side? Roberts barely lasted 50 minutes. The injury resurfaced and he didn't return until mid-December, the problem then flaring up again in late February and ruling him out for the rest of the season. During this time, his already brittle relationship with Megson disintegrated beyond repair.

"I felt really good going into that summer," he said. "I felt good about what I could do as a footballer and I had this feeling we would challenge. The belief was there. I knew I could do it. And I knew if I could do that and we could keep clean sheets, I knew we'd do it, because I had confidence in myself to score. Then I got injured. I jumped up, landed and felt a small crack along my metatarsal. Nobody knew what a metatarsal was until David Beckham got one a year or so later, so I had no idea of the problems it would cause. I broke it in pre-season, missed a couple of months and came back too early. It's such a frustrating injury because there's nothing you can do about it. You just have to rest or you break down again. The fifth metatarsal is the worst as it's on the outside and takes the most pressure. I was told I could have surgery or let it heal naturally. I decided to go for it naturally. It happened again, so we had it pinned. We had a difference of opinion about it. Myself and Cyrille (Roberts's agent) had spoken to our own medical advisors and then there was the manager and the views of the club's medical staff. There was friction between us over that, which happens in football. I've come to appreciate that."

The period between mid-December and late-February was probably Roberts's best Baggies spell. Sixteen games in the League and FA Cup yielded seven goals and three notable moments along the way. And yet it was in a game in which Roberts didn't score that he was to deliver one of his finest performances. The opening weekend of 2002 was FA Cup third-round time and Albion travelled to Sunderland for a midday kick-off. Coaches set off from West Bromwich at 6am in freezing weather. More than 5,000 Albion supporters made the journey in hope, more than expectation. By mid-afternoon, those fans were reflecting on a performance that not only underlined Albion's credentials but thrust Roberts into the spotlight as a striker of genuine top-flight quality. He produced a stunning centre-forward's display against Peter Reid's Premier League side, as did Danny Dichio against the club he had left a few months before. Neil Clement and Andy Johnson were Albion's scorers following Kevin Phillips's opener for Sunderland.

Roberts reflects on the afternoon with a sense of accomplishment. "That was a seminal game for me. It felt like I was operating at a Premier League level and it made me all the more determined to make sure I did what I could to get us into the top flight. I had a really strong relationship and friendship with Daniele Dichio – I'm a Godfather to one of his children – and that game felt really special for me and probably him, too. It felt like we had arrived as a team. The side was set up for me because of Deech's strengths. It was about getting on to the second balls and getting in behind. I felt fit, I felt sharp. I didn't think anyone would stop me that year. That Sunderland game was the one where I thought: 'Yeah, I can do this at the highest level.'"

Albion were building up a momentum that would eventually take them into the Premier League at the expense of Wolves. They were heading for good times. Yet one of the club's greatest players wasn't going to witness the winning of promotion. On the morning of Sunday, January 20, fans woke to the terrible news that 1968 FA Cup hero Jeff Astle had died the previous evening. 'The King' was just 59. Albion were due to play Walsall at The Hawthorns that Sunday in a televised match. Business as usual it might have been for Megson's men but the game was played against a sombre backdrop. Albion's then programme editor Dave Bowler was told the news as he prepared to leave for the game and delayed his departure to rummage through his wardrobe for a long-sleeved t-shirt he had buried away. Emblazoned across the front was a photograph of Astle, with that famous smile, after one of his many Albion goals. A colleague suggested Bowler should pass the shirt to a player in the hope some of the Astle magic may rub off. Bowler's choice was fitting – he called Jason Roberts out of the dressing room and handed it to him. Roberts swiftly took a pair of scissors to the sleeves, to ensure it would fit under his long-sleeved top and continued with his preparations. All he needed now was find a moment…and he did. In the 41st minute, he scored the only goal of the game and, as he turned away to celebrate, he lifted his branded striped shirt to reveal the Astle jersey. It was Albion's first-ever League victory against Walsall; a memorable one at that.

Roberts recalled: "It was a very emotional day. It showed what the King meant not only to the club but the community and the whole country. You could feel the club was grieving. That day, playing local rivals, it felt like it was meant to be. Sometimes, you just have a feeling and I felt especially motivated that afternoon. Dave Bowler is someone who was the heartbeat of the club. There are people you always identify as being the soul and rock of a club – Dave is one of those people. He had a shirt in his hand and asked me to wear it. He said: 'If you score and show that shirt, you'll be a legend forever'. In my youthful confidence, I thought: 'Yes, that's exactly what I'm going to do'. I was absolutely sure it would happen. And then it happened. The ball came in from Jordao, Daniele flicked it on and I got between the defender and the keeper. I hit a shot, it went in and that was that… I ran off and I lifted the shirt. It was a special moment for me."

Albion headed up the M6 twice during February, first for a trip to Burnley – a Sunday teatime televised clash played in an atmosphere more suited to a post-watershed audience. Turf Moor in 2002 was a throwback to a bygone age. Angry, white men hurling abuse towards the black players in the opposition side – it was like a scene from the 1970s; the kind Roberts would have heard about from Uncle Cyrille. It might have been the infancy of a new Millennium but the mood at Burnley on this January night was one of shameful intolerance. Roberts knew exactly how to react. All those stories from the 70s, those tales of hate, with contorted, angry faces glaring down. Suddenly, it had become a living moment for the Albion man. Only this wasn't an anecdote, this was reality; a snapshot from another era. Roberts delivered one of his finest performances for Albion, scoring both their goals in a ten-minute period before half-time. It was a master-class of power, pace and finishing. The irony of those vicious slurs was completely lost among the brain-dead elements of the Turf Moor crowd. Roberts's opponents on the day included Ian Cox and Arthur Gnohere, Burnley's black centre-halves, neither of whom could handle him. It was never established what they thought of their own supporters barracking a black opponent but, for Roberts, it was a throw-back to the abuse his uncle's generation had faced on a weekly basis.

"On the pitch, I was aware of a horrible streak," recalled Roberts. "I hadn't experienced it before and haven't heard it many times since. There was a hostile, vile atmosphere from some of their supporters. I was elbowed off the ball during the game, the atmosphere was nasty and racist. There was a horrible undercurrent and I was so focused on the game that I left it behind, although I was aware it was happening. I was angry and it still rankles that I was trying to do my job and being called all sorts because of my colour. The two defenders against me were black guys – and there were the Burnley fans giving out racist abuse. Looking back now, I'd say there was a real anger to my celebrations. I wanted to show them I wasn't going to let them stop me doing my job."

Albion were picking up form, winning nine of their 11 games in all competitions between December and late February, including a 5-0 victory against Portsmouth – a game in which Roberts scored twice. Sadly, while Albion's form was to continue, Roberts was forced into a watching brief. Just before half-time at Preston on the second of the M6 trips, he picked up his third foot injury of the season, one that effectively ended his campaign there and then. He spent the final two months looking on as his team-mates clawed back an 11-point deficit on Wolves. While all focus was on Albion's incredible run and their neighbours' collapse, Roberts felt increasingly out of the picture. The psychological impact of being sidelined during such a seminal period of the club's modern era lingers…..

Albion's promotion-winning season will always be about Igor Balis, Gary Megson, missed penalties, clean sheets, the Battle of Bramall Lane, Wolves' slump, the passing of Jeff Astle and so much more. And it's an interesting theory delivered by Roberts that many might have forgotten his contribution to the campaign, not least as he missed so many of the more memorable games, including the infamous one away to Sheffield United. Those are the harsh realities of being an injured footballer.

"It's a tough, tough period for any player when they're out for any length of time," admitted Roberts. "Take the Battle of Bramall Lane – I wasn't there. The guys were in on Monday, full of stories, but I didn't feel part of it. You'd be amazed how quickly dressing rooms move on when you're unable to play. It is such an extreme, fickle environment. And not being part of it was so, so difficult. There is a strange phenomenon when you're injured. You effectively become invisible. It's not just an Albion thing. It has happened at every club I've been at. You become invisible to the coaches, invisible to the other players and invisible to the fans. It's all about the here and now and the players available to play. It's understandable and it's how it should be. But, as a young man, I found it so difficult to deal with. My reaction was to hide away. I didn't want to be that invisible man around the club. I worked hard, I got on with my rehab but it was hard to be in the dressing-room environment because it was hurting so much knowing I wasn't contributing. You feel irrelevant. It is every footballer's fear to feel that. If you cannot contribute, you are no longer relevant."

So while Albion players were lauding the adulation of an unlikely promotion, Roberts felt a sense of psychological pain and exclusion – not deliberate by any means, purely by circumstance. What he describes is similar to the 'imposter syndrome' referred to by others; the feeling of detachment when someone doubts their own accomplishments and achievements. Being out of action at such an important time left Roberts looking in on Albion's success from the outside. "Gary was the same as every manager I've played under in that respect," he added. "He isn't interested in me when I'm injured – he's interested in Scott Dobie, he's interested in Bob Taylor, he's interested in Daniele Dichio. Me? I'm injured, so I'm no use to him nor anyone else. I cannot contribute when I'm injured. So, yes, that season was tough in that respect. It was brilliant to have contributed to such a huge success but I often felt I really didn't belong there because I was of no use to anyone.

"I hid away. I wanted as little as possible to do with the team. That was how I dealt with it. I changed later. I wanted to stay and lead, be vocal, encourage my team-mates. But, at West Brom, I was young. And it was the first time I'd experienced this challenge. I just wanted to stay away. I didn't go to the Palace match. I can't recall where I was – but I wasn't at The Hawthorns. Actually, I remember now, I was at home in Stratford watching on TV. That's how it impacted on me – a huge, huge game in the club's history and I needed to think about where I was. But it wasn't about me. It was about the 11 on the pitch. It was a lonely experience but also a learning experience. I felt exactly the same at the end of my career when I retired. I felt useless. You're not important to anyone. There is someone else there to take the limelight. I was ready to take Bob Taylor's shirt, or Dichio's shirt or Dobie's shirt. The same for those guys.

"As a player, you're not waiting on ceremony – you want to play. It's the law of the jungle. As soon as you're injured, you're outside that circle. You need to swallow that feeling and deal with it. And what I learned was to be graceful when it happened. I've been around people who have struggled with that. They can't let go, they cast a shadow over the next cycle of players. I didn't do that. The moment I was injured, or no longer able to play, I got out of the way. Once your career withers, it's important you let the next person grow. And that's tough to deal with."

Roberts's third and final injury of that campaign did little to thaw the increasingly cold relationship between himself and Megson. Although the striker returned for the Premier League adventure in 2002-03, the dynamic between the two didn't improve and Roberts sought a move following Albion's relegation. By then, Megson had fallen out with Jeremy Peace, with their dispute impacting on Roberts's future. Resigned to never playing for Megson again, he wanted a move from The Hawthorns. But Peace had other ideas. The chairman was unwilling to grant Roberts his wish of a permanent summer move to Wigan on the basis that Megson's future was growing increasingly uncertain. It was a fairly clear message: 'We don't want you to go just yet, because the manager might be gone soon'. Instead, Roberts moved to Portsmouth on a three-month loan at the start of 2003-04, wondering whether he would return to The Hawthorns in the New Year with a new manager in place. The feeling was that Megson was one bad run from the sack. Yet that run never came. By January, Albion were looking good for promotion with the strike-force of Rob Hulse and Geoff Horsfield, and Lee Hughes playing against the backdrop of a charge for death by dangerous driving; one which would eventually end with a jail term and dismissal by the club. Having invested heavily in new players – and knowing there would be no financial return on Hughes – Peace softened his stance and reluctantly granted Roberts a permanent move. He joined Wigan for £1.4m in January.

For Roberts, it was a sad end to such a promising period of his career. He accepts he fell short of producing the return that many would have expected – he scored just three times for Albion in the Premier League – but he also feels much of that was down to the defensive system favoured by the manager. "Gary had a way of interacting with people that was confrontational," he said. "It worked for some, not for others. I totally understand that. He achieved success for West Brom, no doubt about that. But I found it tough to deal with him. He created a dynamic where it seemed to be the players versus the manager. It was a hard place to be because of that.

"After those injuries, my relationship with him disintegrated. Listen, he was combative and I understand that side of him. It worked for him, especially with West Brom. It was a great match-up in many respects and nobody can take that away from him. That was what he felt was the best way to get a tune out of players. But because of that, we had a high turnover. That season (in the

Premier League) was difficult because we were a defensive-minded side and there weren't many chances for us to score. We weren't scoring goals and that was my job. So I felt in a very difficult position. I felt I needed more support and I articulated that. I don't think Gary and I had a great relationship anyway but that season exposed the cracks. Yes, there were periods when we were at loggerheads and not getting on. I felt I had more to give to that side.

"But what I can say is this: I never wanted to leave the Albion. It was the last thing I wanted because at that point I had a lot more to give. But I felt I had to do it for my own career. Wigan were a viable option. I appreciated they weren't as big as West Brom but I knew that in Nathan Ellington, I had a player I could build a strong partnership with and it proved to be the case. Ironically, the same thing happened with Nathan some time later. He fell out with Wigan, didn't want to leave, but felt he had to …and ended up at West Brom. It's strange how football works."

Nearly two decades on, Roberts still feels aggrieved and anguished by some of Megson's methods. He claims some of the younger players especially struggled with the caustic, hard-line approach. Roberts continued: "Gary and I have done some TV together since. We got there, did the programme and left – we didn't really chat much. I know from so many other people that he is great company, a lovely man and can be entertaining. But to play for him was tough at times. And for us to put things behind us would be difficult because he created a difficult environment, that not only affected me – I was big enough to take it – but also impacted on some of the younger players. I chalked it down to experience and I turned it to my advantage. All managers have a view on players but I saw people struggle with that environment and that will never sit well with me."

The conversation about Megson brings us back to the beginning of the chapter – the mention of Roberts's surname. It was during his final weeks at the club that he submitted a written transfer request. Due to the formal nature of the document, he signed the form with Robert, the surname he was born with and still uses on legal paperwork. Megson was aware of this but, somewhat mischievously, mentioned the signature ambiguity during a subsequent press conference, implying the striker had failed to spell his name correctly. Roberts, or Robert if you prefer, is now keen to relay his side of the story. He was even willing for me to use the correct spelling throughout this chapter while accepting that using the more common form would cause less confusion.

"I'm glad you've asked me about this because it was a big issue for certain members of my family," he said. "I put in a transfer request through my agent and signed it 'Jason Robert'. Gary came back and I replied: 'Yes, that's my name. The name on my birth certificate is Jason Robert, with no s'. I told him, so he was aware of it. The next thing I know...he said I didn't know how to spell my own name. I thought that was really poor on his part. It was water off a duck's back but I remember my grandma being really upset. It was not really a legitimate way to deal with someone when you're the manager of a club. I just think it lacked class. The disappointing thing is he knew what I'd said was true. There was no need for him to do something so demeaning.

"My surname is Robert. The 's' was added because it became easier. Otherwise you end up correcting everyone a million times. In all of my documentation, including my passport, my name is down as Jason Robert. Obviously, with a formal document like a transfer request, I used my proper name and removed the s. My great, great grandfather had given the family his own name, which was Robert. It happens a lot in the Caribbean. He decided he would give his children his first name. But, you know something, my wife is a stickler for tradition. She writes her name as Carly Robert. My kids also use Robert. So, yeah, maybe I should use it myself."

Roberts severed physical ties with Albion in January, 2004 following 91 League games and 25 goals. Emotionally, the club retains a huge place in his heart. He still refers to Albion as 'my club', even though he played a similar number of games for Wigan and more than 130 times for Blackburn. Yet discussion inevitably returns to his uncle's influence. And, having paid his own t-shirt tribute to another famous no 9 as an Albion player , he was forced to do so again in the most shocking and sudden of circumstances.

Cyrille Regis suffered a fatal heart attack on January 14, 2018. He was weeks away from celebrating his 60th birthday. Family, friends, former colleagues and fans paid their final respects to the club legend at The Hawthorns on January 30, with the cortege leaving the stadium for a private funeral service, before returning for a celebration of his life in front of a packed East Stand. The celebration featured songs, a lively celebration of Cyrille's life and personal tributes from a series of speakers, including Brendon Batson, former Coventry boss John Sillett, Cyrille's widow Julia and Jason himself. A few days later, the club delivered another celebration of his life before the Premier League match against Southampton – the first home game following his death.

Roberts spoke of the impact his uncle had on all the relatives – along with the realisation that the Regis/Roberts family clearly possessed a sporting gene of some significance. He believes his uncle's legacy remains. "That period was so difficult for my family," he added. "It was such a shocking and sudden passing. Nobody saw it coming. And yet the club were brilliant and the fans were amazing. We were so well looked after during that horrible time. My family's relationship with West Bromwich Albion goes from generation to generation. My daughter Nia was open-mouthed when somebody asked me for my autograph because she didn't know much about my career. Albion treat my uncle's legacy so well.It will always be our family's club.

"As well as Cyrille, there was David, my uncle on my father's side (Otis Roberts), John Regis, who was a cousin on my mother's side, and then there was my sister Jasmine, who represented Great Britain in the triple jump. It was in our genes. It seems strange looking back, but we didn't really sit there comparing achievements. We were a family. Having Cyrille as an uncle was amazing. He was so down-to-earth. I came from a big family and yet Uncle Cyrille had no special treatment in my grandfather's house. He was treated as another uncle. But the collective impact he made in one of the poorest neighbourhoods in London was immense. I never had any trouble with gangs or with anyone because I was Cyrille's nephew. My uncle Otis played professional football, as did my Uncle Dave. After my Uncle Cyrille, so many people emerged from these neighbourhoods because they believed they could do it. Les Ferdinand, my uncle Dave, myself, Raheem Sterling… so many others. It left a legacy you could never imagine.

"The thing with Cyrille is that I had the same relationship with him as I had with my other uncles. I feel so blessed to have seen the impact of his life. Somebody pitched a book idea to me some time ago and I was like: 'Why me? I've had a decent career but so have so many others'. But the only interesting angle I can think of is that I ask myself whether, without Cyrille's impact, I'd have become a professional footballer. Would Uncle Dave have made it? Would my other uncle, Otis, have made it? The whole impact he had...I don't think it would have happened without the career he had and the influence he had. The impact he had on the whole diaspora and the Windrush generation made a massive difference. And because of him, and my own playing career, West Bromwich Albion will always have that special connection in our family."

Before moving to the US, Roberts initially relocated to Grenada. Many of his peers have pursued coaching badges or moved into the media and Jason was himself an articulate pundit, chiefly on Match of the Day, before deciding to take a different direction. The father-of-three set up The Jason Roberts Foundation to celebrate diversity, promote respect across the UK and Grenada, and support young people. "I did a Masters in football administration – it was always my thing," he added. "I had been on the PFA management committee, the FIFA anti-discrimination task force and several governance courses. I always knew I wanted to continue in football but from an administrative angle. From my time with Grenada as an international player, I did some work with FIFA and got to work for CONCACAF. The role of director of development became open and I was lucky enough to be offered the role. Essentially, I'm in charge of the agenda of all coaching education, programming, women's football and the corporation social responsibility programmes we run. I feel like I'm giving something back to a region that I have an affinity with, and at an elite level. There is a great opportunity for me to impact change, to make people's lives better.

"I've been in Miami for two years now. I absolutely love it. I have a young family. There is Marley, he's 11. Nia, she is the boss of the family, and then the youngest one (Jason) is seven. They were all there at the game against Southampton and they will never forget that day, nor ever forget Albion for that reason."

Reflecting further on his time at The Hawthorns, he feels a pang of unfinished business. He is proud of his achievements but feels he could have done better and should have made more of his spell there – albeit some of the circumstances were out of his control. "My time was unfulfilled but relatively successful. If someone had told me I'd be part of a promotion-winning side, I'd have snapped their hand off. For West Bromwich as a club, I felt that was success at the time. But for myself, I didn't think I'd written myself into the history books the way I thought I should have. If I had been fit throughout that season, I'd have backed myself to easily score 20-odd goals. And I felt I would have been the focal point of that side. I do think I could have done a lot better in the Premier League but then I feel the side could have been more expansive and ambitious. It was very difficult, as a striker especially, so it was a disappointment for me, even more given how the club treated the death of my uncle and how they looked after my family during those bad weeks.

"I look back at what I did at Wigan, what I did at Blackburn…I just wish I'd done all of that with West Brom. I wish that what happened with those clubs could have happened with Albion. I feel like West Bromwich Albion will forever have a place in my heart, not just because of that promotion, that moment (his tribute to Astle) or because I was a record signing, but also because of the way they honoured my uncle following his passing. The club will always be special to me."

Whether it's Jason Roberts or Jason Robert, the mutual feeling between the man and club will seemingly never diminish. Just don't expect him to wear the no 9 shirt.

Gary Megson

"...Barbara is trying to calm me down, saying: 'You can't bollock players who aren't yours'... the next thing, the waitress has gone over with the biggest cod and chips I've ever seen; the cod was hanging off the bloody plate. I couldn't believe it. It's a couple of nights before their match with Wolves and these two Wednesday players are in the pub..."

Viv Anderson has seen enough. West Bromwich Albion v Tranmere Rovers. March 7, 2000. Sat in the Halfords Lane stand, Middlesbrough's assistant manager shakes his head and leans over to the guy next to him with a pretty grim appraisal: "Lord help anyone who gets this job." 'This job' was that of Albion manager. The club are looking for their eighth manager in nine years. The man sat next to him is Gary Megson. Unbeknown to Anderson, Megson is already Albion's manager-elect and he smiles back at the Nottingham Forest legend without saying a word. Albion win 2-0, with Sean Flynn and Lee Hughes the scorers, but they are far from convincing. Megson knows Anderson is spot-on. Not even the Lord's intervention might be enough to save them.

January, 2020. Gary Megson waits in a side room, preparing to speak to a sell-out audience at the Cradley Heath Sports and Social Club. He has just returned from a trip to the Maldives. It has been a long while since he has spoken candidly to Albion supporters in the Black Country. Some 160 of them will be hanging on his every word. It has also been more than two years since his last proper stint in this part of the world. On that occasion, we met at the Holiday Inn Hotel, next to junction 7 of the M6. He was a week or two away from taking charge of Albion for a second time, albeit in a caretaker capacity, following Tony Pulis's departure. He remained in situ for two games – drawing both, against Spurs and Newcastle. There were calls he should get the job on a full-time basis. The club opted for Alan Pardew instead.....

For now, we are here to speak about the first time. The proper time. The time that nobody will forget, as opposed to the time everyone would sooner forget. Megson cuts a happier figure than some 15 years ago, when he was tired, ruffled, exhausted even. Drained by it all. Metaphorically speaking, he had not only put out the flames at The Hawthorns but climbed back in to rescue the family pet and rebuilt the whole place from scratch. Twice. Naturally, that's an extremely simplistic and brief review of his five years. But the adulation from the public is still there. Even now, a decade and a half on, he remains a heroic figure to supporters. On this particular Friday night, deep in the bowels of the Black Country, he is reluctant to put down the microphone despite knowing he has a two-hour journey back to Sheffield – not helped by the closure of local motorways. He addresses the Cradley Heath audience with 'one last story' for the third time. Nobody wants to leave, least of all Megson. Broadcaster Nigel Pearson, the compere for the evening, addresses him as 'Sir Gary'. And that feels somewhat appropriate. Also, should Megson ever fall on hard times, he could easily carve out a career as an after-dinner speaker. The Albion fans in attendance have chuckled, guffawed and been left open-mouthed at his anecdotes. They consider it £10 well spent.

Bryan Robson, Tony Mowbray, Roberto Di Matteo, Roy Hodgson, Steve Clarke, Pepe Mel, Alan Irvine, Tony Pulis, Alan Pardew, Darren Moore and Slaven Bilic have all managed Albion since Megson left, plus various caretakers. The club might have finished higher up the table on Clarke's watch, beaten Wolves 5-1 under Hodgson and swaggered to the Championship title with Mowbray, but it's unlikely they could have achieved those feats without the foundations laid down by Albion's first managerial appointment of the 21st century. And it's equally unlikely any of those managers are held in the same esteem as the man who flicked the switch in the first place.

By 2020, Albion had spent 12 seasons out of 17 in the top flight and, between 2002 and 2019, did not finish lower than fourth in the Championship. Yet, at the turn of the century, the future looked bleak, with a bloated squad of misfits, a stadium that was only partially fit for the commercial and corporate demands of Premier League football and a training ground that, well, simply didn't exist. Albion's training HQ is now a state-of-the-art complex just off the A34, yet Megson looks back on that opening period of his time as boss by saying: "Everything about the club was an eye-opener. We had no training ground – just imagine that now, a club like West Brom having no training ground. It's unbelievable. And yet we were that club."

Following Brian Little's sacking, Albion wasted no time in finding a successor who could keep the club up. They certainly fulfilled that criteria. And more. Megson continued: "I'd been interviewed for the job at Sheffield United, believe it or not, but it was never going to happen – for all the obvious reasons of me being an ex-Wednesday man. But Paul Thompson asked who they thought Albion should go for. By they, I mean Derek Dooley (the Sheffield chairman), who gave me a really good reference. I met the board in a hotel next to a service station on the M1. Several of them turned up – Thompson, John Wile, Barry Hurst, Clive Stapleton, Joe Brandrick among them. We went into this room for a chat and they asked me what I knew about West Brom. I replied: 'I know you've had a glorious past with the likes of Bobby Hope, Jeff Astle, Bomber Brown, etc…and I also know that you're always falling out among yourselves on the board.' That went down as badly as you can imagine but Paul Thompson said: 'Actually, it's probably true' and that was that. They offered me the job."

And so it was that Megson was whisked to The Hawthorns for a watching brief as Albion played Tranmere. By then, speculation was rife but not everyone was fully aware of Albion's intended choice and Viv Anderson clearly wasn't one for gossip. "I went to the game before I was named as manager," said Megson. "Cyrille and John Trewick were in caretaker charge. Viv Anderson was sat next to me and when he said 'Lord help anyone who gets this job', I couldn't say anything! When I did get it, Viv called me and said: 'You bastard…you never said anything!' At the first game, I parked on Halfords Lane on some dog-rough car park. But it felt like a proper club. There were crowds milling, the floodlights were on. It felt good, even though the club was in a bad way. I remember a young lad came up and said: 'Can you sign this, please?' His dad leaned over and said: 'Aye, get him to sign that quickly because he'll be going the same way as the others'. One of the papers had 'Gary Who?' as a headline. Did it bother me? Not really. It was better to come in like that and make a name. Once the fans saw what I was about, I think they got an idea what I wanted for them. Until then, it had been like a rest home for footballers. That was a culture I didn't want because it would have sent us down."

Megson was appointed, on a three-year deal, as the club's 31st manager. Speaking to the press at the time, he said: "I'm just like the fans. I don't just sit and watch the match – I get involved and want the team to do everything they can to win. If players always give their best and with a great deal of honesty, they won't get any complaints from me or anyone else. But we've got to wake up and smell the roses…we are in a situation where every game is critical, every point is critical and every goal is critical."

Megson's opening game was at Stockport – a club he had left just nine months earlier. The Baggies won courtesy of Lee Hughes's goal in the opening 20-odd seconds. The new manager missed what proved to be the best bit of the game. "At Stockport, you have to walk along the stand to the dug-out. I didn't want to walk there, get slaughtered by their supporters and have real animosity in the ground, so I waited until the game had started. It never crossed my mind we would score after 20 seconds. We went with three centre-halves but poor Larus (Sigurdsson) got injured and it was a bad one [he ruptured his cruciate ligament]. I looked at the team and hoped we could hold out for a win, which we did. It was a great result but that was just the start of it. You usually get a job when the circumstances are bad at a club. That was certainly the case with us."

Good results didn't follow. Albion lost the next three – at home to Huddersfield and away to Portsmouth and Manchester City, with the defeat at Maine Road particularly galling. Albion took the lead on the hour, again through Hughes, before Shaun Goater scored a cruel injury-time winner following Mark Kennedy's leveller. For the first time, relegation was looking more a reality than a possibility. For the opening few weeks, Megson pretty much worked alone, albeit assisted by Regis and other backroom staff. He knew who he wanted with him and there was a sequence of events that he can laugh about now but which he didn't find amusing at the time. Not only did he end up with his no 2 but the new man had to assume a 'managerial' role before he'd even signed on the dotted line with Albion.

The setting was Fratton Park for a game against Tony Pulis's Portsmouth, refereed by Graham Poll. What could possibly go wrong? Megson, shaking his head while laughing, adds: "I knew I needed an assistant. I didn't know who I wanted but knew the type of person I wanted. I had experience, I'm someone who wants everything done yesterday, I'm a 'roll-your-sleeves-up' type, and I've got enthusiasm, so I needed a cooler head. The call came through telling me Frank Burrows was available. I didn't know him from Adam, so I arranged to pick him up and have a chat on the way down to Portsmouth. We'd never even met and he turns up with his daft cap and suit. He sits down, we're talking football and we got on really well.

"I told him to watch the game with me on the touchline. He had a suit on, which I thought would look stupid next to me wearing a tracksuit, so I told him to get some kit sorted out. To cut a long story short, we were struggling and had a few decisions against us – then Poll sent me off. It was ridiculous. He was having one of those games and I knew the only way I'd get his attention would be if I crossed the line, so I did and knew the minute I said what I said, that he would come across and send me off. So, we're losing and Frank is now in charge, bearing in mind I'd only met him for the first time a few hours before. He went to 4-4-1 – Matt Carbon had been sent off – in a game we needed to win. I'm sat next to Dr John (Evans) in the stand, screaming down to the dug-out, full of bad language, acting like an idiot. God knows what Dr John was thinking. Anyway, we lost and Frank said: 'Well, that's a first. I've come down to meet a manager about a job, I can't sit in the directors' box, I have to borrow some kit, I end up in charge, then I get a bollocking for going to the wrong formation. And I'm not even getting paid!'"

Frank Burrows, welcome to West Bromwich Albion. The Scot was a savvy appointment. A former boss of Pompey (twice), Cardiff (twice) and Swansea, he had more than 21 years as coach under his trademark flat cap by the time he pitched up alongside Megson. He was a likeable and knowledgeable character – the archetype of the so-called 'football man', bandied around by so many in the industry. Immersed in old-school values but working in a changing landscape, Burrows was to become a useful eyes-and-ears for Megson during the next four and a half years. Each of his scouting reports, of which there were many, apparently began with the line: 'The boy is…', followed by a description of the individual's attributes and anything else about his playing style. By some coincidence, he returned to Albion as a part-time scout during Pulis's time as boss, although his spell didn't overlap with Megson's period as assistant.

In 2000, Burrows wasted no time in returning a brutal assessment of Albion's predicament. Megson added: "In the first training session after Frank joined, I didn't want to ostracise anyone, so we did a 15-a-side. It was ridiculous, really, but I wanted everyone to be judged. We were all involved –

coaches, too, apart from Frank. I told him I wanted his feedback. The whistle goes at the end, everyone runs off and I'm thinking: 'What kind of place is this?' I go over to Frank and ask what he thought. He said: 'We've got three players: you, Cyrille and Lee Hughes.' I thought: 'Fuck me, Cyrille and I can't help… Lee Hughes is our only hope'. And bear in mind there were 30-odd players."

With Burrows's 'endorsement' eating away at him, the Baggies boss knew he needed players. Quickly. Transfer windows, as we know them, were still three seasons away. Players needed to be signed or sold by the third Thursday of March. That was transfer deadline day. Nevertheless, time was running out. So in they came. A group of five: Neil Clement on loan from Chelsea, Watford's Des Lyttle, Tony Butler from Port Vale, Tranmere's Georges Santos on a short-term deal and Bob Taylor, returning from Bolton. "On the way back in after that training session, I remember I told Frank we would go down with the players we had. This was two days before the deadline, so we had to make the changes quickly but not for changes' sake. Des arrived slightly over-weight, big Georges Santos turned up, Tony Butler – who was in the reserves at Port Vale – young Neil Clement, who I'd seen on TV, and Bob, who obviously we thought would give the place a lift, which it did. He made the most of that. He got a lovely long contract out of it."

All five made their debuts in that defeat at Manchester City. The next three games were draws – against Ipswich, when Albion lost Lee Hughes to injury for the remainder of the campaign, Barnsley and Bolton, the latter in a ridiculous 4-4 draw in the kind of match fans love but coaches hate. Off the field, Megson was trying to shift a culture embedded in the past and, worse, accepting of mediocrity. The club was stumbling towards decay because it had been allowed to by a series of poor managerial appointments, poorly-structured playing contracts and a board with little conviction or desire to improve. Paul Thompson as chairman, alongside John Wile as chief executive, started to address the weeping malaise by making big changes, not least in the way Albion players would be remunerated under newly-structured contracts. But that would take time to bed in. That was to Albion's future benefit. This was now. Megson's arrival provided that front-line jolt on and off the pitch. Although Albion fans weren't to know it, the club was starting to show promise, if only they could achieve their first pressing aim and stay up…

Megson noted the state of the Albion nation before reaching for the wrecking ball and introducing it to the bits that mattered. "It was a big club totally consumed and obsessed by the past and talking about the future – all of these great players who were supposedly going to come through, but actually didn't," he said. "Nobody was talking about the present. It was a big club, where nobody was on particularly big money and it had a lot going for it. I felt people were coming to the club to treat it like a rest home. I don't mean that nastily but it was way, way too easy for them. When I joined, we were starting training at 11. I got in touch with other managers I knew and they were generally saying 10am… we were the only ones starting at 11. So that changed straightaway. My big thing was to change the culture to one about what players could do for the club, not what the club could do for players. The year we got promoted, we had, I think, the 17th highest wage bill. We weren't a club who could spend their way to promotion. We had to gradually build up standards. And that's what it was all about. Standards. Ours were absolutely nowhere near what they should have been."

Albion survived 1999-2000 but only just. Defeat against Walsall, four matches from the end, left them with much to do to have a fighting chance of survival. The balls fell kindly. With Port Vale and Swindon long gone, the final place was between Albion and the Saddlers. Albion next faced a Grimsby side who were all but safe. Taylor's double saw to them. Walsall were at play-off chasers Birmingham, who left it late to score twice. The penultimate match saw Albion grind out a 0-0 draw at Queens Park Rangers while Walsall beat a Portsmouth side featuring Russell Hoult and Darren Moore. The scene for the final weekend was thus: Albion and Walsall were both on 46 points. The Baggies, hosting title winners Charlton, needed to match whatever result Walsall managed at Ipswich, who still had a slight chance of automatic promotion. A superior goal difference was Albion's ace card. As it happens, Albion completed the job emphatically in front of 22,000 at The Hawthorns against a weary, some-might-say hungover Charlton side. Walsall were rolled over by a side defensively marshalled by Tony Mowbray. The victory over Charlton was rightly lauded by supporters but less so on the touchline.

Survival, while considered a milestone when he took over, was hardly the barometer of success for Megson. "We had some really good players," he said. "But they needed to be mentally right, honest and wanting to succeed. Yeah, I upset players. I don't apologise for that. I was there to be successful, not give people a cushy life. There were some who thought they were the club's crown jewels – they still criticise me now – but I was brought in to raise the bar, make the club better. They weren't on board with that. That day we played Walsall… .I walked into the dressing room and Fabian (De Freitas) was sat there, legs outstretched, reading a paper. We're about to play one of our biggest games of the season and he's there looking like he's sat on a park bench relaxing. He was a nice guy but he wasn't my type of player. The fans might have been celebrating our survival but, for me, it was failure that Albion were down there in the first place. I had to break some eggs to make an omelette and there were too many bad eggs to make that possible."

Sorry, Gary, but the elephant has been in the room long enough. Mention of players who were moved on brings us to those who exited with what might be called 'parting shots' against the manager. Bob Taylor and Richard Sneekes have been vociferous with their criticism in the past. Others chipped in. One player was offered a blistering, withering insight into how he wouldn't be allowed to get away with undermining the manager. That player was Lee Marshall. Back in 2003, at the height of the animosity between he and Megson, mere mention of his name would have earned any journalist a robust rebuke from the manager and club's media staff. This led to an amusing incident at a supporters club meeting, attended by Megson, with a fan raising his hand and asking: 'Gary, I just wanted to ask you about West Bromwich Albion's forgotten man…' While the attending media held their collective breath, the gentleman completed his question with the underwhelming, but valid: '…That forgotten man being Michael Appleton. What's happened to him since his injury?'

Marshall's lack of discipline and poor time-keeping infuriated his manager. Such was the rift that he eventually involved the PFA in a bid to resolve the dispute. There was innuendo that Megson was unwilling to play certain players, notably Marshall, no matter what. He denied those allegations at the time, saying: "Rumours start but there is no player on our payroll that I would say isn't part of our plans. I expect all players to be doing their very best for West Brom and doing all they can to get into our starting line-up." Despite the passage of time, Megson doesn't hold back, even nearly two decades on. He still has little time for the dissenters and agitators during his time as Baggies boss. "You can't keep everyone happy," he continued. "Bob wanted to play all the time. I think we played Blackburn in our first season in the Premier League and he couldn't hack it. He had been given a four-year contract (in 2000) when I only wanted him for a few months. I wasn't going to let people like that run the club and that was my fear at the time. Richard Sneekes I got rid of after the play-off defeat…but we got promoted the year after.

"As for Lee Marshall, he simply didn't behave in the manner I expected. He turned up in black jeans, black t-shirt, his cap askew. His legs were dangling over the side of the chair. If I'd been more experienced, I'd have said thanks but no thanks. I shouldn't have signed him. I wasn't a disciplinarian. I wanted people to be professional. If I upset people, fine. In terms of compliments or comments, I couldn't give a monkey's what they think of me. I knew, for instance, we'd be better without Sneekes. But some players were smashing. I remember when we were in Denmark and I read some names out. Des was one, Clem was another. Their body fat measurements were too high, so I sat them down and Des said: 'We're the fat boys club, aren't we…?' Neil Clement looked ok but his body fat wasn't – it was just over. After that, he never had any problems. We needed players like that to move us on; people who were professional, willing to listen, be honest and willing to push us on as a club. Clem was a great professional for me and Des did everything he could to get into the side. Both were good pros."

One of the biggest disappointments on Megson's watch was the injury and subsequent retirement of Michael Appleton. Signed from Preston – ironically due to Derek McInnes's major knee injury in 2000 – the former Manchester United midfielder was showing signs of forging a very strong career alongside the fit-again McInnes and returning to the Premier League. Sadly, his career ground to a sudden halt in November, 2001 when a training pitch collision with Des Lyttle left him with a torn cruciate. It was a 50-50 challenge for which no blame was attributed. Subsequent surgical mistakes forced him to quit. Since then, Appleton, happily, has become a respected coach and is managing Lincoln at the time of writing. "Appy was an unfortunate case," admits Megson, immediately softening his demeanour. "He turned out to be a miles better player than I thought when we signed him. I was so disappointed, for us and for him especially, when he picked up that injury. Myself and the physio Nick

Worth had to carry him off and all the problems he had afterwards you wouldn't wish on anyone, not least somebody like him who would work all he could to get back in. It used to really piss me off seeing the efforts he would put in trying to get fit – he'd be in the gym all the time, working hard – when others flounced around without a care in the world. It's great to see him coaching now."

Rebuilding for the 2000-01 season started immediately. Jason Roberts arrived for £2m from Bristol Rovers and Albion's record signing was joined by Jordao from Sporting Braga and Tottenham's Ruel Fox, while Clement completed his permanent move from Chelsea. Igor Balis, Russell Hoult, Phil Gilchrist and Appleton were added during the season. Perhaps the seminal Megson signing was McInnes. Arriving from French club Toulouse, the Scot quickly established himself as the leader Albion had so sorely missed for so long. He even took a significant pay drop in swapping the south of France for the Black Country. It wasn't an overnight success. Albion lost their opening three games of the season – at Nottingham Forest, at home to Bolton and then a thumping 4-1 defeat at Barnsley. Megson returned to the tactics board.

"We were awful, playing 4-4-2, and it just wasn't working," he added. "We were stuck near the bottom and when you're in that position, you can end up isolated. I said to Frank we would go with three centre-halves. We played on the Monday against QPR and had to win, which we did. We looked better with each game. That shape was to become the basis for us because it suited us. We brought in better players to suit that system – people like Igor, Phil Gilchrist, Houltie. We went from losing the first three games to reaching the play-offs. The standard of player got better and better. Honesty and effort were improving and, importantly, so was the culture. That was the big thing. It wasn't perfect, though. Far from it. We had no training ground. In the first pre-season, we were given half a rugby pitch at the University and it had ruts where the tractors had gone through it. That never happened again, I made sure of it. We were a Championship club in name only. We were behaving like a non-League club. To be fair, Paul Thompson made a pledge to break the transfer record, which he did, bring in the training ground and improve the stadium… all of which he did. But the club needed a massive shake-up. We had too many players faffing around on a Saturday, so, yes, there were clashes. I wanted players who would do what I wanted to do. It was important to blend ability and attitude. Up front, we had probably the most lethal player at that level, Lee Hughes. He messed up big style later but I absolutely loved him. Really loved him. He was a good player and defenders couldn't handle him. Jason did very well for us in the first season, too. We made ourselves strong at the back and moved the club forward on and off the pitch."

Plans were put in place for a new training ground just off the A34 near the Great Barr-Walsall border. A previous application to build on the old St Margaret's Hospital site off the Queslett Road in Great Barr had been thrown out following objections from nearby residents citing potential traffic problems. Ironically, the base was eventually sold to Bovis for £13m, with some 450 new homes built during the mid-2000s. No such traffic problems there, then! At The Hawthorns, the club got busy with clearing out the Rainbow Stand. The venue's oldest stand was no longer fit for purpose, not for Thompson's vision of Premier League football anyway. The bulldozers moved in during the New Year, leaving Albion with a building site behind one touchline.

Results continued to improve. By spring, Albion were realistic challengers for a top-six finish – a feat they achieved, for the first time since 1993, with the 2-1 victory against Gillingham. A brilliant opening 60 minutes then saw them lead Bolton 2-0 in the play-off semi-final, courtesy of goals by Roberts and Hughes. But a collapse in the final ten minutes left them as underdogs for the second leg, which they lost 3-0. Megson believes his plans and ambitions were undermined by the lingering culture of mediocrity he was trying to banish. He claims some players were aware they were playing out their final games for the club – with promotion of little personal benefit to them. They are strong claims but Megson offers the theory with conviction. And his pre-match preparations at Bolton were not helped by a bust-up between two players he declines to identify.

"We got into the play-offs and made an arse of it. We were 2-0 up and wasted it. There were still players there that weren't mine and I am absolutely convinced to this day some knew that, if we were promoted, they would be out of the club. They knew I would have moved them on. We were a shadow of ourselves in that second leg. On the morning of the game, I had to break up a fight between two players. For me, it showed a total lack of focus. What were they thinking of? It was something childish, too. And they were going to move on anyway. I made sure of that. Bolton were favourites but we had got so close in the first leg that I felt disappointed we couldn't make it harder for them. It was our fans I really felt for. The away end at Bolton is great for supporters – the acoustics are brilliant. I was so, so disappointed that night because I felt it was our supporters who should be in the Premier League. But, that season, I felt we lit a fire up the arse of the club, the fans, the players, everyone. To do that after losing the first three games and with a team that wasn't yet my own.... I thought we did ok."

The summer of 2001 brought new challenges. Roberts suffered a major ankle injury that troubled him throughout the campaign. He was a big miss. Taylor, now 34, was joined by new recruit Scott Dobie, who signed from Carlisle. Hughes was one of football's hottest properties and it was widely circulated that he could leave should anyone offer £5m for him. There was little interest from the Premier League, opening the door for big-spending Coventry. He struggled to deliver there, scoring just 15 times for a side whose under-achievement and failure to win promotion back to the top flight enabled Albion to snare the player back for £2.5m the following season.

In the early hours of November 22, 2003, Hughes fled the scene of a fatal crash in Meriden that involved his Mercedes Coupé and a Renault Megane. A passenger in the Renault was killed instantly. The deceased victim's wife was to die in her sleep 13 months later, with another passenger confined to a wheelchair. Hughes went into hiding after the accident, prompting police to take the unusual step of naming the person they would like to speak to in connection with the accident. The following day, Albion were preparing for a game against Cardiff. Megson recalled the week and the invaluable guidance he received from one of football's most distinguished statesmen.

"It was a tough period. We knew something had gone on and he'd gone missing. I had to do a press conference and was trying to concentrate on that while being very mindful of the whole thing involving Lee. It was then I got a phone call from my mate Micky Phelan, who was a coach at Manchester United. He said: 'The gaffer wants a word'. It was Sir Alex Ferguson, who said a few things but the one that stuck with me was: 'Just remember somebody has died in this'. I was perfectly aware of that but he was used to press conferences where there is immense pressure. He was trying to help me and I'll always be grateful for that. I was getting all of this advice on what to say or what I shouldn't say. I went into the press conference and there must have been 80-90 people. I recognised some from the news, usually dealing with big stories. The first question I get is: 'Will Lee Hughes be in the squad tomorrow?' I remembered Sir Alex's advice straightaway and voiced a reminder that someone had died."

At 10am on Monday, November 24, Hughes walked into Little Park Street police station and gave himself up. He appeared in court the following summer. "I didn't know whether to go to the trial or not," admitted Megson. "I didn't want to look like I was condoning it but, equally, Lee was one of my players, so I felt a duty to him. In the end, I went. I've stayed in touch with him and he does regret it so much. It was all very sad for all concerned." Hughes was found guilty on August 9, 2004 of causing death by dangerous driving. He was sentenced to six years in prison. His Albion contract was terminated with immediate effect.

Typically, Albion started 2001-02 with a stumble and stutter. That was no major surprise. Two defeats were followed by a draw and four back-to-back victories. The momentum was back. And, by then, Megson had brought in Danny Dichio. Inadvertently, it was the pursuit of the Sunderland striker that sowed the seeds for discontent later in the season. His salary was the issue, with the top-flight man understandably demanding a figure that was out of step with Albion's means. The Hawthorns wage bill was having difficulty keeping up with progress on the pitch and Megson feels the club was struggling to maintain the same impetus as the team. "We only lost the first two in 2001-02, which was slightly better!" he said. "I wanted any new players to arrive earlier. We couldn't get that done but once we did get those in that I wanted, things came together. We weren't favourites for anything that year. (Manchester) City came into it and blew everyone away, Wolves were spending big, Coventry spent big and took our striker, of course. We lost Lee, Bob was older, Jason got a bad injury. We had to cope with that. There were aspects of the club where we moved quickly, on other things the club kept labouring and things were held up.

"Scott Dobie came in and did brilliantly. He was a good signing but he could have been a better player. He was painfully shy, a lovely player – the opposite to Lee – but he was terrific for the club. We had a strong backline and had a thread of honesty going through the club. We were still training on pitches that weren't fit for purpose. It's a testament to the players they won promotion when they didn't even have proper facilities. On the pitch, we went from nothing to sprinting. But, off it, we were way behind. Where we trained had no laundry, no canteen. It was basically a building. It needed a lot of work and it can't be right that on the first day back to training, your players are walking down to The Bell pub for lunch. That's what we were dealing with."

The first hints that all was starting to unravel behind the scenes came during the opening months of 2002. Megson, as he continued to do throughout his spell at the club, was commuting from his Sheffield home. His chairman Paul Thompson owned a business in Rotherham and also lived near Sheffield, meaning that much of Albion's high-end business in 2001-02 was being conducted 100 miles up the road in South Yorkshire. "Paul Thompson wanted meetings once a week, said Megson "We would meet in Rotherham, discuss what was going on with the team and other business. When we met once, we were doing ok with about 14 games to go. He started talking about clubs going up too early, not having the infrastructure, etc… I threw in the name of a club who were up there at the time and said: 'They will struggle if they go up' and Paul came back with: 'Well, that's why I don't want to go up this year…our foundations aren't there either'. I just smiled and said: 'You cannot choose when you go up'. But it told me a lot. I couldn't get out of the room quickly enough. I knew we were a decent side. But I also knew who we still had to play and who Wolves had to play…and I felt we had the better run."

Albion versus Wolves was to become the intriguing backdrop to the season. They had drawn their Hawthorns meeting before a bad-tempered game at Molineux, on the second day of December, was won 1-0 by Megson's side, courtesy of Jordao's strike. Off the pitch, things were about to hot up. Megson continued: "When we beat them, it was a great derby and Dave Jones (Wolves manager) said: 'They've had their day, we'll have ours'. That was wonderful to hear. I knew the work we were doing meant we would probably end the season well – that's how I set my teams up work-wise. It's the business end of the season when you want to do well. When other teams are doing five-a-sides, we're still working hard. I knew we had a really good chance to keep going if Wolves slipped up."

March 16, 2002 is a milestone date for any Albion fan. It was the day they travelled to Sheffield United for a routine second-tier match. Only it wasn't.

Megson and United boss Neil Warnock could barely hide their contempt for each other. Twelve months earlier, Andy Johnson – then at Nottingham Forest – was involved in an incident with Sheffield's Georges Santos, who was caught by Johnson's elbow during an aerial challenge. He suffered a double fracture of the eye socket, necessitating a five-and-a-half-hour operation to insert a titanium plate. Albion were leading 2-0 against the Blades, who were down to ten men following the ninth minute dismissal of Simon Tracey for handling outside his area. Scott Dobie had already scored and Derek McInnes struck the best goal of his career to make it two. Then United made a double substitution. Off came Michael Tonge and Gus Uhlenbeek, on went Patrick Suffo and Santos. Within seconds, chaos ensued. McInnes's pass across the pitch fell short, leaving Johnson having to sprint to the ball. As he arrived, he was pitched into the air by a violent, reckless challenge from Santos. As referee Eddie Wolstenholme tried to restore some order – Santos had already been given a red card – Suffo aimed his head at McInnes. He, too, was dismissed. Albion scored a third before Michael Brown and Rob Ullathorne went off injured, leaving United with six men – insufficient for the game to continue.

The match was abandoned at 3-0 after 82 minutes but, the following Thursday, Albion were awarded the three points. Recriminations followed. Anecdotal claims from the away dressing room including racial abuse directed at Albion players, Sheffield captain Keith Curle trying to bully Danny Dichio in order to force another red card – presumably to get the game abandoned earlier – and Warnock instructing players to become lame. For Megson, it was an uncomfortable period, not least as he still lived in Sheffield. And his resentment remains to this day, even at the mere mention of 'The Battle of Bramall Lane'. "Why are you calling it that? Why are you calling it a battle?" he asks. "That is the thing that really irks me. There is a newspaper article in the East Stand that's framed and hanging up with other photos – it has the 'Battle of Bramall Lane' as its headline. A battle is between two fighters. We weren't fighting. One team was fighting, we weren't. We were trying to play football.

"I'm the wrong person to ask about this, really. You'd have to ask Sheffield United what happened. I've never seen anything like it. It seemed to me that it had all been organised beforehand. What I can say is that I had to leave the touchline because I could hear what he (Warnock) was saying. I had to go and sit in the directors' box and as I get there, the ref has blown his whistle…I went to see the ref and he said: 'Game's abandoned'. I went to the dressing room and told the players to keep their kit on. I wanted the ref to play the final few minutes. The next day, my son was playing Sunday football and I heard Warnock on the radio talking about the game being replayed. So I rang them up… 'Get me on that show'. I got myself in trouble with John Barnwell (the League Managers' Association chairman) for doing that but I wasn't going to let it lie. I told the radio station: 'If the FA say we have to replay it, we will play it and we will get five sent off…the points simply have to come to West Brom'. Everybody knew what went on. We know who was involved. We won fair and square. Some of the things that went on – disgraceful challenges, our captain being assaulted, racist comments, players trying to get sent off, other things… it was madness and it winds me up that it is called a 'battle' because it wasn't us doing the fighting. We were the ones playing football."

While the Bramall Lane hostilities gave the impression of a united West Bromwich Albion, all wasn't well behind the scenes. Paul Thompson was now openly critical of the club's scouting system, using the match-day programme to deliver his vision of Albion's future. Speaking at the time, he said: "For the club to progress, I believe we need to buy younger players. This is one of the reasons we are determined to see an integrated scouting system which will identify the right players to develop the squad. In the past, this club has concentrated on short-term fixes to problems without looking at longer-term health, a policy that has kept us out of the top division for 16 years. We need to balance the immediate demands of the manager with the longer-term needs of the club."

Megson took the comments as a personal affront. His recruitment policy was indeed a paradox. While openly admitting to having a small scouting network, the success of signings during his opening two seasons suggested the system was working just fine. "They were doing things that I didn't agree with," he added. "The whole issue of integration was about them getting involved with it, which I was fine about – they are involved in that process anyway. My concern was that if I want to sign a player, they can just say: 'We can't afford him'. But if they want to sign a player, I will stick him in the reserves if I don't want him. I told them I would go elsewhere – we could shake hands and call it a day. But we were going well at the time, so they didn't want to do that. When they came to talk about the integrated scouting system, ok, so let's talk about my scouting: I brought in Johnson, McInnes, Hoult, big Mooro, Gilchrist, Appleton – I think I did ok. Thompson said only two clubs had scouting right. One of those was Manchester United. I asked someone there what their set-up was like… they said they had something like 30 scouts. They had a massive budget for scouting. We had my dad, one other scout and that was pretty much it… but we were expected to go head to head with United? It was madness."

Following an Albion victory over Cheltenham in the FA Cup fifth round, Megson came out fighting, defending his signings record and firing back at suggestions that his recruitment had fallen short. Despite the differences, Albion were to win promotion, courtesy of their incredible run at the end of the campaign. Yet the bickering persisted. May, 2002 should have been the greatest moment in the club's modern history – certainly the best for four decades. Instead, The Hawthorns resembled a battleground, with tensions between manager and chairman escalating. Megson or Thompson. One of the two would be leaving. As we now know, it was the employee, rather than the employer, who came out on top. Thompson quit, with Jeremy Peace hastily seizing control from interim chairman Clive Stapleton. Appreciating the value of Megson's achievements and standing among Albion fans, Peace threw his support behind his manager. It caused the destruction of the board. Barry Hurst and Stapleton were ousted, as was chief executive John Wile. Coming in as managing director and chief executive respectively were Brendon Batson and Mike O'Leary, the latter working without a salary.

"It was pathetic," recalled Megson. "They wanted to run the club totally differently, which is fine. That's up to them and I was quite prepared to step aside. I didn't want to work like that and as a result of Thompson's stance, Peace got in. Don't forget we had just gone up. I had never seen anything like it. Everyone was down when they should have been celebrating this incredible achievement. It was like we'd been relegated. On the Tuesday after we went up, somebody put a notice up on the pin-board that read: 'Remember! It is PROMOTION, not RELEGATION'. There was no Champagne after we beat Palace – we had to find our own and the sponsors of the League gave us some. It was as if the club didn't want to go up. It was flat. It's like we'd done wrong. On the Monday, the board wanted a photo with the players. One of the lads got wind of it and said: 'We're not going on it…they've done nothing for us'. They were also mindful of the bonuses Wolves players were promised compared with what they were getting, which was pretty much nothing. I had to convince them to go on the photo – in the end, I threatened to fine them. They came back: 'We will go on the photo but we're not smiling'. I've never seen that photograph to this day. It was such a shame, totally pathetic. I'd said it when I arrived…it was a club that liked to argue.

"When we went up under Thompson, they re-signed all the players I'd released. I told them I wouldn't be offering them anything. I went on holiday, came back and the board had re-signed the lot. Other than Des Lyttle, I don't think any of them played for me in the Premier League. It's hard work when you're being constantly undermined. It makes it doubly hard. They gave new contracts to players who were never going to play for us in the Premier League. It was ridiculous." And what of Thompson's assertion that all was well between them now? "Is that right? That's news to me. When I got the job at Sheffield Wednesday, I got a letter from him as if nothing had ever happened. But the fact is that had Paul stayed, I'd have gone. And I was prepared to go. By the end, I simply couldn't work with him."

And yet 2002 could easily have gone a different way. By the time Megson's side pitched up at Bradford, they had missed eight out of 11 penalties. Had they converted just half of those, the narrative would have been about Albion's promotion and little else. They would have been on course to be sure two or three games earlier, although we will never know how the Baggies would have fared from a position of pressure, rather than chasing. Instead, there was drama with each game. It was only expected that, in a season of such high tension, there would be one more twist. With Albion seemingly heading for a 0-0 draw at Valley Parade, Bob Taylor found himself bundled over and young referee Mike Dean pointed to the spot. With a glowing smile, Megson said: "Igor was the nicest bloke in the world. I'd want my daughter to marry him. Somehow, we've got it into our heads that he takes penalties for his national team. He'd been here for however long and then announces he also takes penalties – and has never missed one! For God's sake, Igor! We'd have scored all 12 had he taken them. We knew it was a big one. It was the most important kick of the ball all season. Had he missed, the momentum might have gone away from us. We were supposed to have supporters in one end of the ground… it was packed everywhere. I'm trying to keep calm and then Igor scored…oh, wow, bloody hell!"

But Megson's job wasn't done. The week between the Bradford and Crystal Palace games was surreal. Promotion could have been secured had Wolves lost to Wimbledon on the day after Albion's win in West Yorkshire. But they won. Clinton Morrison, then of Palace, stirred the pot by claiming he would be doing all he could to help his Republic of Ireland team-mate Mark Kennedy, who was playing for Wolves. Albion players were banned from speaking in the media but details had emerged a few weeks earlier of Wolves' players being promised a huge promotion bonus and a trip to the Bahamas if they went up. Megson merely lapped it up, pinning more and more examples of Wolves' entitlement to success on the dressing-room pin-board. In one final dramatic twist, the Albion boss had to be restrained by Mrs Megson after spotting two Wednesday players tucking into the kind of food that would have left football nutritionists shaking their heads.

Megson declined to name the Wednesday duo as he recalled, with clarity, the events of the week commencing April 15, 2002, which began with Albion as a second-tier club and ended with them in the Premier League. "Clinton Morrison did my team talk, saying he wanted to beat us for the Ireland lads at Wolves – nice one, Clinton!" laughed Megson. "He ended up playing for me and is a lovely lad but I did thank him for that. We played on a Sunday, so on the Friday, I suggested we all (wife and son) go to this pub in Sheffield. We're sat minding our own business when I notice two Wednesday players, seemingly waiting to have a meal. I couldn't believe it. I was going mental. Barbara was telling me to calm down and I'm thinking: 'What the hell are they doing in a pub so close to a game?' The weekend was massive for us and Wolves but not for those two. I was stewing, wanting to say something. Barbara is trying to calm me down, saying: 'You can't bollock players who aren't yours'. So I just kept my eye on them. The next thing I see, the waitress has gone over to their table with the biggest cod and chips I've ever seen; the cod was hanging off the bloody plate. I couldn't believe it. It's a couple of nights before their match with Wolves and these two Wednesday players are in the pub. I was fuming but stuck to my word. I didn't say anything. [Of the two players, only one featured against Wolves, the other wasn't involved].

"I stayed over at the Village Hotel in Dudley on the Saturday night and was up really early, about 5am. There was nobody around but the cleaner. He said: 'Can't you sleep? Bet you're nervous, aren't you?' and I replied, laughing: 'Yeah, how did you guess?' Too right I was nervous." And so to the match…

Megson continued: "I asked (manager's secretary) Alison Matthews to invite all of the kids and families in. But I said: 'If the players find out, it's a waste of time, so they mustn't know'. Thankfully, they didn't suspect anything. I wrote that Dave Jones quote on the board – 'They've had their day, we'll have ours' – and underneath I said: 'Not fucking today, they won't'. When the players were ready, I asked: 'Who do you play for? You've played for myself and other managers. You don't just play for West Bromwich Albion, you play for others'. Then I said: 'This is who you play for? These people are there for you when you're rubbish, when you're injured, when you've been sent off or lost.' And with that, the wives, children and other family members walked in. So I'm there giving this speech and I could see one of the kids out of the corner of my eye. He was shaking his mum's hand. 'Mum, mum, look, he's written fucking on the board'… so I went and rubbed it off, much to the amusement of everyone. After all that build-up, one of the kids stole my thunder!" Albion won 2-0, with Darren Moore and Bob Taylor scoring, to secure top-flight football for the first time since 1986.

Megson had to deal with other challenges. During his first year at the club, his wife Barbara was struck down with illness. Then his no 2 Frank Burrows was diagnosed with kidney cancer in autumn, 2001. Both recovered well. "My wife was in a serious way with stomach problems but she had great treatment," said Megson. "When I spoke to Paul Thompson about the job, I told him I wouldn't leave Sheffield but said I'd be first in every morning. And I was. It did take its toll driving up and down every day, on top of dealing with her illness. The travelling was the thing that might have seen me pack in. The driving would sometimes be robotic, auto-pilot. That can't be good but I was pleased that I was there first thing before anyone else. And then there was Frank. He called me in… 'Can I have a word please, Gary…I've got kidney cancer'. That put everything into perspective. He didn't want to make a fuss of it. He wanted to disappear and get well, which thankfully he did.

"Manchester City also went up that year. I wasn't really getting on with

West Brom by this point. Anyway, I got an invite to the LMA awards do. I don't usually go and certainly didn't fancy this one because I knew the board were going. John Barnwell called and said: 'I notice you're not coming. You need to come…do I need to spell it out for you?' So I went but made it clear I didn't want to sit on our board's table. I ended up next to Stevie Coppell and was chatting to him when they told me I'd won the Manager of the Year for the Championship. I thought Kevin Keegan should have got it. It doesn't matter what you spend, if you finish champions, you're the best team. Kevin was terrific about it. I collected this award and mentioned Frank in my speech: 'We've had 27 clean sheets and got promoted…but the best news I had all season was Frank getting the all-clear from cancer'. Sir Alex Ferguson was there and came across to say: 'I didn't realise Burrows was ill' – typical of the man, he called him there and then to see how he was. That was a good night."

Megson had an unexpected dice with his own mortality in the most unusual circumstances some years later. In January, 2011, talkSPORT breakfast show presenter Alan Brazil shocked listeners when he announced: "After the break, we will have more on the sad, sad death of Gary Megson." As social media went into meltdown, I was contacted by my news and sports editors at the Birmingham Mail, demanding several pages of copy for a tribute 'special'. Broadcaster Tom Ross, aware of the same announcement, took it upon himself to make a check call. "I had a call and was surprised to hear Tom's voice," Megson said. "And then he explained. I'd had no idea that talkSPORT or Brazil had even reported that." Thankfully, Megson's well-being was confirmed there and then. The ex-Baggies boss was, indeed, fit, well and somewhat alarmed to learn of his premature passing. Brazil's subsequent comments and news bulletins confirmed that it was former boxer Gary Mason who had died following a cycling accident. Megson added: "What disappoints me is that it was not only poor, but somebody else's loved ones were coming to terms with some tragic, horrible news and there they (talkSPORT) were making that awful mistake. I never received an apology from Brazil."

Albion's first-ever campaign under the Premier League banner ended predictably. They finished 19th. The following season, Megson guided them to a second promotion, as runners-up to Norwich. And that triumph wasn't without dramas either. In autumn, 2003, there were strong suggestions Megson was about to be dismissed, with speculation that Albion had already lined up his replacement. The rumour was at its peak during the weekend Albion travelled to West Ham, where it was felt a defeat would finish Megson off. As it happened, Albion came from three down to win a dramatic match 4-3. The name mentioned at the time was Mark Hughes, who was then managing Wales and looking for a move to the club circuit. The so-called pursuit never came to fruition and Megson claims Hughes's name wasn't the one suggested to him at the time. Seventeen years on, he opts against naming the man who was being touted as his successor.

"I was aware people were briefing the press," he continued. "I had a call from a huge name in terms of management, to tell me a mate of his had been offered the job. Yet I was still in the job. I just got to the point where I'd had enough. That second promotion was a lot harder because people expected us to go up. But we did have a better team and it was still a difficult club to manage. We did it with three or four games to spare but, make no mistake, that was some achievement. Have a look at how many sides go back up first time. Not many. We did. We were promoted without kicking a ball (Sunderland, Albion's nearest rivals, failed to win a lunchtime kick-off against Wigan). We gave the lads a glass of Champagne – it worked because we won 3-0. It was very satisfying but not as much as the first one.

"The Premier League first time had been a tough one for us. We were planning for relegation before the season started. We had the lowest budget in the division – we were the 17th highest in the Championship for goodness sake, so what chance did we have in the Premier League? The assumption was the club would come back. Most clubs don't but we managed that. I wanted to work in the Premier League by getting there with a club. And I managed that. But the season we went down was the hardest I've ever had because we didn't have the money many had. We had the most incredible talent in Jason Koumas. He was phenomenally talented but he had to deal with a lot of things that others don't. He was the most naturally two-footed player I ever saw. He had so much ability. The things he could do were amazing. But he didn't want to do the other things, like the running."

Megson's final throes at The Hawthorns were as a Premier League manager. In one week during the summer of 2004, he welcomed three players who would become iconic signings in their own way. Jonathan Greening, from

Middlesbrough, became a title-winning captain four years later while Zoltan Gera became possibly the club's finest overseas player. And then there was Kanu, the high-profile Bosman free transfer from Arsenal. He was the club's first £20,000-a-week player at a time when all others were earning four-figure sums. Rob Earnshaw became the club's record signing a few weeks later.

"I went home from a pre-season trip to Denmark in an attempt to sign some players," Megson added. "Kanu was one. I recall having a meeting and saying we needed a signing that wasn't just a player but one who would make other clubs and players realise we'd changed. I met him in London and we managed to get him in. That opened opportunities for other players. We wanted to show people we were serious about it. Kanu was a great lad, very enthusiastic. I went with my son to meet him and there was my son taking pics. I apologised but he said 'no problem' and took some for us. I only wish we'd got him earlier in his career. But he was a player we needed so as to show we could move the club on. What a wonderful footballer he was! It was important for us to try and change. We hadn't tried a leg after our first promotion, so I was keen to ensure we were more prepared to stay up. He opened the door to other players. Zoltan was also a lovely lad. He was so, so happy to sign. He'd had this troubled past and coming to England was a dream come true for him. He actually had tears in his eyes when he signed because he just couldn't believe he'd joined a Premier League club. He asked: 'Am I now a West Brom player?' I said: 'Yes, you are, Zoltan'. And he just gave his other half a big hug. He was that happy. And then there was (Rob) Earnshaw. Sod's Law when I left, he couldn't stop scoring. He was a proper goalscorer. It's difficult enough being in the Premier League and trying to kick on where you want it to be. We still weren't behaving like a Premier League club in many respects. There were things going on behind the scenes."

Megson decides against going on the record about those 'things'. He left Albion on October 25, 2004, his relationship with the board having gone beyond repair. Over the course of his career, he managed nine clubs between 1995 and 2012, with a couple of weeks as caretaker at Albion in 2017. Albion were the fifth club he had been in charge of. In his time at The Hawthorns, he presided over 197 League games, winning 83, drawing 47 and losing 67. Given the Premier League campaign of 2002-03, that is certainly no bad return. He reflects on his time in the Black Country with fondness, albeit tempered by frustration at Albion's inability to keep pace with the on-pitch progress. "I loved what we achieved," he continued. "The lowest we finished in the Championship was in the play-offs. I didn't like the stuff that went on above me. It was a real us v them. But in terms of on the pitch and with the crowd, that was brilliant. We managed to move the club forward very quickly. I look back on that period with fondness and appreciate how lucky I was."

Megson is asked whether he had any regrets. Would he have done anything differently? "No, no, I wouldn't," he said after a brief pause. "One or two things maybe but I always did what I thought was right for the club, even though it wasn't always what people wanted to hear. I said it before: I was a steward of the club. I came in every day – I'd be first in after driving from Sheffield – and I'd generally be the last to leave. I used to write my own programme notes and there was one notable time when I noticed they'd been changed. I remember writing: 'Every single decision I've made has been what I felt was the best decision for the club…and I hope everyone else can say that'. It was pulled out. Why? I have no idea. People can draw their own conclusions.

"I know I wasn't the obvious choice for the fans at first but I was fortunate to get the job. I took Stockport to their highest finish, Stoke were second when I left, Blackpool I took from the bottom to seventh. I wasn't that bad, was I? I'd like to think when people look back on my time in charge, they'll generally be quite pleased with how it worked out."

So Viv Anderson was wrong: Megson didn't need the Lord's intervention after all.

Igor Balis

*"...I knew I had to score and also knew it would be very, very bad
if I missed...if you had measured my blood pressure, it would
have blown the instruments..."*

And, after all that, it was the greatest of fibs. Igor Balis doesn't seem the kind to tell porkies but we should be grateful he did. Without it, we wouldn't be here now. 'From Buzaglo to …Taylor', or 'From Buzaglo to …Moore' just doesn't sound right. Alliteration can be everything in this game. Balis nailed it. One shot, one goal, one moment of glory. His life would never be the same again, certainly not among Baggies fans. The Slovakian is the most unwilling of heroes. That penalty shifted West Bromwich Albion's destiny to unprecedented territory in the modern era.

For any Albion fan over a certain age, the mere mention of the name 'Igor' brings back certain emotions and memories. Glory, success, tears of joy, nerves, celebrations. Plenty of celebrations. Those who were too young can only imagine from the stories and anecdotes they have heard from a mad Saturday.

'Igor', has its place in the Albion lexicon. Much like 'The King' means Astle, much like 'Bomber' means your record goalscorer, much like 'Big C' means Regis, much like 'Colin' means… you get the drift. Igor is one penalty, one goal, one afternoon, one never-to-be-repeated moment. It was TV pundit and Liverpool legend Jamie Carragher who once said nobody ever grew up wanting to be a right-back like Gary Neville. He was so wrong. I defy any Albion fan not to want to have stepped into the boots of Igor Balis, if only for 30 seconds of their lives. One kick was enough. Balis played another 30 or so games for Albion after this. Would anyone remember any of those? Probably not. Time remains suspended for him; suspended to a few seconds in Bradford.

That was then. This is now. It's November, 2019 and a dozen or so Albion fans have made the journey from the Black Country to seek out their hero.

Joined by Steve Madeley from football website The Athletic and me, the group are in Slovakia for no other reason than to break bread and share merriment with one of Albion's most celebrated heroes. On one half of the table sit a group of fans, none of whom speak Slovakian. On the other side sit the Balis family, led by Igor. The common language is football. It is 6pm in Trnava. Balis has already given us a guided tour of the national stadium, a purpose-built arena that would look at home in the Championship. Now we have moved to a restaurant. It could easily be a lot later. The nights are drawing in, people are losing track of time. That'll be the alcohol. The following day, Trnava will host Slovakia's game with Azerbaijan which the hosts will win 2-0. None of us are bothered about that despite several having tickets. The Balis family certainly don't care and don't bother to go. They know it won't be enough to secure Euro qualification and are spot-on. Tonight, there is only one show in town.

Understated to the point of shyness, Balis has dropped his guard. We are in a hostelry bearing resemblance to a large dining room in a stately home and he is playing mine host. The vision and spatial awareness you'd associate with an international footballer remains. The moment a glass empties, he is on his feet, rushing with a bottle of Borovicka to top it up. In these parts, it is the height of bad form for anyone's glass to be empty. Borovicka is a spirit made from juniper berries. The first sip prompts facial contortion, some spluttering, a burning throat, flushed cheeks and the synchronised shaking of heads from a clientele more used to English ale and draught lager. The spirit is a Slovakian delicacy, yet wouldn't be out of place in a giant steel tank, pump-operated, on a petrol station forecourt. One bottle of this stuff could run a small hatchback for two days. By the fourth or fifth shot – and some are well past that particular point of no return – it starts to go down easier and quicker. Some of these fans will be in for a long night and an extremely fuzzy morning.

Balis is adored because of one moment; one you could feasibly have blinked and missed. And because of that, he could walk into any watering hole in West Bromwich and have his choice of beverage. All paid for. All on the house. But not tonight. He is looking after us.

The Balis story began just 30 miles away in Bratislava during the back end of summer, 2000. Frank Burrows, Albion's assistant manager, went to watch Slovakia play FYR Macedonia in a qualifier for the 2002 World Cup. Of particular interest to the Baggies was Inter Bratislava striker Szilard Nemeth, who played reasonably well in the hosts' comfortable 2-0 win. But the club were not in a financial position to pounce. He was definitely one for the 'files'. He would eventually get his move to England, signing for Middlesbrough a year or so later. But Burrows's eye was also caught by the right-sided midfielder, who dropped back to assist the defence and played like a makeshift right-back. His diligence, effort and reading of the game impressed. Burrows reported back to Megson that the player, Igor Balis, was worth pursuing.

Balis arrived in England in November, 2000 for a trial after being granted permission by his club Slovan Bratislava. He completed a £150,000 signing shortly after. "It was Frank Burrows who spotted me," recalls Balis through his English-speaking friend and translator. "It was kind of funny because there was a national team game in Bratislava and they came to see another player, not me. But they liked me and asked if I can go for a trial. I went but the West Bromwich chairman Paul Thompson was not there, so they asked me to go for a second time. The coach (Gary Megson) said he liked me and when he saw Paul Thompson, they sorted out the finances of the transfer."

On his first day of training, Albion staff reported seeing Balis marching down the Birmingham Road clutching his boots in a brown paper bag. He looked more like a manual worker heading to a factory for his early-morning shift, than a pro footballer. He was staying at the Moat House Hotel, a mile from the ground. Word quickly got around that he was walking in, so, rather than have their new signing running the gauntlet across the M5 slip roads, Albion's coaching team asked around for team-mates willing to swing by to pick him up. Derek McInnes's hand went up. "I stayed at that hotel for three months, which was tough at times, but also quite comfortable for me. It had everything I needed, apart from my family," added Balis. "Derek McInnes would come and pick me up – he was very good and helpful. My English wasn't good then and still isn't. That's the one thing I've never been able to do. But everyone in the team was very friendly to me. They knew I didn't speak English, so every single one tried to help. The foreign players (Jordao, Brian Jensen) were especially helpful because they knew the struggle I faced. They had probably been in a similar situation but at least they spoke English. It was the first time I had experienced something like that."

Our trip to visit Balis coincides with the 30th anniversary of the 'Gentle

Revolution', which brought to an end communist rule and led ultimately to the split of Czechoslovakia and creation of two new countries, Slovakia and the Czech Republic. Growing up in an Eastern Bloc country before the dismantling of the Berlin Wall was a different experience – Communist dictats, queues for limited produce and the mainlining of values that rejected the democratic governance and market economies of the West. State-run shops, known as Tuzex, did not accept local currency, selling luxury items and foreign goods, but only for vouchers that had to be exchanged for foreign currency (usually US Dollars) in certain banks. Although Czechoslovakia was among the more prosperous of Eastern Bloc states, the true Soviet values remained. Those days were long gone by 2000 but Balis's upbringing in the pre-1989 days were a world away from the riches he would earn in the Premier League.

"They were different times," he added. "I was very young, so I didn't care much about politics or know much about it. But the language was a disadvantage for me when I came to England because I had only learned Russian at school, apart from my own language. That was very common at that time. These days, children learn English but not when I was growing up. I wanted to talk to the fans all the time when I was there but I didn't speak English and maybe the fans were thinking something bad about me because I never spoke to them or answered them. It is a reason why I want to go back but only if someone can translate. I am still not quite comfortable. Life in this country was different before because we learned Russian only and the country was different. But since then (1989), Slovakia has only gone up. It is not as good as in the Czech Republic because they are still a little ahead of us, but we have everything here. I wouldn't change anything. We are doing well. I have everything I need – my kids, my family and my health. That is all I want and all I need. So, yes, adjusting to England was difficult at first because of the language but also because Adriana (his wife) and our children weren't there. They joined me at Christmas."

Having spent three months at the hotel, Balis moved with his family to a detached property in Cottesmore Close, in the Wigmore area of West Bromwich. It is doubtful any professional footballer would live in the town these days but Balis maintained a humble lifestyle in his new surroundings. The very address had Albion connections as it was the same cul-de-sac that Jeff Astle had lived in for most of his time at The Hawthorns. And while many of Balis's team-mates were cruising round in the newly-launched BMW X5 4x4s, he opted for a more practical Mazda 323 five-door hatchback. As he adjusted to his new life, sons Denis and Boris began as pupils at nearby Hollyhedge Primary School and, in their spare time, played football for renowned local side Bustleholme. It was, in many respects, the ideal lifestyle for a young family trying to find their feet in a new country. Gary Megson really couldn't have asked for a better professional.

Meanwhile, in Trnava, Balis is on good form as he continues serving drinks to increasingly fuel-injected but jubilant Albion fans. Every now and again, an 'Igor…Igor…Igor…' breaks out as the alternative to a more traditional toast of 'cheers'. Shot glasses are raised each time. The Borovicka is going down well. Balis remains in his element, ensuring nobody runs dry. It's fairly clear that by tomorrow morning, the result will read: Borovicka 1 Albion fans 0. Yet, in the dressing room, Balis was the quiet one who went unnoticed. Match reports seldom mentioned him, he rarely scored (he managed four in his two and a half years at Albion) and he was a steady seven out of 10 in the ratings. Indeed, it requires some searching to establish whether the most low-key member of Albion's squad had played at Sheffield United in another highly memorable game of 2001-02. Indeed, he had.

While all hell broke loose around him, it is of little surprise to note Balis retained his usual calm and dignity. If you type 'Battle of Bramall Lane' into a Google photos search, you'll struggle to see him on any of the pictures. Yet he was there. "It was the first time I had experienced something like that," he added. "I didn't know the rule that the game would be abandoned if more than four or five players were injured or sent off. So it was a big shock for me to see this happen. Were they injured? I don't think they were. They acted like they were injured because they wanted the game to be called off."

And, so, to the very reason we are here. Balis played 75 times for Albion. Although he barely let them down, he rarely stood out either. Yet it took one moment – of less than 10 seconds – to write himself into Hawthorns folklore. On April 13, 2002, Albion travelled to Bradford for the penultimate game of the Division One season. The game was teetering towards a goalless draw, which would have kept Albion two points ahead of Wolves, who were due to play Wimbledon the following day at Molineux. Step forward Mike Dean. By

2019, he was one of the Premier League's most established and best-known officials. Back in 2002, he was carving out a career. In the final throes of the game, he changed the destiny of the promotion race. Bob Taylor was caught just below the knee by a rash and clumsy Andy Myers challenge. Dean, with the game deep into stoppage time, pointed straight to the spot.

A penalty with pretty much the final kick of the afternoon would put Albion four points ahead of Wolves, leaving them in control of their own destiny. What could possibly go wrong? Sadly, Albion had a nervous disposition to penalties throughout the campaign. They had been awarded 11 and converted only three. Derek McInnes, Bob Taylor, Scott Dobie, Jason Roberts and Neil Clement had all missed....so, who next? Step forward Balis. The defender had only taken one previously – in a successful shoot-out in a League Cup game at Cambridge. With Albion desperate to end their aversion, Megson was seeking a new taker. During a training session some weeks earlier, he had asked Balis whether he had ever taken one. Not realising his manager was being serious, Balis joked that he was Slovakia's regular penalty-taker. Thankfully, 2002 was a time before search engines had the capacity to bring up Slovakian results, line-ups and goalscorers of that period. Had Albion's staff done so, Megson and his Internet-savvy staff might have spotted that Balis's only goal for Slovakia had come from open play and that Szilard Nemeth was the national side's designated taker. Still, what were the chances of him being needed? And then his little white lie became serious.

"I told him I had taken penalties before but had never taken any," laughed Balis. "I had taken maybe two or three in my whole career but no more than that. It was after a game six weeks before, he asked if I wanted to take the penalties and whether I had taken any. I replied: 'Yes, why not?' We ended up not having a penalty for a while, so I forgot all about it...until it actually happened. It would have been slightly different if the score had been 3-0 but I did not expect it to be the second last game of the season in that situation."

The lengthy wait for a penalty was extended further while the stricken Taylor – 'There's no way I'm taking this penalty' – received treatment and bought some valuable time. So how was Balis feeling? "I realised very quickly that it was all on me. I took the ball and focused only on the penalty spot. I knew Megson wasn't looking – I think he was more nervous than me. I knew I had to score and also knew it would be very, very bad if I missed. I would have been home a year earlier. If you had measured my blood pressure, it would have blown the instruments. I could see all the faces behind the goal, of fans holding their heads because we had missed so many penalties. There was so much fear."

Balis dispatched his penalty, prompting an incredible outpouring of celebration from not only the away end, but other sections of the stadium. "The feeling I had after scoring was magic," recalled Balis. "Everyone was happy and cheering. It was the biggest moment of my life and I realised a big moment in West Bromwich history. I don't think I will ever forget that magic feeling. My children were at home in Cottesmore Close and listening on the radio. Then I came home and told them how crazy it was." Which is why we are here now.

These days, Balis earns his living as a driver for a big company in Trnava, although he was signed off due to high blood pressure at the time of our visit. "One thing I got from my family is high blood pressure," he added. "Most people inherit money but I got high blood pressure. Actually, when I came to England, my blood pressure dropped because of the change of scenery and the different lifestyle. I'm not sure my blood pressure was as good on that day at Bradford."

Albion completed the job a week later. They beat Crystal Palace 2-0 thanks to goals from Darren Moore and Taylor, although not before an impromptu change to Megson's pre-match plans. As the players went through the final stages of preparation, the manager invited the players' families into the dressing room to remind them who else all their efforts were for. Balis was somewhat surprised to find himself preparing for the biggest match of his career, with his grandma stood in front of him, waving at him. "Before the last match against Palace, Megson prepared a surprise. We were in the cabin and our wives and children walked in. I remember our grandma was there – my mother's mother. She came to England for a few weeks, so the whole family was at the match. At the final whistle, there was just this amazing wave of happiness. Fans ran on to the pitch and enjoyed that moment with us.

"I never knew we could do it but we played great at that time and did everything that our coach wanted us to do. We wanted to go to the Premier League. At one point, the gap was really big – it was 11 points or something like that. But we had a good coach. Megson was good. He wanted 100 per cent all the time and if you did, he would be calm. But if you didn't, he would tell you. You want to win every game but you don't really have your hopes high that you can catch a team that are so far above you. But they (Wolves) stopped playing because they lost a couple of games and we started winning and it was also about luck. It was lucky that West Bromwich started winning and Wolves started losing."

Life in the Premier League brought new challenges for Albion as a club and Balis as a player. With Slovakia not integrated into the European Union until 2004, he was still in a position where his work permit was dependent on his place in the national team. Having lost his international spot, though, he was counting on Albion to make a case to have it extended. Sadly, it wasn't to be. Towards the end of that 2002-03 campaign, he was struck down by debilitating tinnitus. He was released at the end of that season following Albion's relegation back to the Championship and returned to Slovakia at the age of 33.

A VIP trip to The Hawthorns remains on the cards for Albion's most lauded penalty-taker of the 21st century. He has avoided returning in the past because of a lack of confidence in his patchy English. Yet if and when that time comes, Balis can be sure of a hero's reception from Albion supporters and a royal welcome from the WBA FPA, Albion's former players' association. It will be a stark difference to how ex-players are treated in his homeland. It is at this point that Igor's son Boris pipes up to bemoan the lack of pomp and respect awarded to former footballers in Slovakia. His father will undoubtedly be given full military honours when he visits the Black Country – in one half of the region at least. But Boris claimed: "Footballers (in Slovakia) are forgotten a couple of years after they finish." For a man who was capped 41 times and played in a globally-lauded Premier League, that lack of recognition is difficult to comprehend.

Igor added: "I still do a lot of interviews but they are calling from betting companies wanting tips for games. It is different to England where older players are appreciated. They forget about us here and that's a shame. That year in the Premier League was big for me even though we didn't do as well on the pitch [Albion finished 19th]. It was a big time for West Bromwich, being part of the Premier League. We saw David Beckham, the great Manchester United and Arsenal teams. I could only dream of this before and here I was playing in those games. But I had the problem with my ear. I still have it and it will never go away. I just have to learn to live with it. It wasn't just that it disrupted my hearing. It made a difference to my balance, which obviously isn't good if you play football."

Reflecting on life in England, he continued: 'My wife would have stayed there because she still likes all the architecture and everything in England. It's something I will remember for the rest of my life and I would remember it even if I had missed the penalty. That made it more special for me. Over there, I learned what it means to be a professional football player because it is slightly different here. I had to learn how to behave there because everything about football there is far, far from how it is here. It is fantastic and it is my best memories from my career. And the fans are fantastic. The stadiums are always full. In Slovakia, we go to church, you go the stadium."

It's the end of our meal in Trnava. Amid the protestations from the Albion fans, Balis has already sneaked off to pay the bill. One supporter wanders off and reappears with a bottle of white wine as a gift. The following day, fans club together and order a bouquet of flowers for Mrs Balis as thanks for the hospitality. The hangovers are bad but the memories will linger for so many.

It's unlikely any other Albion player has been defined in a positive way by one such moment. That isn't to demean Balis's career, more to emphasise the gravitas of that one right-footed swing at goal. The photo of that celebration at Bradford, with Balis open-mouthed and right fist clenched, with a blurred Derek McInnes cheering behind him, will forever be among the club's most cherished iconography. The little-known Slovakian, who came to play in the Championship, ended up checking out as a Premier League star and Hawthorns hero; all down to one little fib.

And finally....

See, it wasn't that bad after all. That horrible start, a slightly meandering middle and then an enthralling apex right at the end. Perfectly scripted. West Bromwich Albion, I thank you for the narrative.

As with any book, a number of people gave up their time to assist or contribute.

I thank the 18 former players, ex-managers and directors who offered their insights, including Andy Hunt, whose story will have to wait for another day. I am also indebted to Alan Miller for giving me exclusive access to his unpublished diary from the 1997-98 period. A big thumbs up to Daryl Burgess for dusting off his holiday photo album and to Paul Thompson for his generosity and kindness. Ian Hamilton also spoke at length, with much of his detail adding colour and insight to several chapters. Nobody ever credits those responsible for the assists but Hammy deserves a big cheer for his role as provider of stories and anecdotes. And then there is Jason Roberts and his thriving Foundation (https://www.jasonrobertsfoundation.com/). Please give generously.

I extend a huge shout-out to members of the S4A book sub-committee who backed this project financially and offered invaluable support throughout the process. The inner sanctum were Bill Smith, Spiro Marcetic, Reg Jones, Martin Grange, Len Smith, David Baker and Chris Saunders, the latter of whom designed the covers. David Instone edited the book. Laurie Rampling, the one who wears the shorts, provided the pics, along with contributions from West Ham United, talkSPORT broadcaster Nigel Pearson, Albion fan Dave Smallwood and Andy Walker at the FA.

Others due a significant acknowledgement include Dr John Evans, Mel

Eves, Stuart Curtis, Ben Campbell of West Ham United, the Birmingham Post & Mail, the Express & Star, WBA Former Players Association chairman Geoff Snape, David Holmes from Woking, the Balis family, journalist Graham Hill, author Dave Bowler, Daily Telegraph reporter John Percy, Steve Madeley and Stuart James of The Athletic, Express & Star journalist Matt Maher, Radio WM, broadcaster Adrian Goldberg and the very talented Paul Ridley of @subbuteolegends. Our thanks also to supporters John Homer, Mick Coldicott, Kieran Handley, Anil Shiyal, Dean Walton and his Slovakian posse, and Richard Jefferson for his 1990s soundtrack guidance.

Three cheers to those who supported the @BuzagloToBalis Twitter account, who offered kind words on Facebook, Instagram or bought the book.

And, finally, a big thanks for the support of my family, especially my teenage daughter Renia, who is still not quite getting football. Given that my memories of watching Albion at her age were of a struggling side, I cannot really blame her.

Chris Lepkowski
Summer, 2020

Roll of Honour

Jess Ackroyd
Paul Affron
Paul Eamonn Ager
Charles Allen
Mark (Alf) and Jake Allport,
'Smethwick Enders'
Franc Andrews
Lee Armstrong
Carl Ashford
Jonathan (Rick) and Noah Astley,
'Smethwick Enders'
Sue Aston
Ian Atkins, Deborah, David,
Daniel & Matthew

Baggiebrookesie
Baggie Joe
Gordon Baker
Trevor Bailey
Jon Barber, Albion through and
through
Vincent Barber, Albion through
and through
Gillian Barker
Paul Barker
Norman Bartlam
Dave Bassett
Dave Baxendale
Andy Baylis
Baynes (father and son)
Tim Beech
Thomas Beetison
Scott Bell
Andrew Benbow
Ed Benbow
Dave, Chris & Adam Bending
Tim Bennett, aged 44, lifelong
Baggies fan
The Benton Sisters
Matthew Biddle
Lyndon Bird
Janice Bissell RIP

Pete Black - Tamworth
George Blackham
Ian Blackham
Shane Blaney
Thomas Blundell
Stian Bøe
Will Bolton
Peter Bone (Beestonbaggie)
Maureen Bourne
Trevor Bowler
Peter, David & Poppy Brackley -
3 generations of Albion fans
Simon Bradbury
The Bradley family
Nick, Maria & Natascha Bramwell
Garry Brandrick
Paul Bridges
The Brindley family
Peter Brinton
Mike Brooke
Kay Brookes
Lisa Brown
Brian J Burnet
David Burrell.... so many
memorable days...
Keith Burrows
Jason, Megan & Amos Burt -
Edinburgh Albion
David Butler - Albion til I die (not
too soon though!)
Ray Butler, over 50 years a
Baggie

Chris Cadman
Mark, Sam, Ben and Jemma
Cadwallader
Emma and Sophie Caldwell
Sean Calvert
Mike Campbell, Gary Campbell,
George Russell Campbell
Daniel Carpenter
Roy Carr

Matt Carter
Steve Carter
David Cartwright
Gareth 'Hank' Cartwright
Graham Cartwright
Sharon Cartwright
Martin Cashmore
Kerry Cassidy
Iain Chambers
John Robert Chambers
Dave Chantry
Brian Chappell
Paul Chappell
John Clapham
Andrew Clarke
A A E F Clarkson Sisters
Alan J Clements
Tom Clempson
Derek and Stuart Cliff
John F Clinton
Dave Coates
Mike Coates
Steve Coates
Chris Cochrane
Mick Cochrane
Tom Coles
Peter Colley (1958-forever)
Paul Collins
Sid Collins
Ken Conway
Michael Cook
Mark Cooper
The Corfield family ATWD
Elliott Cox, boing boing
Ken Cox, a lifelong Baggie
Alison, Evie, Hector & Wilfred
Crow-Marcetic
Crowy

Joe Dabbs
David Dallaway
Eric Dandy
Ray Dangerfield, Mike Nicklin,
Chris Damms, great memories
Bob Davies
Michael Davies

Simon Davies
Toby Davies
Paul and Eleanor Davis
Pete Shaggy Daw
Brett Dawson
Scott Deakin
James Derrer
David Derricott
Bal and Brendan Dhadda. Well
done, Chris!
Brian Dimmock
Mark Dixon - when I learned to
boing boing
Hudson John Downes
Martin Draper
Eddie Duffield
The Dunn family

In loving memory of Ian Edmunds
Christine and David Edwards
Derek Edwards
Jonathan Ellis
Kelvin Elson-Whittaker
Jack Elvin, Albion through and
through
Mark Elvin
Bob Elvins
Chris Ewing

Rob Fain
John 'Faz' Farrington and baby
bump June 2020
Paul & Mick Faulkner RIP Dad
Raymond Faulkner
Ian Fellows, will always love Gary
Megson very much
Matt Ferguson
Bob Fisher
Craig Edward Fisher
Paul Fisher
Stuart Fisher
Richard Fitzpatrick
Andy Fletcher. Was there for
Woking and Bradford. ATID
Fletcher family
Neil Floyd

Alexander Forty
Harry Forty
Paul Foster
John Freeman - Albion since 18th
May 1968
Pat Frost

Mark Bamber Gascoigne - former
kit-man
The Geddes family
Peter George
Peter George
Rachael Gibson
Andy Gittins
Steven Goodhall
David J Goodman
Geoffrey S Goodman
Paul Goodwin
Grandad Gorby!!
Brian Goredema-Braid
Leonard Granger
Neil Greatholder
Les Green
Peter J Gregory
For David Griffin
Dave Griffiths
Andy Grigg
Kirk Guest
Peter, David & Martin Guest
The Gwilts

Andrew Haddleton
David Haddleton
John Haddleton
Simon Haddleton
From Graham Haines to his
brother Geoff
Katy Hale
Mike Hampson
Steven Harris
Phil Harrison - My Dad who made
me love the Albion
Tim Haskey
Ashley Hayward
Michael Hazlehurst
Herville Hector

Robert Hennefer
Mike Henry
Jack, Paula & Rod Hepworth
Luke Heritage
David Higgins
Ross Higgins
Tim Higgs
David & Ronnie Hill
Dominic Hill
John Hill. It's a privilege sharing
the Albion journey with you
Miles Hill
Rob Hindley
Aubrey Hodder, displaying the
colours with pride to all from
SO41
Richard Hodgkins
For Dad - M J Holder
Matt Holding
Richard Hollyhead
Gil Holmes
Jake, Toby & Dave Homer
Grampy Jim, Andy Hood and
Alistair Hood. WBA make us
happy
Paul Hoper
Alex Horton
Mark Howard
Stefan Hubscher
Daria Hudson
Stuart Hudson
David Hughes
Michael Hughes
To Tom and Mick Humphreys. For
showing me the Baggies way
Rob Humphries
Brad Hurst

Roy Ingram

Simon Jaffa
Clive James, vice-chairman WBA
David James
Peter James
Jean Jeanes, loved by all who
knew her. Craig & Mike Jeanes

Luke Jerromes
Steve Jinks
Gavin Johnson
Alan and Alan Andrew Jones
Caspar Jones
David J Jones & David G Jones
Gary Jones 1.7.1962 - 13.4.2020
Roy Jones
The Jones boys, who live in hope...

Olle Kannö
Antony Kefalas
Lee Kelly
Rob Kelly
Ray Kemp
Adam Kemshall and Tony Kemshall (RIP)
Leigh Kent
Paul Kent
Stewart Kerins
Mike Kinson
Brian Kirkham
Dave Knott
Jon Kordas

Phil Lancaster
Thanks to my Grandad Tom Lane
Dave Langran
Emma Lardner Albion till I die!
Mark Lardner
Paul Large
Dave Law
James Leadbeater
Elfa Leather
Richard Lester
Frazer Lewis
Ian Lewis
Pete Lewis
David Lissimore
Kev Lowbridge
Dan Lowe
Graeme T Lowe (1945 - 2020)
Matt Lucas. COYB
Aaron Luxton

Alex Macvie
Bob Macvie
Elliot Macvie
Michael Macvie
Frank Malcolm, Albion Shakespeare
Jim Male
Tom Manly
Jovan Marcetic
Marija & Jovan Marcetic; fantastic parents!
Stefan Marcetic
Nigel Lee Marriott
Howard Martin
Derek Masters RIP, lifelong fan who lived in the Balis era
Stuart Matthews
Richard May
David Maydew
Pete, Matt & Aidan McArdle
Christy McCann
Ian McCart. To my dad, love ya.
John McDermott
John Mckeon
Thelma McLeod, lifelong Albion fan
Tommy McMullan
Andrew McVicar
Fraser McVicar
Jamie McVicar
Matt Merrick
Mick Mills
Chris Moore
Helen Moore
Peter Moore
Jeff Morris
Michael Morris (baggiemick)
Dave Morgan - Mementos Memorabilia Ltd
Bob Moseley, 73 years a Baggie
Mr E Mu
Brian Mulcahy
Andy Munn
Steve Murray

Dave Neale

Shaun & Matt Newman - Albion
Till We Die
John R Nicholls (Jonty)
Mike Nicklin
Owen Noakes
David Norman
Richard North (Sedgley Albion)

JP
Ian Page
John Painter
Stephen Parish
Arthur "AG" Parsons
Leena Patel
Gavin Paul
Chris Pearce
Garth Pearce, a 1950's addict...
and still hooked
Harvey Peniket
Mike Perkins
Richard Perkins
Stuart Mark Perkins
Thomas John Perry RIP
Alan Phillips
Kevin Phillips
Robert Phillips
Garry Pitt (1956-2018)
Martyn Pope
Gary Powell
The Power family
John Preece
Jeff 'Baggie for life' Prestridge
Bob Price
David Price
Lorraine Price, she loved the
Baggies! XXXXX Darren Price
Dedicated to Micheal Anthony
Price
Colin Pritchard
John Pritchard

Magnus Quist

Tim Radford
In memory of Ray Rawlins, leader
of the Four Generations x

Janet Mary Rayner
Reader & Kendrick family
Jon Reeve
David Reeves
Kevin Reynolds
Mark Reynolds
Martin Reynolds
Neil Reynolds
Tony Ridgway, 61 years of
Baggies pain
Simon Ridler
Jim Riley
Dr Roger Rimmer, life member &
WBA medical officer from 1958 to
1995
Ian Rivers
Stephen Rivers
Alan A Roberts
Geoff Rollason
@rollsie7
In Loving Memory Of Dorothy
Rowbottom 3.11.41 to 24.3.2020
Julian Rowe
Dave Royle
John Russell
Mark Ryder

Peter Sandland
Liam Sargent
Andrew Saunders
Greg Saunders
James Richard Saunders, 1932 -
2013
Stevan Savkovic
James Seaborne
In remembrance of Joseph
Sherwood 1940-1991
Martin and Daniel Shilvock
Laurence Silvester
Inderjit Singh, DesiBaggie
Jadeen, Jeevan, Joshan Singh
Noah & Kellan Sirrell
Mark Skellon
Matt Slater
Mathew Smart
Andrew Guy Smith

David, Eva & Benji Smith "Up the Baggies" ♥
Eric Smith
Gemma Smith
John 'Smiler' Smith
Jonathan Smith
Mark K G Smith
Martin John Smith
Riley John Smith 08/11/2011
Snarka
Ewan and Anya Snell - future Baggies
Michael Snell
Reg and Val Snell
Ross Snell
Charlie Spear
Luke Stanley
Steve Stanley
Matt Stephens
Warren Stephens
David Stokes
John Stokes
Stourdave
Chris and Adi Stowell
Joseph Stubbs
The Sutton family
Callum Swain
Craig Swain
John Swain and Johnny Swain - Baggies both
Swedenbaggie

Andy Taylor
Kevin Taylor
Laura Taylor
Mark Taylor (Taz)
Mark Taylor
Roger, Phillip, Matthew & Cameron Taylor
Michael Thomas
Jonathan Thombs
Robert & Janet Timmins
John Tkaczuk
Martyn Todd
Darren Tomlinson in Poland
Paul Trattles

David Trumper (Baggie from 7, STH from '96)
Olivia & Ben Trumpeter
Alan Turner
Andy Turner
Carl, Ben, Lottie & Grandpa Turner
Joseph & Harry Turner
Richard Turner - Love you dad x
Russ Turton
Paul Tuxworth

Kieran Unitt

Vansports

Jake Wain
Luke Walford
Nick Walker
Scott Walker
Christiaan Wallett
Nicholas Wallett
Dean 'Deano' Walton
Jonathan "Mozza" Ward
Sam Ward
Tom Waterhouse
Hannah Weaver
Nick Weaver
Dougie Webb
Matthew D H Wesson
Greg 'heart rate is 122 & not even kicked off yet' Westwood
Neil Wetherall boing boing
Arron White
Neil White
Tom Whitehorn
Neil Whitehouse
Rupert Whitehouse
Steve Whitehouse
Mark Wickets, happy 60th, love Craig, Nicky & the girls
Lee Wickstead
Rich Wilkinson COYB
Geoff Willetts
Michael Willetts
Brian Windsor

Jon Winwood
Malcolm Woodhall
Josh Wooding
Taylor Woolridge
Nick Worth - WBA physio 1998-2007
Luke Wozniak
Chris Wright
Gary Wright
Simon Wright

Danny, Nicki and Ryan Yardley
Andrew Young

You are my Albion, my only Albion
We cor watch. Duncan & Mary
Thanks for introducing the
Baggies to me, Dad - love Will x
Baggies Forever - Clair & Steve
To Grandad, Happy Birthday. Lots
& lots of love, Stu & Leanne x
Danielle's Husband & Elyssia's
Dad
Choose Life, Choose WBA
For Phil, Leah & Asa: little
Baggies who lived most of this

WifiMarxist: still wary of Shef's
driving
Congratulations to my brother on
his second book
These years are not best
forgotten, better remembered
clearly
Boing boing!
Perfect book to read on a beach
in Maine, top bloke Chris!
Lifelong Baggies supporter from
Czech Republic
To Tess and Alex - a lifetime's
addiction, sorry
Boing Boing SP
The two Adrians and Sue - boing
boing!
Jacob, Zach & the Demon Van
Crew
11.11.67 8-1
Geoff, Dawn, Steven and
Kathryn... Baggies in our blood
In memory of my Dad, who first
took me to the Albion in 1960

WBA Former Players Association are delighted to support
Chris Lepkowski in the writing of this book and wish
him huge success with it.

ABOUT THE AUTHOR: Chris Lepkowski is a sports journalist, having covered West Bromwich Albion for 13 years at the Birmingham Mail and served as head of media at The Hawthorns. Now a freelance writer and sports journalism lecturer, Chris's work has been published in several titles, including The Blizzard, Backpass, FourFourTwo and a number of national newspapers. He is also the author of In Pastures Green and a contributor to several others.

COVER DESIGN: By Chris Saunders.